C000150479

1 MONTH OF
FREE
READING

at
www.ForgottenBooks.com

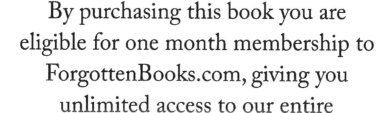

By purchasing this book you are
eligible for one month membership to
ForgottenBooks.com, giving you
unlimited access to our entire
collection of over 1,000,000 titles via
our web site and mobile apps.

To claim your free month visit:
www.forgottenbooks.com/free952193

* Offer is valid for 45 days from date of purchase. Terms and conditions apply.

ISBN 978-0-260-49832-8
PIBN 10952193

This book is a reproduction of an important historical work. Forgotten Books uses
state-of-the-art technology to digitally reconstruct the work, preserving the original format
whilst repairing imperfections present in the aged copy. In rare cases, an imperfection in
the original, such as a blemish or missing page, may be replicated in our edition. We do,
however, repair the vast majority of imperfections successfully; any imperfections that
remain are intentionally left to preserve the state of such historical works.

Forgotten Books is a registered trademark of FB &c Ltd.
Copyright © 2018 FB &c Ltd.
FB &c Ltd, Dalton House, 60 Windsor Avenue, London, SW19 2RR.
Company number 08720141. Registered in England and Wales.

For support please visit www.forgottenbooks.com

Y 4.Ag 8/1: 98-50

AGRICULTURAL PRODUCTIVITY ACT OF 1983

HEARING

BEFORE THE

SUBCOMMITTEE ON DEPARTMENT OPERATIONS,
RESEARCH, AND FOREIGN AGRICULTURE

OF THE

COMMITTEE ON AGRICULTURE
HOUSE OF REPRESENTATIVES

NINETY-EIGHTH CONGRESS

FIRST SESSION

ON

H.R. 2714

AUGUST 3, 1983

Serial No. 98–50

CIS RECORD ONLY:

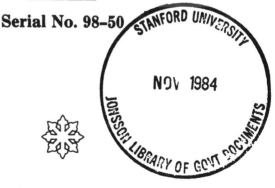

STANFORD UNIVERSITY
NOV 1984
JONSSON LIBRARY OF GOVT DOCUMENTS

COMMITTEE ON AGRICULTURE

E (KIKA) DE LA GARZA, Texas, *Chairman*

THOMAS S. FOLEY, Washington,
Vice Chairman
WALTER B. JONES, North Carolina
ED JONES, Tennessee
GEORGE E. BROWN, JR., California
CHARLES ROSE, North Carolina
JIM WEAVER, Oregon
TOM HARKIN, Iowa
BERKLEY BEDELL, Iowa
GLENN ENGLISH, Oklahoma
LEON E. PANETTA, California
JERRY HUCKABY, Louisiana
DAN GLICKMAN, Kansas
CHARLES WHITLEY, North Carolina
TONY COELHO, California
TOM DASCHLE, South Dakota
CHARLES W. STENHOLM, Texas
HAROLD L. VOLKMER, Missouri
CHARLES HATCHER, Georgia
ROBIN TALLON, South Carolina
HARLEY O. STAGGERS, JR., West Virginia
RICHARD J. DURBIN, Illinois
LANE EVANS, Illinois
ROBERT LINDSAY THOMAS, Georgia
JAMES R. OLIN, Virginia
TIMOTHY J. PENNY, Minnesota

EDWARD R. MADIGAN, Illinois,
Ranking Minority Member
JAMES M. JEFFORDS, Vermont
E. THOMAS COLEMAN, Missouri
RON MARLENEE, Montana
LARRY J. HOPKINS, Kentucky
GEORGE HANSEN, Idaho
ARLAN STANGELAND, Minnesota
PAT ROBERTS, Kansas
BILL EMERSON, Missouri
JOE SKEEN, New Mexico
SID MORRISON, Washington
STEVE GUNDERSON, Wisconsin
COOPER EVANS, Iowa
GENE CHAPPIE, California
WEBB FRANKLIN, Mississippi

PROFESSIONAL STAFF

A. MARIO CASTILLO, *Staff Director*
ROBERT M. BOR, *Chief Counsel*
JOHN E. HOGAN, *Minority Counsel*
BERNARD BRENNER, *Press Secretary*

SUBCOMMITTEE ON DEPARTMENT OPERATIONS, RESEARCH, AND FOREIGN AGRICULTURE

GEORGE E. BROWN, JR., California, *Chairman*

HARLEY O. STAGGERS, JR., West Virginia
TIMOTHY J. PENNY, Minnesota
LEON E. PANETTA, California
THOMAS S. FOLEY, Washington
TONY COELHO, California
HAROLD L. VOLKMER, Missouri
JAMES R. OLIN, Virginia

PAT ROBERTS, Kansas
STEVE GUNDERSON, Wisconsin
COOPER EVANS, Iowa
WEBB FRANKLIN, Mississippi

CONTENTS

(III)

53 440SU 3411
      XL
9/98 31150-200 MULB

AGRICULTURAL PRODUCTIVITY ACT OF 1983

WEDNESDAY, AUGUST 3, 1983

House of Representatives,
Subcommittee on Department Operations,
Research, and Foreign Agriculture,
Committee on Agriculture,
Washington, D.C.

The subcommittee met, pursuant to call, at 10 a.m., in room 1302, Longworth House Office Building, Hon. George E. Brown, Jr. (chairman of the subcommittee) presiding.

Present: Representatives Penny, Roberts, Gunderson, Evans of Iowa, and Franklin.

Also present: Representatives Weaver and Jeffords, members of the full committee.

Staff present: Cristobal P. Aldrete, special counsel; Peggy L. Pecore, clerk; Charles Benbrook, Gerald R. Jorgensen, and Thomas E. Adams, Jr.

OPENING STATEMENT OF HON. GEORGE E. BROWN, JR., A REPRESENTATIVE IN CONGRESS FROM THE STATE OF CALIFORNIA

Mr. Brown. The subcommittee will come to order.

I have a brief opening statement which I will read in the hopes that will allow more time for a few more members to show up.

I would like to welcome everyone today to these important legislative hearings on H.R. 2714, the Agricultural Productivity Act of 1983. As most of you are aware, this subcommittee has been conducting oversight of the agricultural research system. We are engaged in an exciting dialog now on how the Department should establish national priorities and long-range plans to achieve those priorities.

An important issue within the context of national research priorities is the question of how agricultural research can foster sustainable agricultural systems that have the potential to increase agricultural productivity, improve the profitability of farm operations, and promote environmental quality. Research to reduce soil erosion, to reduce losses of water and plant nutrients, and to conserve energy and natural resources are among the areas in need of greater attention.

The subcommittee has developed a record that suggests the need for the Department of Agriculture to invest in research to support a diversity of approaches to agricultural productivity. Hearings before this subcommittee on sustainable agricultural systems, held in 1982, made it clear that the research, teaching, and extension agenda of the USDA is not responsive to the needs of a substantial

(1)

number of farmers relying on unconventional, but nonetheless productive, farming methods. I am attaching comments I recently made on the floor of the House on this general subject.

I view the legislation before us today as potentially a positive step. This bill would direct the Department of Agriculture to set up a number of pilot studies to evaluate, in an objective manner, the effectiveness of moving from energy intensive practices to farm systems that do not rely so heavily on purchased inputs.

We have an impressive list of individuals who wish to offer testimony on the proposed legislation.

So I will not extend my statement further, except I should comment that this legislation is sponsored by a large number of our colleagues in the Congress, including nearly a dozen from the Agriculture Committee, and I think this is a good indication that the legislation does have broad support.

[The extension of remarks of Mr. Brown, H.R. 2714, and the report from U.S. Department of Agriculture follows:]

EXTENSION OF REMARKS

July 25, 1983

ORGANIC AND CONVENTIONAL AGRICULTURE: NEW COMMON GROUND

MR. BROWN of Calif. Mr. Speaker, recently I described for my
colleagues a new consensus on priorities for agricultural
research and development which is beginning to emerge. Today, I
want to report further on the 'Agriculture Committee, Department
Operations, Research, and Foreign Agriculture Subcommittee's
recent hearings, and describe some very interesting testimony on
the subject of organic agriculture.

American farmers are having a tough time lately. Caught
between low prices and high costs, they are struggling
financially, and federal programs to control surpluses and
maintain farm income are imposing unprecedented costs on the
taxpayer. According to witnesses at our recent hearings on
research, farmers presently lack the kind of flexible management
options that would enable them to control the variable costs of
production in order to obtain maximum profit. Instead, they
almost universally go for maximum yields, and we end up with huge
surpluses, increased erosion, and other problems.

Getting information to the farmer is part of the solution.
The minicomputer, coupled with advances in economic research, may
soon give individual farmers the ability to develop management
strategies that give higher profits and spare our resources of
soil, energy, and water. But some physical limitations remain.
There are problems in shifting from heavy use of fertilizer,
water, and pesticides, to low-input approaches, and this
discourages many farmers from trying. Even though we now have a
number of studies which show that organic farmers, who use few,
or no, synthetic fertilizers and pesticides, are generally about
as profitable as conventional farmers, we lack scientific
information on the problems of making a transition to such
methods.

We also don't understand the long-term possibilities for
flexible strategies that would combine the low-input,
resource-conserving practices of organic farmers with the
intensive methods developed over the years by our state and
federal agricultural research programs. We learned at our
hearings, however, that there is an increasing sense among
agricultural scientists that we need to investigate these issues.
We need to increase research on agro-ecosystems, to look closely
at how farming practices influence long-term soil fertility and
nutrient relations. We need to study the dynamics of populations
of weeds, fungi, bacteria, insects, and other animals. And most
important, we need to study this as a total system, under

different types of management. For instance, much needs to be
done to comprehend the long-term implications of reduced tillage
and no-till farming systems, which are becoming much more common.

One of our witnesses was Mr. Robert Rodale, President of the
Regenerative Agriculture Association, publisher of Organic
Gardening magazine, and the leader of a large private research
program in organic farming. He reported on his recent
participation in a meeting of the American Phytopathological
Society, in Ames, Iowa. At a plenary session on the
sustainability of agricultural systems, specialists in the study
of plant disease discussed the need for new paradigms for
agriculture, both to find better ways to control plant diseases,
and to improve the economics of farming.

It appeared to some at that meeting of scientific experts
that the present, intensive, chemically-based approach is not
working very well. Organic farming is beginning to be seen as a
serious alternative, indeed as the only alternative presently
available. Mr. Rodale reported that one representative of a
large agriculture company told him privately, "Look, we have to
meet you halfway."

I believe these statements, which would have been considered
utterly heretical by mainstream agricultural scientists not long
ago, reflect a growing consensus on the need for new approaches.

We cannot continue to consume our resources to produce huge food surpluses that deplete our treasury. Despite the attractive appeal to produce all we can, because the world is hungry, we must reconsider our approach. Mr. Rodale also told us of his work with Tanzania, funded by AID. They succeeded in developing sustainable agriculture systems, based on regenerative principles, rather than large amounts of synthetic inputs, in a nation which has very severe food problems.

We are getting beyond the time when a secretary of agriculture could say that organic farming was okay as long as somebody decides which 50 million people are going to starve. We are ready to begin learning from successful organic farmers and to study management strategies that sustain production without destroying irreplaceable resources or contaminating our environment.

The scientists, at least, seem to be moving to meet halfway on this, but I'm not sure that our agricultural leaders in Washington have the message. ARS has not included funds for organic farming research in its six-year plan, and it isn't clear if USDA policymakers really understand the issue at all. We are not seeing efforts to develop these alternative, reduced input management approaches being supported at the federal level.

Mr. Speaker, the Department Operations, Research, and
Foreign Agriculture Subcommittee will hold a hearing August 3rd
on the Agricultural Productivity Act of 1983, introduced by my
colleague Mr. Weaver and numerous cosponsors. This bill will
create a program of research, using demonstration farms located
throughout the country. The research will focus on ways to
enable producers to switch to low-input management techniques and
regenerative methods without loss of profitability. I intend to
give this proposal a thorough examination and to support an
enhanced program of research in this area.

It is time we put aside the differences that have divided
proponents of differing approaches to food production, and begin
to use our scientific and farming knowledge and skills to help
solve our production and resource conservation problems. I
believe some very promising new ways are beginning to open up,
and I hope we in Congress will do all we can to encourage these
exciting developments.

98TH CONGRESS
1ST SESSION

H. R. 2714

To direct the Secretary of Agriculture to take certain actions to improve the productivity of American farmers, and for other purposes.

IN THE HOUSE OF REPRESENTATIVES

APRIL 21, 1983

Mr. WEAVER (for himself, Mr. FOLEY, Mr. HARKIN, Mr. ROSE, Mr. BEDELL, Mr. DASCHLE, Mr. JEFFORDS, Mr. PENNY, Mr. EVANS of Illinois, Mr. TAUKE, Mr. BEREUTER, Mr. FUQUA, Mr. BEILENSON, Mr. GEJDENSON, Mr. SIMON, Mr. NEAL, Mr. HUGHES, Ms. MIKULSKI, Mr. WILLIAMS of Montana, Mr. SABO, Mr. VENTO, Mr. FORD of Tennessee, Mr. KASTEN-MEIER, Mr. FAUNTROY, Mr. SEIBERLING, Mr. DELLUMS, Mr. OBERSTAR, Mr. DE LUGO, Mr. FRANK, Mr. BARNES, Mr. HORTON, Mr. FAZIO, Mr. SWIFT, Mr. SCHEUER, Mrs. SCHROEDER, Mr. KOLTER, Mrs. SCHNEIDER, Mr. GINGRICH, Mr. BOSCO, Mr. OTTINGER, Mr. LOWRY of Washington, Mr. BONIOR of Michigan, Mr. HOWARD, Mr. MOAKLEY, Ms. KAPTUR, Mr. SUNIA, Mr. LUNDINE, Mr. ROE, Mr. WIRTH, Mr. LEHMAN of California, and Mrs. KENNELLY) introduced the following bill; which was referred to the Committee on Agriculture

---

A BILL

To direct the Secretary of Agriculture to take certain actions to improve the productivity of American farmers, and for other purposes.

1   *Be it enacted by the Senate and House of Representa-*

2   *tives of the United States of America in Congress assembled,*

3   That this Act may be cited as the "Agricultural Productivity

4   Act of 1983".

2

2   SEC. 2. The Congress finds that—

3   (1) highly productive agricultural systems which

4   include sound conservation practices are essential to

5   ensure long-term agricultural sustainability and profit-

6   ability;

7   (2) agricultural research and technology transfer

8   activities of the Department of Agriculture (including

9   the Extension Service of the Department of Agricul-

10   ture), Cooperative State Research Service, cooperative

11   extension services of the States, land-grant and other

12   colleges and universities, and State agricultural experi-

13   ment stations have contributed greatly to innovation in

14   agriculture, and have a continuing role to play in fos-

15   tering more efficient and sustainable agricultural pro-

16   duction systems;

17   (3) the annual irretrievable loss of billions of tons

18   of precious topsoil through wind and water erosion re-

19   duces agricultural productivity and raises the spectre of

20   another dust bowl;

21   (4) energy-intensive agricultural practices are

22   needlessly dependent on limited global reserves of oil

23   and natural gas, heightening the economic vulnerability

24   of the United States agricultural system;

3

1   (5) public funding of a properly planned and bal-

2 anced agricultural research program is essential to im-

3 proving agricultural productivity and conservation

4 practices; and

5   (6) expanded agricultural research and extension

6 efforts in certain key areas are needed to assist farmers

7 in improving agricultural productivity and implement-

8 ing soil, water, and energy conservation practices.

9   PURPOSES OF ACT

10 SEC. 3. It is the purpose of this Act to—

11   (1) facilitate and promote, within the context of

12 modern agricultural technologies, the scientific investi-

13 gation and understanding of farming systems with the

14 potential to increase agricultural productivity without

15 serious degradation of the land, reduce soil erosion and

16 losses of water and plant nutrients, conserve energy

17 and natural resources, and maintain high quantity and

18 quality yields of agricultural commodities without rely-

19 ing on energy-intensive agricultural practices; and

20   (2) provide assistance to family farmers and other

21 producers to use such systems in a manner which is

22 consistent with other provisions of law relating to

23 family farms and which complements the use of

24 modern agricultural technology in agricultural produc-

25 tion.

4

SEC. 4. (a) The Secretary shall inventory and classify by subject matter all studies, reports and other materials developed by the Secretary or by any person or government with the participation or financial assistance of the Department of Agriculture, which could be used to further the purposes of this Act.

(b) In carrying out such project, the Secretary shall—

(1) identify, assess, and classify existing information and research reports which will further the purposes of this Act, including, but not limited to, information and research relating to legume-based crop rotations, the use of green manure, animal manures, and municipal wastes in agricultural production, soil acidity, liming in relation to nutrient release, intercropping, the role of organic matter in soil productivity and erosion control, the effect of topsoil loss on soil productivity, and nonchemical or biological methods of weed, disease, and insect control;

(2) identify existing information and research reports which are currently useful or require revision, and make these available to further the purposes of this Act; and

(3) identify gaps in the information available to the Extension Service for distribution to farmers and

12

5

1   other members of the public in order to achieve the

2   purposes of this Act, and establish a plan to carry out

3   a program of research and education to fill those gaps.

4   PILOT RESEARCH PROJECTS

5   SEC. 5. (a)(1) The Secretary shall, pursuant to section 8

6   and with the cooperation of willing producers, conduct twelve

7   pilot research projects on farms for the purpose of examining

8   the effects of the transition from—

9   (A) farm practices which rely on synthetically

10   compounded fertilizers, pesticides, growth regulators,

11   livestock feed additives, and tillage practices which fail

12   to control erosion; to

13   (B) farm systems which rely on legume and other

14   sod-based crop rotations, the efficient use of crop resi-

15   dues, green manures, animal manures, off-farm organic

16   wastes and mineral bearing rocks, and the utilization of

17   sound, efficient production practices including conserva-

18   tion tillage, conservation irrigation (including low-pres-

19   sure systems and irrigation scheduling), and nonchemi-

20   cal or biological methods of weed and pest control.

21   (2) The Secretary shall select farms on which to conduct

22   the pilot research projects as follows:

23   (A) Six farms shall be selected which grow crops

24   and raise livestock. Two of such farms shall be dairy

25   farms and four of such farms shall be nondairy farms.

6

1   (B) Six farms shall be selected which grow crops

2   but do not raise livestock. Four of such farms shall be

3   farms that grow wheat, feed grains, upland cotton, or

4   rice, or any combination thereof. Two of such farms

5   shall be farms that grow fruits or vegetables, or both.

6   (b) In order to examine and assess the consequences of

7 farm systems referred to in subsection (a)(1)(B) of this sec-

8 tion, the Secretary shall also study twelve farms which have

9 been employing such farm systems for at least five years

10 prior to the effective date of this Act. The Secretary shall

11 select farms on which to conduct these pilot research projects

12 on the same basis as described in subsection (a)(2) of this

13 section.

14   (c)(1) Within one hundred and twenty days after the ef-

15 fective date of this Act, the Secretary shall select farms for

16 participation in the pilot research projects required under this

17 section with as diverse characteristics as practicable, includ-

18 ing diversity in size, soil type, and climatic conditions.

19   (2) The pilot research projects shall be conducted pursu-

20 ant to agreements which are entered into between the Secre-

21 tary and producers operating the farms at which the pilot

22 research projects are conducted and which provide that such

23 farms shall serve as demonstration farms. The agreements

24 may include limitations as to the hours during which the

25 farms shall be open to the public for demonstration purposes.

1   (3) Each pilot research project shall extend for a five-
2 year period.

3   (4) During the one-year period following the selection of
4 pilot research project participants, comprehensive data con-
5 cerning all aspects of the farming operations carried out on
6 such farms shall be collected and analyzed in order to provide
7 a baseline from which the effects of the project can be as-
8 sessed. Such data shall include, but not be limited to, infor-
9 mation with respect to—

10   (A) the type, quantity, and cost of production
11   inputs used in such farming operations, including capi-
12   tal, energy, fertilizers, pesticides, and water;

13   (B) the quality and quantity of production outputs
14   of such farming operations, including information on
15   crop yields, nutritional value of such crops, and rates
16   of production in livestock operations;

17   (C) the characteristics of the soil of such farm, in-
18   cluding the thickness of the topsoil on such farm, the
19   rate of loss of such topsoil as a result of such farming
20   operations, the level of organic nutrient matter in soil
21   on such farm, the water-holding capacity of such soil,
22   and the rooting depth of plants in such soil;

23   (D) the characteristics of other natural resources
24   of such farm, including water quantity and quality;

8

1   (E) the net income derived from such farming op-

2 erations; and

3   (F) such other factors as the Secretary deems ap-

4 propriate to fully assess the effects of the project.

5 (5) During the last four years of such pilot research proj-

6 ects—

7   (A) in the case of a farm selected under subsection

8 (a)(1), the transition described in subsection (a) shall be

9 carried out as directed by the Secretary or the Secre-

10 tary's designee;

11   (B) if a farm on which a pilot research project is

12 conducted is located in a local conservation district, the

13 owner or operator of the farm must have a conserva-

14 tion plan approved by and on file with the district. If

15 such farm is not located in a local conservation district,

16 the owner or operator of the farm must have a conser-

17 vation plan approved by and on file with the Secretary;

18 and

19   (C) data similar to the data collected in the first

20 year of such pilot research project under paragraph (4)

21 shall be collected and analyzed for all farms selected

22 for participation in the pilot research projects in order

23 to fully assess—

24   (i) the effects of the transition on the farms

25 selected under subsection (a)(1); and

9

1   (ii) the efficiency of the operations on farms

2   selected under subsection (b).

3   (6) The Secretary, in coordination with the Extension

4 Service and the cooperative extension services of the States,

5 shall take steps to ensure that farmers are aware of the exist-

6 ence of the demonstration farms.

7   (d)(1) The Secretary shall, subject to paragraph (2) of

8 this subsection, make payments to producers who operate

9 farms selected under subsection (a)(1) at which the transition

10 pilot research projects are conducted if the Secretary deter-

11 mines that such payments are justified to compensate farmers

12 for any responsibilities assumed in order to carry out the

13 projects agreed upon pursuant to this Act.

14   (2) Any payments so made by the Secretary—

15   (A) shall be made only during the last four years

16   of such project; and

17   (B) in any such year, shall not exceed any differ-

18   ence between—

19   (i) the net income received by such producer

20   with respect to farming operations carried out on

21   such farm in the first year of such project, adjust-

22   ed by the Secretary to compensate for any ex-

23   traordinary economic condition, natural occur-

24   rence, or other situation which significantly affect-

10

1   ed net income from such operations in the first

2   year of such project; and

3   (ii) the net income received by such producer

4   with respect to farming operations carried out on

5   such farm in the year for which payments are

6   being made, adjusted by the Secretary to compen-

7   sate for any extraordinary economic condition,

8   natural occurrence, or other situation which sig-

9   nificantly affected net income from such oper-

10   ations in the year for which payments are being

11   made.

12   COORDINATION

13   SEC. 6. In order to fully effectuate the purposes of this

14 Act, the Secretary shall take steps to ensure that the pilot

15 research projects are designed and carried out in coordination

16 with the Agricultural Research Service, Agricultural Stabili-

17 zation and Conservation Service, Soil Conservation Service,

18 Extension Service, cooperative extensive services of the

19 States, land-grant colleges and universities, State agricultur-

20 al experiment stations, the National Association of Farmer

21 Elected Committeemen, and the farmers participating in such

22 projects.

23   REPORTS

24   SEC. 7. The Secretary shall submit to the Committee on

25 Agriculture of the House of Representatives and the Com-

18

11

1 mittee on Agriculture, Nutrition, and Forestry of the

2 Senate—

3   (1) not later than fifteen months after the effective

4   date of this Act a report describing the results of the

5   project carried out under section 4 of this Act;

6   (2) not later than April 1 of each of the calendar

7   years 1985, 1986, 1987, and 1988, a report describing

8   the progress of the pilot research projects; and

9   (3) not later than April 1, 1989, a report contain-

10 ing—

11   (A) a summary of the data collected under

12   the pilot research projects;

13   (B) analyses of, and conclusions drawn from,

14   such data; and

15   (C) recommendations for new basic or ap-

16   plied research from such conclusions.

17   AGREEMENTS

18   SEC. 8. (a)(1) The Secretary may carry out the project

19 under section 4, conduct any pilot research project, and col-

20 lect and analyze information developed under the pilot re-

21 search projects through any agency in the Department of Ag-

22 riculture or through agreements with any land-grant college

23 or university or any other university or nonprofit organization

24 which has demonstrated expertise in the areas of agricultural

25 research and policy.

12

1   (2) The Secretary may not require matching funds for
2 any such agreements.

3   DISSEMINATION OF DATA

4   SEC. 9. The Secretary shall make available through the
5 Extension Service and the cooperative extension services of
6 the States the information and research reports identified
7 under section 4, the data collected under the pilot research
8 projects, and analyses of, and conclusions drawn from, such
9 data, and shall otherwise take such steps as are necessary to
10 assure that such material is made available to farmers and
11 other members of the public.

12   INTERCROPPING ASSISTANCE

13   SEC. 10. Beginning on the effective date, of this Act
14 and ending five years after such date intercropping shall be
15 considered an enduring conservation measure which is eligi-
16 ble for financial assistance under section 8(b) of the Soil Con-
17 servation and Domestic Allotment Act (16 U.S.C. 590h(b)).

18   DEFINITIONS

19   SEC. 11. For the purposes of this Act—
20   (1) the term "extension" shall have the meaning
21   given to such term by section 1404(7) of the National
22   Agricultural Research, Extension, and Teaching Policy
23   Act of 1977 (7 U.S.C. 3103(7));
24   (2) the term "conservation plan" means a plan
25   which describes and outlines a schedule for the imple-

13

1 mentation of conservation measures or practices on a

2 farm which are designed—

3   (A) to prevent significant degradation of the

4   soil, water, and other natural resources of such

5   farm; and

6   (B) to meet the management objectives of

7   the farmer operating such farm;

8   (3) the term "intercropping" means a crop pro-

9 duction practice which involves establishing and culti-

10 vating a soil-conserving crop (such as alfalfa, clover,

11 trefoil, hairy vetch, grass, winter wheat, or oats) on

12 land on which, at the same time, a row crop (such as

13 corn, soybeans, or cotton) is established and cultivated;

14   (4) the term "land-grant colleges and universities"

15 shall have the meaning given to such term by section

16 1404(10) of such Act (7 U.S.C. 3103(10));

17   (5) the term "demonstration farm" means a farm

18 participating in a pilot research project conducted

19 under section 5, which shall be open to the public in

20 order to demonstrate the applicability of the farm sys-

21 tems being practiced on such farms;

22   (6) the term "Secretary" means the Secretary of

23 Agriculture;

14

1   (7) the term "State agricultural experiment sta-
2 tions" shall have the meaning given to such term by
3 section 1404(13) of such Act (7 U.S.C. 3103(13));
4   (8) the term "transition pilot research project"
5 means the pilot research projects conducted pursuant
6 to section 5(a) of this Act; and
7   (9) the term "United States" means the several
8 States, the District of Columbia, the Commonwealth of
9 Puerto Rico, the Commonwealth of the Northern Mari-
10 ana Islands, and the territories and possessions of the
11 United States.

12   AUTHORIZATION OF APPROPRIATIONS

13   SEC. 12. For purposes of carrying out this Act, there is
14 authorized to be appropriated a sum not to exceed
15 $2,100,000 for each of the fiscal years 1984, 1985, 1986,
16 1987, and 1988.

17   EFFECTIVE DATE

18   SEC. 13. This Act shall take effect October 1, 1983.

DEPARTMENT OF AGRICULTURE
OFFICE OF THE SECRETARY
WASHINGTON D C 20250

AUG 2 1983

Honorable E. (Kika) de la Garza
Chairman, Committee on Agriculture
U. S. House of Representatives
Washington, D. C. 20515

Dear Mr. Chairman:

This is in response to your request for a report on H.R. 2714, a bill, "To direct the Secretary of Agriculture to take certain actions to improve the productivity of American farmers, and for other purposes."

The Department opposes enactment of the bill.

We are sympathetic with the purposes of this bill and the attempt to address one objective of research on natural resources as set forth in Section 1402 (10)(D)(v) of the National Agricultural Research, Extension, and Teaching Policy Act of 1977, as amended. However, we believe that enactment of this bill is not necessary. State and USDA scientists are currently conducting research that will be providing a continually updated source of technological information to the Nation's farmers and ranchers through the cooperative extension services of the States. This includes research on the following technologies: crop rotations; improved tillage methods; roles of legumes in crop sequence; biological nitrogen fixation; crop varieties and associated management to avoid potential diseases and insects; soil and residue management for erosion control; use of animal manures; and biological weed control. In addition there are several problems with certain provisions of the bill and the cost of the program would both exceed the proposed authorization level and the President's budget request.

Section 4 provides for an information study which, if conducted through jointly coordinated efforts of the Extension Service (ES), the cooperative extension services of the States, and the National Agricultural Library (NAL), would require funding for additional staff, microcomputer equipment and materials, and enrichment of book collections and services by NAL or a significant redirection of existing programs. Section 5(c)(6) and Section 9 would require the ES and the cooperative extension services of the States to engage in certain educational programs and the dissemination of results, which similarly would require additional funds or redirection of existing programs.

Section 5(a) provides for the conduct of twelve pilot research projects on (operating) farms to evaluate the effects of transitions from ("conventional") farming systems that utilize chemically-intensive practices along with nonconserving soil management, to alternative farming systems that rely on legume-based rotations, and other considerations. In addition, Section 5(b) specifies the selection and study of twelve other farms that have been managed according to alternative systems. This would make a total of 24 farms under study consisting of 12 matched pairs. Measured changes would be as paired comparisons, assuming it is possible to match the natural resource bases for each farm pair. This statistical basis is weak. There needs to be a larger sample size with very careful matching to achieve acceptable statistical confidence in the results.

The bill as written is restrictive, leaving the scientists and research managers little opportunity to design the studies in ways to produce results more meaningful in responding to the objectives and problem needs. For example, although large diversity in farm size, soil type, and climate characteristics are specified for farm selection under Section 5(c), which could be thought to be an advantage by some, these same features would dramatically complicate the research and could likely result in data of minimum value.

It is specified the projects shall extend for a five-year period. This is much too short for the anticipated changes to occur. With the first year "specified" as a data base establishment year, only four remain for measurement of effects. Then, if a four-year crop rotation is employed, for example, only one cycle could be completed in that four years, and biased data would result. The bias would likely be unfavorable to the alternative farming system.

If it is necessary to study whole farm systems, it must be recognized that the combinations of logical choices by farmers who use either "conventional" or alternate farming systems are many. This complicates the research and the interpretations of data, and the application of conclusions to real world conditions becomes questionable. This application is influenced to the extreme by a farmer's own preference, his financial flexibility, the characteristics of available soil and water resources, and the kind of farming system to be utilized.

In contrast, problems of changing farming systems that include effects of crop rotations, sequences of crops, livestock, manure, and other variables on soils, soil erosion, productivity, food and feed quality, income, and other factors can and are being researched in interdisciplinary projects. Utilizing numerous locations to sample differences in climate, soil, customs, and other variables can produce results which have excellent direct educational and demonstration value to farmers.

Section 6 provides for coordination among agencies and other parties in the design and coordination of the pilot research projects. The Cooperative State Research Service (CSRS) should be included because of its role with Federally funded research at the State agricultural experiment stations and because this part of the program could be administered by CSRS through Special Research Grants. CSRS administers Special Research Grants which are designed to further the programs of the Department of Agriculture at land-grant colleges and universities, State agricultural experiment stations, and all colleges and universities having a demonstrable capacity in food and agricultural research.

Section 10 provides for intercropping assistance under Section 8(b) of the Soil Conservation and Domestic Allotment Act (16 U.S.C. 590 h(b)). This would be in conflict with fiscal year 1984 budget limitations if the practice were to be mandated.

Section 12 provides funding authorizations not to exceed $2,100,000 for each of five fiscal years from 1984 through 1988. The Department believes the program envisioned by H.R. 2714 would, in fact, cost $14.3 million for this same period. As a point of reference this could be compared to the ARS projected expenditures for fiscal year 1983 on research areas related to organic farming of approximately $18.8 million.

In summary, while we are sympathetic to the purposes of H.R. 2714, we are opposed to this legislation because: Current work is underway that relates well to the purpose of the bill; we feel the authorities are duplicative; the bill would impose overly restrictive requirements on the conduct of such research; and the costs are excessive.

The Office of Management and Budget advises that there is no objection to the presentation of this report from the standpoint of the Administration's program.

Sincerely,

John R. Block
Secretary

Mr. BROWN. At this point I will ask Mr. Franklin if he cares to make an opening statement.

Mr. FRANKLIN. No, Mr. Chairman.

Mr. BROWN. I will, without objection, reserve a place in the record for any opening statement of our ranking minority member, Mr. Roberts, if he submits one.

We will also place in the record the statement of Senator Patrick Leahy.

[The prepared statement of Senator Leahy follows:]

Statement of Senator Patrick Leahy
The Agricultural Productivity Act of 1983
House Agriculture Committee
August 3, 1983

Mr. Chairman, I want to first commend you for holding this
important hearing today. Organic farming holds great potential
for American agriculture. I am very pleased that you are going
to explore this subject in detail.

I also want to congratulate Congressman Jim Weaver for his
leadership on this issue. His initiative in this area over the
past two years has done a great deal to make many people aware
of the benefits of organic farming.

Mr. Chairman, the American farmer is the backbone of this
country's economy.

American agriculture employs 23 million people, generates tens
of billions of dollars in exports each year, and feeds the people
of this country and millions throughout the world.

Despite this impressive record of achievement, traditional
American agriculture is in trouble.

Farm debt passed the $200 billion mark last year while farm
income will remain flat this year, after three straight years of
decline. You have to go back to the Great Depression to find
corresponding income statistics.

Commodity prices remain at record lows, forcing farmers to plant
fence row to fence row in an effort to keep their cash flow above
bankruptcy levels.

THIS KIND OF INTENSE PLANTING, OFTEN ON MARGINAL AND VULNERABLE SOILS, NECESSITATES THE USE OF MILLIONS OF TONS OF FERTILIZERS AND PESTICIDES IN A DESPARATE ATTEMPT TO WRING BIGGER AND BIGGER YIELDS FROM TIRED, WORN SOILS.

THESE RECORD HARVESTS ONLY FURTHER DEPRESS COMMODITY PRICES, COMPLETING THE VICIOUS CYCLE THAT MANY FARMERS FIND THEMSELVES IN TODAY.

WE MUST PURSUE POLICIES DESIGNED TO BREAK THIS DEPRESSING TREND IN AGRICULTURE.

ORGANIC FARMING PRESENTS SUCH A POLICY. IT IS A VIABLE, WORKABLE ALTERNATIVE METHOD OF FOOD PRODUCTION THAT HAS THE POTENTIAL OF TURNING THE CURRENT FARM SITUATION AROUND.

ORGANIC FARMING IS A SYSTEM OF AGRICULTURE.

IT WORKS WITH -- NOT AGAINST -- THE FORCES IN NATURE ALREADY AT WORK IN OUR SOILS.

IT STRESSES AGRICULTURAL TECHNIQUES THAT COMPLEMENT -- NOT DESTROY -- THE NATURAL NUTRIENT BUILDING AND PEST CONTROL PROCESSES ON THE FARM.

THE USE OF PESTICIDES, HERBICIDES, AND OTHER SYNTHETIC ADDITIVES ARE LARGELY AVOIDED. THIS NOT ONLY SIGNIFICANTLY REDUCES A FARMER'S COST OF PRODUCTION, BUT ALSO REDUCES DAMAGING RUN-OFF FROM FIELDS AND STREAMS.

FARMERS AND THEIR WORKERS ARE NOT EXPOSED TO LARGE AMOUNTS OF TOXICS IN THE AIR AND WATER NOR ARE THE PEOPLE WHO CONSUME THE FOOD.

IT IS A PROVEN METHOD OF AGRICULTURE, EMPLOYED ON SOME 40,000
FARMS OF ALL SIZES.

TWO OF THE BIGGEST OBSTACLES TO MORE WIDESPREAD USE OF THESE
TECHNIQUES ARE LACK OF INFORMATION AND AN ABUNDANCE OF MISINFORMATION.

AGRICULTURE SECRETARY JOHN BLOCK HAS CALLED ORGANIC FARMING A
"DEAD END".

FORMER AGRICULTURE SECRETARY EARL BUTZ ONCE SAID THAT IF ORGANIC
FARMING PRACTICES WERE EMPLOYED WORLDWIDE, 50 MILLION PEOPLE WOULD
STARVE!

TALK ABOUT MISINFORMATION!

IN AN EFFORT TO REDIRECT THE DISCUSSION, I INTRODUCED IN THE
SENATE THE AGRICULTURAL PRODUCTIVITY ACT OF 1983. I AM PLEASED
TO REPORT THAT THIS BILL HAS 15 SENATE CO-SPONSORS.

IN ORDER TO CONVINCE SKEPTICS LIKE AGRICULTURE SECRETARY BLOCK
THAT ORGANIC FARMING DOES NOT MEAN THE END OF FOOD PRODUCTION AS
WE KNOW IT, THE AGRICULTURAL PRODUCTIVITY ACT OF 1983 WOULD
ESTABLISH 12 ON-FARM STUDIES.

DAIRY FARMS, CROP FARMS, INTEGRATED OPERATIONS WITH CROPS
AND LIVESTOCK, AND FRUIT AND VEGETABLE FARMS WOULD BE EXAMINED.

EACH WOULD BE STUDIED OVER A FIVE YEAR PERIOD AS IT MADE THE
TRANSITION FROM CHEMICAL-ENERGY INTENSIVE AGRICULTURE TO ORGANIC
TECHNIQUES.

SOIL PROFILE, FARM INCOME, CROP YIELDS, PRODUCTION COSTS --
ALL WOULD BE STUDIED IN AN ON-FARM SITUATION.

TWELVE ADDITIONAL FARMS ALREADY USING ORGANIC TECHNIQUES
WOULD BE STUDIED AS A CONTROL GROUP.

THE SECRETARY OF AGRICULTURE MUST INVENTORY EXISTING RESEARCH
RESEARCH MATERIALS ON FILE AND ENSURE THAT THEY ARE MADE AVAILABLE
TO INTERESTED PERSONS AS WELL.

THIS BILL WOULD COST APPROXIMATELY $2 MILLION PER YEAR, OR
TWO TENTHS OF ONE PERCENT OF THE TOTAL USDA RESEARCH BUDGET.

YOU WOULD THINK SUCH A PROPOSAL TO IMPROVE THE BASIC HEALTH
OF AMERICAN AGRICULTURE WOULD BE RECEIVED WITH OPEN ARMS.

WELL, THE DEPARTMENT OF AGRICULTURE, PURPORTEDLY AN AGENCY
SERVING THE INTERESTS OF THE FARMER, HAS OPPOSED THIS LEGISLATION
IN THE PAST, AND I EXPECT IT WILL CONTINUE TO DO SO.

IT CITES THE COST -- WHICH ABSOLUTELY PALES IN THE FACE OF THE
ADMINISTRATION'S DEFENSE SPENDING PROPOSALS.

IT CLAIMS THAT THE RESEARCH WOULD DUPLICATE ON-GOING EFFORTS
AT USDA ON THIS VERY SUBJECT.

BUT THE AGENCY FIRED THE ONLY ORGANIC FARMING EXPERT IN
THE DEPARTMENT LAST YEAR, DR. GARTH YOUNGBERG.

IT IS TIME THAT THIS ADMINISTRATION REALIZE THAT ORGANIC
FARMING HOLDS GREAT POTENTIAL FOR AMERICAN AGRICULTURE.

ORGANIC FARMING DESERVES A CHANCE. IT IS HIGH TIME THAT THE
DEPARTMENT OF AGRICULTURE RECOGNIZES THIS FACT.

Mr. Brown. I will now turn to the author of the legislation, our distinguished colleague from Oregon, Congressman Weaver, and you may proceed with your statement, Mr. Weaver.

STATEMENT OF HON. JIM WEAVER, A REPRESENTATIVE IN CONGRESS FROM THE STATE OF OREGON

Mr. Weaver. Thank you, Mr. Chairman and Congressman Franklin.

I appreciate the opportunity to appear before the subcommittee this morning and commend you for your great leadership in calling this hearing and all the work that you have done in agricultural research. Your record is of the greatest in this Congress, and I appreciate the hearing on H.R. 2714, the Agricultural Productivity Act of 1983.

Without doubt, agricultural research is the cornerstone of American farm productivity. We have made tremendous progress in the past 30 years in our ability to produce food and fiber.

Before the technological revolution swept across America's farmlands, our farmers produced enough food, on the average, for 16 people. Today they can feed 68. This increase is due, in large part, to rapid technological advances in machinery, plant germplasm, and fertilizers. The USDA's publicly funded research programs fostered many of these productivity improvements, and they clearly have an important role to play in helping farmers in the future.

But the technological improvements of the past quarter century, beneficial though they are, have brought with them their own problems. They have ushered in a new era—an era of industrial farming in which short-term yield increases often take precedence over long-term sustainability.

We now live in an era of limits—limited soil, limited water, and limited energy. It is important, therefore, to devote some of our limited agricultural research budget to the examination and development of farming systems which, within the context of modern agricultural technologies, will insure the long-term sustainability of our food and fiber production system.

In 1950, 90 percent of all agricultural research was publicly funded. Today, it has dropped to 45 percent. The reason for this dramatic shift is, of course, that the private sector has a commercial interest in performing certain types of agricultural research: they have a product to sell.

For example, the chemical industry spent $450 million on pesticide and herbicide research alone in 1981—more than was spent during that year by the entire Agricultural Research Service at USDA.

I point this out only to demonstrate that the primary obligation to perform agricultural research which does not promote specific commercial products must lie with the Government. If the Government does not do it, it is not likely to get done.

Fortunately, the need for public funding of this type of research is well-recognized. Unfortunately, that need often goes unfulfilled.

In 1977 Congress directed the USDA to investigate and analyze the feasibility and practicability of using organic wastes such as manures, crop residues, and sewage sludge to improve soil fertility on American farms.

Three years later, the Department released a "Report and Recommendations on Organic Farming" which examined a variety of innovative methods of fertilization, soil conservation, and enhanced crop production. The report concluded that even a partial shift away from energy intensive farming practices would significantly help farmers improve their operations. Most importantly, the report suggests that these methods are cost effective.

In the wake of this report, many questions were raised about what USDA meant by organic farming systems. Did it require the complete elimination of all synthetic pesticides and fertilizers from American farms? Would it mean a return to the horse and buggy days of farming? The answer is, of course, no.

Like a musical score or a work of art, organic farming systems typically means different things to different people. When the Department of Agriculture uses it, however, it means productive agricultural systems that avoid or minimize the use of nonrenewable resources, conserve soil and water resources, maintain or increase soil productivity, and produce high quality products. Finding the right combination of farming practices to achieve these objectives is not unlike the skillful, dedicated effort required to create a priceless painting or a superb symphony.

The urgent need to embark on a research program specifically designed to find that combination was expressly recognized when, in October 1980, 3 months after the Organic Farming Report was released, the National Agricultural Research and Extension Users Advisory Board [UAB] recommended that USDA significantly redirect current levels of research and extension work to expand and improve the use of economic organic methods.

The UAB was established by Congress to prepare independent opinions on needs and budget priorities for research and extension in the food and agricultural sciences. In fulfilling that role, the board regularly makes recommendations for short- and long-term national policies, priorities, and strategies for agricultural research and extension programs conducted by USDA.

The USDA's fiscal year 1982 budget ignored the board's recommendation, however, and sought no funding for organic systems research.

In its fiscal year 1982 report, the UAB chastised the Department for failing to heed its advice, and again recommended that funds be redirected from other agricultural production related work. In addition, the board expressed its concern that the Office of Management and Budget could override or ignore the consensus of expert, research user, and political opinion by arbitrarily reversing the priorities established in the USDA's 1980 report on organic farming.

Despite these recommendations by its own experts and advisors, however, the Department again refused in fiscal year 1983 to seek even modest funding for what it described as "organic farming systems" research. In fact, the Department has never requested funding for "organic farming systems" research. In a July 1982 memo entitled "Reducing Farmers Production Costs," Acting Agricultural Research Service [ARS] Administrator Mary Carter reported that: "there is no research presently being conducted by ARS that conforms to the concept of holistic research as described in the July 1980 'Organic Farming Report.' "

By "holistic research," Ms. Carter was referring to integrated, multidisciplinary research that would examine and develop productive agricultural systems. Such research focuses not just on the actions and reactions of specific farming practices, but also examines the interactions between the various practices used in the farmer's management system.

By conducting systems research, the Department is better equipped to help farmers integrate techniques into their operations that will enhance productivity and conserve their precious soil and water resources.

If there is no objection, Mr. Chairman, I would like to submit for the record a copy of a letter I received from the Department of Agriculture, as well as a letter from the Congressional Research Service which confirms that specific appropriations to the Agricultural Research Service for "organic farming systems" research have never been sought or provided.

Mr. BROWN. Without objection, they will be made a part of the record.

Mr. WEAVER. Thank you, Mr. Chairman.

[The letters referred to above follow:]

 **United States
Department of
Agriculture**

**Agricultural
Research
Service**

**Office of the
Administrator**

**Washington, D.C.
20250**

APR 20 1983

Honorable Jim Weaver
House of Representatives
Washington, D. C. 20515

Dear Congressman Weaver:

Thank you for your letter of March 30 regarding organic farming research in the
Agricultural Research Service (ARS). Our responses to your questions are
numbered in the same order as cited in your letter.

1. There are no special authorizations existing now or needed for ARS to
   conduct research on organic farming. The general authorizations that cover
   all of our research activities are adequate.

2. ARS did not spend any funding for organic farming "systems" research in
   Fiscal Years 1978-1983. The ARS 6-Year Implementation Plan reflects zero
   dollar allocations for the Fiscal Year 1982 base period and projected for
   the period 1984 to 1990.

3. In an attachment to this letter, I am duplicating the list of 9 research
   areas and total ARS funds that you provided. For each of these areas, I
   have added the amount and percent of total funds that relate to organic
   systems research. Also included, as you requested, are statements on criteria
   on what types of research are classified as relating to organic farming
   systems.

4. ARS has not used or relied on any specific reports or analysis of organic
   farming for development of policies, redirections, or budgets pertaining
   to organic systems research. The ARS Program Plan and 6-Year Implementation
   Plan, with which you are already familiar, state in broad terms our program
   directions with respect to soil and crop research components that will be
   applicable to both organic and conventional farming systems. Reference is
   also made to the USDA "Report and Recommendations on Organic Farming." A
   copy of this document is enclosed for your information.

We appreciate your interest in ARS research programs.

Sincerely,

T. B. KINNEY, JR.
Administrator

2 Enclosures

ARS Research Funds that Support Organic Farming Systems

	Total	Support Organic Systems	Percent
		----------$1,000----------	
1. Horticultural crops, insect control	8,584	1,716	20
2. Field crops, insect control	7,585	1,896	25
3. Basic insect control technology	12,768	1,300	10
4. Biocontrol and taxonomy	10,036	8,817	89
5. Disease and nematode control	9,766	525	-
6. Weed control technology	11,079	610	-
7. Tillage practices	3,489	1,400	40
8. Water use efficiency	9,254	700	-
9. Soil fertility	7,866	1,910	24

Criteria used to classify research components of insect-related research (items 1-4) as organic systems are studies which rely on such nonchemical means of insect management as insect-resistant plants and biological control

Criteria used to classify research components of disease and nematode control (item 5) as "organic systems" are: any study in which amounts kinds effects of, decomposition, and methods of application of any organic material — such as crop residues municipal wastes or innocuous industrial organic wastes — are determined on plant diseases or nematodes. Examples of research include: effec of sludge on plant disease, of crop residues on diseases or of naturally high versus low organic soils on diseases and nematodes efficacy of nematicides and effectiveness of biocontrol fungi which destroy parasitic crop fungi that live in various soil types; and effects of beneficial fungi such as mycorrhizae in various soils.

Criteria used to classify weed research (item 6) that supports organic systems include: (1) mulches for weed control, (2) reduced tillage practices, (3) crop residues on the surface in combination with selective herbicides and reduced tillage, and (4) crop rotations, cultural practices, and other ecological practices of weed control.

Criteria used that can provide useful results for organic systems from soil fertility, water-use efficiency and tillage results items 7-9) include research that addresses mechanisms of largely self-sustaining nutrient cycles for crop production; mechanisms and principles whereby organic matter and residues improve water-use efficiency for crop production; and mechanisms and principles whereby tillage practices enhance the maintenance of organic matter and sustained soil productivity, respectively.

Congressional Research Service
The Library of Congress

Washington, DC 20540

April 6, 1983

TO   : Honorable James Weaver
               Attention: Kevin Kirschner

FROM   : Jeffrey Zinn
               Specialist
               Food and Agriculture Section (ENR)

SUBJECT   : Organic Farming

In a March 24, 1983 letter, you requested we obtain information in response
to three questions about organic farming as an activity of the Agricultural Research
Service (ARS). The questions and responses are presented below. The information
was supplied by the budget office in the Agricultural Research Service. I can
provide you with a contact if you wish to follow up on any aspect of these questions
and responses.

   1. From what law or laws does the Agricultural Research Service derive its
authority to conduct research in organic farming?

   The basic authorities under which ARS conducts research on organic farming
are the Organic Act of 1862 and the Research and Marketing Act of 1946. Under
these laws, the Service can conduct research on any aspect of agricutlure that
would enhance farm productivity. The language of the law is broad. It does not
not mention organic farming or any similar terminology, but organic farming is
generally interpreted to fall within the general responsibilities of ARS.

2. What is the dollar amount spent for "organic systems", as outlined in
the (ARS Program) Plan, for Fiscal Years 78-83?

Specific appropriations to ARS for "organic systems" have never been sought
or provided. Many of the research projects undoubtedly address aspects of organic
systems, but this work has not been specifically identified as benefiting organic
systems in the past.

3. How much money is actually spent on "organic systems" research? What
criteria are used to classify various research components within each area as
"organic systems?"

In June 10, 1982, testimony before your subcommittee, Dr. Kinney, Acting
Assistant Secretary for Science and Education, identified several general topics
where the research results could apply to organic farming. ARS staff I have
talked with informally define organic farming as "absence of any chemicals","no
use of chemicals to enhance productivity", or other similar concepts. Using these
concepts, the following projects and funding levels for FY83 were identified by
the ARS budget office as applying to organic farming.

Projects	Funding Level
Effects of nitrogen fixation	$ 625,000
Use of municipal waste on cropland	100,000
Effects of soil fertility and tilth on production of economic crops	2,000,000
Relationship of organic matter content in soil to soil moisture and soil erosion	1,150,000
Use of animal manure as nutrients	250,000
Use of crop rotation and crop manure systems	560,000
Development of pest-resistant plants	17,700,000
Development of biological pest control techniques	8,800,000
Effects of organic matter on the growth and survival of soil-borne plant pathogens	62,000

If, after you review this material, you have additional questions, please
call me at 287-7296.

Mr. WEAVER. In January 1983, the Agricultural Research Service proposed its 6-year program plan. In the plan, ARS advocates developing farming systems "characterized by less costly methods and by technologies that are safe, sustainable, and environmentally sound."

The plan further recommends innovative research "to reduce farm production costs while maintaining a high level of sustainable productivity through the development of efficient and diversified crop- and animal-production systems," and "to insure conservation of our natural resources."

Once again, however, no funding was proposed by ARS to carry out this research. The plan recommended zero funding for "organic farming systems" research during fiscal years 1984–90. In fact, contrary to some statements emanating from USDA, the plan actually proposed to reduce, by 78 percent, funding for integration of knowledge about alternative agricultural systems into current production practices.

The Agricultural Productivity Act would remedy this problem. It would establish 12 onfarm pilot research projects to collect and analyze data about the effects of a transition from energy intensive farming practices to systems which reduce production costs, conserve water and energy, and control erosion. Each project would span a 5-year period.

Twelve additional studies would analyze similar data on farms which have been using the low energy systems for at least 5 years, and therefore are past the critical transition period, in order to examine the efficiency of their operations.

It is important to point out, Mr. Chairman that the pilot research projects established by this act are not intended to provide a comparative analysis between so-called "conventional" and "organic" farming operations. Rather, they are designed as case studies which will, as the Organic Farming Report recommended, investigate the highly complex and poorly understood chemical and microbiological interactions which take place during and after the transition period.

Although USDA has conducted some research which has applications to "organic farming systems," it has been fragmentary and piecemeal. None of it has examined these types of systems, or the transitional barriers to implementing these systems, using an integrated, multidisciplinary approach. It is precisely this type of approach which the Department's experts and advisers have been requesting in vain, and it is precisely this type of approach that the Agricultural Productivity Act would require.

While I would certainly support the initiation of a full comparative analysis of "conventional" and "organic" systems covering a broad range of farm operations and locations, such a study would be highly complex and extremely expensive.

The case study approach adopted in the Agricultural Productivity Act, on the other hand, is an important first step that will provide the Department, and the farmers who rely upon it, with sound data about the effects of a transition on different types of farm operations, including dairy farms, mixed crop and livestock farms, and specialty crop farms.

The bill also establishes a program to assist farmers who utilize intercropping systems to establish a vegetative cover that improves nitrogen fixation, rebuilds the soil, and controls erosion. Intercropping is the practice of planting legumes, grasses, or other soil-conserving crops between rows of crops such as corn, wheat, or soybeans.

Finally, H.R. 2714 directs the Department of Agriculture to inventory and assess existing research and extension materials, and to subsequently recommend new research that will help farmers achieve a better understanding of innovative farming practices. The USDA already has initiated a minimal effort in this direction, but it has been funded only at a fraction of what a full study would cost. Our bill would help guarantee that the Department's survey is adequately funded and properly conducted.

The bill authorizes the USDA to spend up to $2.1 million annually for 5 years to implement these programs. That figure represents less than one-half of 1 percent of the fiscal year 1983 ARS budget. In addition, because it carries its own authorization, H.R. 2714 would not divert any funds from existing research programs at USDA.

Mr. Chairman, the Agricultural Productivity Act has the broad bipartisan support of 64 Members of Congress. An identical companion bill introduced by Senator Patrick Leahy, S. 1128, has 17 cosponsors. In addition, it is supported by the National Farmers Union and the National Grange, both of whom have submitted written statements today, as well as by the National Farmers Organization, which has endorsed the bill in a letter that I would like to submit for the record.

Mr. BROWN. Without objection, the letter will be made a part of the record.

Mr. WEAVER. Thank you, Mr. Chairman.

[The letter referred to above follows:]

PRESIDENT
DeVon R. Woodland
Blackfoot, Idaho

VICE-PRESIDENT
Robert W. Arndt
Echo, Minnesota

DIRECTOR,
WASHINGTON OFFICE
Charles L. Frazier

NATIONAL FARMERS ORGANIZATION

WASHINGTON OFFICE
SUITE 2200
475 L'ENFANT PLAZA, S.W
WASHINGTON, D.C. 20024
202-484-7075

July 28, 1983

Honorable Jim Weaver
U.S. House of Representatives
Washington, DC 20515

Dear Mr. Weaver:

First, let me compliment you and many of your
colleagues in the House who have joined in the development
and introduction of the Agricultural Productivity Act
of 1983. We are pleased that you will have a hearing
on this bill, H.R. 2714, August, 3, 1983. It will be
impossible for us to arrange a personal appearance to
testify at that time, but we do wish to comment on the
bill and urge favorable action by the Committee.

The members of the National Farmers Organization are
modern-day producers who utilize the best available
technology that they can afford in the current prevailing
farm economy. I can most accurately reflect their
expressions of viewpoint in our national conventions
and through other lines of communication by citing
their concerns with soil and water loss from erosion,
the ever increasing costs of producing the major farm
commodities and the absolute necessity of getting
our commodity prices up to profitable levels. If we
work toward those goals, however, it is important to
remember that soil and water are our basic resources
upon which all agriculture is dependent.

Even though we may be using modern-day fertilizers,
pesticides and herbicides effectively, there is another
side of the coin. It is high time that more attention
be given to the importance of the old-fashioned crop
rotation concept and conservation tillage. It is no
longer speculative conversation or starry-eyed dreaming

COLLECTIVE BARGAINING FOR AGRICULTURE

40

to think seriously of expanding the application of these desirable farming practices that work so well in conjunction with the application of chemical technology. A substantial number of average size, or larger, producers are in such programs today and they are profitable. They are also contributing to conservation of our natural resources.

We think it is ridiculous that the Department of Agriculture abolished the job of the one full-time staff member who was responsible for tracking the progress of organic agriculture. One is forced to think of the greedy, and perhaps inordinate, influence exercised by the advocates of more chemicals and fertilizers in our scheme of production.

As we see it, your bill would not seriously derail any commercial sales of fertilizers or chemicals, but it would provide some direction and encouragement to those responsible for research and demonstration activities in the USDA that would be highly desirable.

The modest amount of funds required to establish the pilot project and demonstration is clearly justifiable.

Please let us sum up our attitude toward this legislation in this manner -- considering the budget necessary to operate the Department of Agriculture in the current Fiscal Year, this bill offers the best bargain before the House Agriculture Committee in a long time.

Sincerely,

Charles L. Frazier
Director
Washington Office

Mr. WEAVER. A broad coalition of scientific, conservation, consumer, and health groups are also supporting the bill.

Finally, and perhaps most importantly, the Agricultural Productivity Act is supported by farmers from all across the country. I have received more than 700 letters endorsing this bill, many of which were from farmers. I have one such letter, Mr. Chairman, which I believe is representative of the rest and which I would also like to submit for the record, from a Mr. Douglas Fields, from Withee, Wis.

[The letter referred to above follows:]

42

7-10-83

Douglas Fields
Rt. 2 Box 338
Withee, WI 54498

Rep. Jim Weaver
Rm. 1301 Longworth House Office Bldg.
Washington, D.C. 20515

Dear Representative Weaver,

    I am writing to thank you for your support of H.R. 2714,
the Agricultural Productivity Act. As a small farmer who is
concerned that the productivity of our soils may be dropping,
I find that it is very difficult to get the information that
I need to farm in a less energy intensive way. In other words,
I don't feel that I'm getting my tax moneys' worth of research
and information from the extension service.
    I believe that the relatively small amount that would be
spent under the Act has the potential to produce substantial
benefits to American agriculture. It would be money well spent
which is not always the case with our governments' expenditures
these days.
    Please do all that you can to get this bill moving and
before Congress as soon as possible. Thank you.

Sincerely,

RECEIVED

JUL 1 3 1983

WASHINGTON OFFICE

Mr. WEAVER. In closing, Mr. Chairman, I would simply like to say that the Agricultural Productivity Act is a modest but, I believe, extremely important piece of legislation. Although the USDA already has the authority to implement the research and extension projects mandated by this bill, it has chosen not to do so, in spite of the recommendations of many of its top experts and advisers.

The costs of this bill are minimal, while the benefits to American agriculture are substantial. I believe that the Agricultural Productivity Act will help guarantee that our farmers continue to have the land, water, and energy they need to maintain their preeminent role in food and fiber production.

Thank you very much, Mr. Chairman, for allowing me to testify.

Mr. BROWN. Thank you for an excellent statement, Mr. Weaver, and for continuing to focus attention on this extremely important issue in American agriculture.

As you pointed out in your statement, the Department probably has and probably will contend that it doesn't need this legislation because it could conduct the research and demonstration activities that you have set forth in your bill under existing authority.

Obviously they haven't done it and the purpose of the bill would be to encourage them to do so, but I would like to know how you calculated or came to the amounts that you have authorized in this legislation. In the event of its passage, I think this will help to clarify the way the funds ought to be expended.

Mr. WEAVER. Mr. Chairman, we discussed the project costs with various experts and scientists involved in agricultural research. It was agreed that we needed about $100,000 a year for the transition farms, and about $60,000 for the post-transition farms, so we came up with a general figure of around $2 million per year. This seemed to us to be the minimum amount needed, and we felt it wise in these days of fiscal prudence to keep it to the minimum amount needed.

Mr. BROWN. Mr. Roberts, do you have any questions?

Mr. ROBERTS. None, Mr. Chairman, except to welcome my colleague and friend to the subcommittee, and I appreciate having the benefit of his views and his statement. He has worked very diligently in behalf of this particular area of interest on his bill with the same perseverance as he runs laps in the House gymnasium.

Mr. WEAVER. That is a great compliment. However, I point to my crutches over there. I ran one too many times around the track.

Mr. ROBERTS. You will be on the track again, I am sure.

Mr. BROWN. Mr. Franklin.

Mr. FRANKLIN. No questions.

Mr. BROWN. Mr. Penny.

Mr. PENNY. I have no questions. I do want to commend Mr. Weaver for his testimony.

Mr. WEAVER. Thank you very much.

Mr. BROWN. Thank you very much. Do you have any knowledge of Senator Leahy's schedule?

Mr. WEAVER. Only that he is in an Intelligence Committee meeting and hopes to be here around 11 to 11:30.

Mr. BROWN. We will welcome him whenever he can show up.

Our next witness will be Dr. Clare Harris, Acting Administrator for the CSRS, Department of Agriculture, who will be accompanied by various colleagues.

Dr. Harris, we are pleased to have you here this morning. We have the text of your statement and if you wish to summarize or abbreviate it, why, that will be satisfactory. The full text will be inserted in the record at this point. If my information is correct, you have with you Dr. Charles Smith, whom we welcome, Dr. Ed Knipling, Ms. Jayne Maclean, and Mr. Rick Gomez. We are pleased to have all of you here this morning. You may proceed.

STATEMENT OF CLARE I. HARRIS, ACTING ADMINISTRATOR, CO-OPERATIVE STATE RESEARCH SERVICE, U.S. DEPARTMENT OF AGRICULTURE, ACCOMPANIED BY CHARLES SMITH, CSRS; ED KNIPLING, AGRICULTURAL RESEARCH SERVICE; JAYNE Mac-LEAN, NATIONAL AGRICULTURAL LIBRARY; AND RICK GOMEZ, EXTENSION SERVICE

Mr. HARRIS. Thank you, Mr. Chairman, members of the subcommittee. We appreciate the opportunity to participate in your hearing on H.R. 2714, the Agricultural Productivity Act of 1983.

I would state at the outset that the mechanisms already exist to permit the types of research and extension education programs advocated in the bill. State and USDA scientists are conducting research that provides a continually updated source of technological information to the Nation's farmers and ranchers through the cooperative extension services of the States.

These efforts apply to the concerns and problems of producers regardless of the farming system they choose to use. We are aware of the purposes of this bill and the attempt to address one objective of research on natural resources as set forth in section 1402(10)(D)(v) of the National Agricultural Research, Extension, and Teaching Policy Act of 1977, as amended in 1981, however, the Department opposes enactment of the bill.

Our Nation's publicly supported agricultural research and extension education system is unique. This system, which has worked so effectively for many decades, is a combination of a centrally directed Federal research institution within the U.S. Department of Agriculture, and strong, independent, yet responsive State institutions engaged in research and extension education programs addressing the needs of agriculture.

It is the primary responsibility of the Agricultural Research Service [ARS] to conduct research on problems that apply to agriculture on a regional or national scale. Primary factors are identified that limit production in agricultural systems regardless of size of operation or other unique characteristics and those concerns are addressed to the extent resources allow. The knowledge gained provides a scientific basis for developing new technologies to increase or maintain agricultural productivity.

The State agricultural experiment stations [SAES] respond to local, State, national, and international needs, covering all the agricultural sciences including soils, water, and other natural resources, plant an animal sciences, economics and the social sciences. The Cooperative State Research Service [CSRS] provides the linkage between Federal and State components of the cooperative agricultural research system.

Recent advances in computer technology have increased the capacities of Federal and State scientists to deal more effectively with complex agricultural production systems. Understanding the interrelationships among the variable parts of these systems permits simulation, analysis, and manipulation of farming practices in ways not previously possible. Research on basic properties of the biological and physical processes that make up these components, conducted under a wide range of soil, climate, and crop conditions, facilitates application of the results to specific problems.

Thus, by focusing on individual components and interactions among them, research findings can be integrated into production systems whether they are organic or conventional, small or commercial, major commodity or specialty crop. It should be noted that not only is this approach being used by both State and Federal scientists, it is consistent with the ARS program plan of 1983.

ARS and the SAES conduct research that supports alternative or organic farming systems. For example, in the area of biocontrol of pests, researchers are finding natural biological enemies of insects, diseases, and weeds, and are developing ways to manage them to increase productivity. In another area, conservation tillage, cultural and management practices are being developed that emphasize the use of crop residues to protect the soil from erosion and enhance nutrient status, waterholding capacity, and soil physical condition.

Extensive research is underway to develop improved germplasm that can be used for resistance in plants to diseases and insects, to develop plants that grow rapidly and competitively with weeds in altered ecological conditions produced by residues, direct seeding, and intercropping, for plants and associated organisms that fix large amounts of nitrogen, and for plant products having high nutritional value.

Some immediately applicable information from ongoing research covers crop rotation systems which, in numerous cases, have been underway for many years and several cycles of crops. Of the experiments having modern design, one example is the crop rotations at the Lancaster Experiment Station, in Wisconsin, that were instituted in 1967. These contain the essential plot treatments needed for comparisons of crop yield resulting from fertilizer and cropping sequence variables. The effects of different cropping systems develop over several years of time. Data of this type provide the basis for cropping systems models and for farmers' decisions as to the technologies they will adopt.

The Cooperative Extension System is structured to be responsive to the needs of people because the majority of its programs address local and/or State problems as determined by various citizens advisory boards. The resulting agricultural programs encompass crop and animal production and marketing in all their aspects.

Generally, these educational programs are not differentiated because of use of synthetic chemicals or natural chemicals. However, many program components are applicable to both the traditional—with synthetic chemicals—and the alternative systems of agricultural production.

Extension programs emphasize the conservation of natural and non-renewable resources and the protection of the environment through appropriate production practices. Crop production programs include the following: Selection of varieties resistant to diseases and other pests; adaptation of varieties to the environment; value of soil organic matter and its conservation, maintenance, or increase; pest monitoring and control through integrated pest management [IPM] systems; irrigation and water use to minimize environmental pollution; and others.

Gardening publications include topics on composting, soil amendments, and use of manures and other organic materials. Pest identification is included, although pest control by use of synthetic chemicals is usually presented in separate fact sheets.

The State universities provide education programs for the training of most of the future agricultural scientists for the research, extension, and teaching professions. Therefore, it is significant to the issues and problems associated with alternative farming systems that several universities have developed courses and have graduate students in these areas of emphasis.

Special programs have been organized such as a workshop in February 1983 on management alternatives for biological farming, a combined effort of the Iowa Agricultural Experiment Station, Cooperative Extension Service, ARS, and certain other Federal agencies. This successful workshop involved farmers and other private enterpreneurs, biologists, researchers, and educators. A course in this area of emphasis offered in the agronomy department at Iowa State University last year, however, did not have enough registrants to permit it to be taught

The National Agricultural Library's [NAL] involvement in providing information on the various aspects of alternative agriculture or organic farming spans several years. Along with the extension service, and often in cooperation with it, NAL has been a major resource for the agricultural community. The information NAL relays to inquirers is often based on the published research findings of the ARS, SAES, and CSRS.

NAL publishes many bibliographies on topics of current interest. The Quick Bibliography series, based on searches of NAL's automated bibliographic database, Agricola, has been an important vehicle. There are over 16 titles relating directly to resource conserving crop production systems including, for example: "Double Cropping and Inter-planting;" "Composts and Composting of Organic Wastes;" "Organic Farming and Gardening;" "Minimum/Zero/ Conservation Tillage;" "Nitrogen Fixation in Soybeans;" "Allelopathy—the harmful effects of chemicals produced by one plant upon another—Cropping Systems;" "Integrated Pest Management;" and others.

Current activities of NAL include selection of published materials for purchase, to augment the collection of literature relating to all the alternative approaches to agriculture. They also include continuing to provide information in response to reference inquiries, and to fulfill special needs for literature searches on particular topics.

An example of the latter was the information package sent to North Carolina State University, which has a team working under a cooperative agreement with CSRS on evaluating the applicability of the alternative farming literature to current issues and concerns. Also, a bibliography is being developed by NAL on crop rotations with legumes, for the North Carolina team, which will eventually emerge as a Quick Bibliography for general distribution.

Although many more examples of applicable research and education programs could be cited, I will now make some comments more specific to the bill being considered. We have identified the following problems with H.R. 2714. Enactment of the bill could require the Federal and State extension services to engage in certain activities requiring new programs that are duplicative and unnecessarily costly.

Section 5 provides for 12 pilot farms utilizing four different management systems to be converted to the alternative non-chemical systems. The conditions of selection, the subsequent treatments, and small sample size and the omission of conventional systems make the statistical basis weak for needed comparisons. This means that after the projects are completed it would be difficult, if not impossible, to have much confidence that the results have real meaning.

The bill as written is restrictive, leaving the scientists and onsite research managers, who are located where the research would be conducted, little opportunity to design the studies in ways to produce more meaningful results in responding to the objectives and problem needs.

For example, although large diversity in farm size, soil type, and climate characteristics are specified for farm selection in section 5, which could be thought to be an advantage by some, these characteristics would dramatically complicate the research and could likely result in data of minimum value.

It is specified the projects shall extend for a 5-year period. This time frame is much too short for the anticipated changes to be expressed. With the first year specified as a data base establishment year, only four remain for measurement of effects. Then, if a 4-year crop rotation is employed, for example, only one cycle could be completed in that 4 years, and biased data would result. The bias would likely be unfavorable to the alternative farming system.

If it is necessary to study whole farm systems, it must be recognized that the combinations of logical choices by farmers who might use either conventional or alternate farming systems are many. This complicates the research and the interpretation of data. Subsequently, unless the research utilizes sound statistical procedure, the application of conclusions to real world conditions can be questionable.

This application is influenced to the extreme by a farmer's own preference, his financial flexibility, the characteristics of available soil and water resources, and the kind of farming system to be utilized. Problems of changing farming systems, however, can and are being researched in carefully planned interdisciplinary projects.

Let me emphasize that the research and extension education arms of USDA and the cooperating State institutions are very concerned about the high cost of production faced by farmers. We are committed to continuing research and education activities to address the problems of all farmers. To combine all the variables comprising a farming system is an imposing task. Not only is it difficult and expensive, only one system of many possible options would be evaluated in each unit as described in this bill.

In summary, while we are sympathetic to the purposes of H.R. 2714, we are opposed to this legislation because much of this work is currently underway; the bill would impose overly restrictive requirements on the conduct of such research and the costs are excessive.

Mr. Chairman, this completes my prepared statement. I will be pleased to respond to questions or refer them to our resource scientists from CSRS, ARS, ES, and NAL who have accompanied me.

Mr. BROWN. Thank you very much, Dr. Harris, for your testimony.

Just a brief question; then I will turn to my colleagues.

Dr. Harris, you mentioned on page 4 an example which you cite as an experiment having modern design on crop rotation at the Lancaster Experiment Station in Wisconsin. I don't want any further elaboration on that, but I am familiar with a fairly substantial number of farmers who are using organic methods in the area of Lancaster, Pa., which is what struck my notice.

I wonder if you have participated in, or the Department has, or know of any research on the cost-effectiveness of the type of farming that the Amish farmers are doing up there in Pennsylvania, which I understand is largely based upon practices of maybe 100 or 200 years ago, largely does not use mechanical or chemical inputs, and should be a classic case for comparison between organic and nonorganic farming?

Mr. HARRIS. That is certainly a good example of some continuing work in that area. I am personally not familiar whether we have any work in that or not.

Mr. SMITH. I, too, would have to defer an answer on that and suggest that we would need to pose that question to our colleagues at Pennsylvania State University. I suspect studies have been conducted but do not have the information on them.

Mr. BROWN. If anything has been published, I am sure Ms. MacLean would have it somewhere.

Ms. MACLEAN. Somewhere.

Mr. BROWN. Maybe you could look and see if there is anything that has been published on that, and I would appreciate it if some inquiry could be made to the Pennsylvania Extension Station, and see if they have anything in terms of comparison of that farming system to others.

The general mystique is that despite their antiquated ways, that they have profitable farming operations. That could be due to a lot of different factors. They have very good land and water resources there and cheap labor and a lot of other things that may not be duplicated in other farms. But it is pertinent to the subject of this bill and would be interesting information.

[The information follows:]

Response to Congressman Brown's request for information about organic farms near Lancaster, Pa.

The most comprehensive study on a largely "organic" farm in Pennsylvania is one conducted cooperatively by the Pennsylvania Agricultural Experiment Station and the Rodale Research Center on a farm adjacent to the Rodale Research Center, operated by a Mennonite family. The broad report including an economic analysis was participated in by Dr. Patrick Madden, Pennsylvania State University, and others. This report was referred to, we believe, by Dr. Richard Harwood in his testimony at the August 3 hearings.

An additional study of that farm is the basis for a thesis by Mr. Victor Wegrzyn, a student of Dr. Dale Baker, Agronomy Department, Pennsylvania State University. Also, Dr. Pat Madden served on the thesis and examining committee. The thesis evaluates in a comprehensive way the nitrogen (N) balance and the N cycling that exists on the farm. He also evaluated the management practices considering the questions of whether adequate fertility was achieved with the labor-intensive farming operation, whether weed control is adequate without herbicides, adequacy of machinery, and other factors. The thesis is completed with final typing and reproduction still to be accomplished. Incidentally Mr. Wegrzyn was involved in the initial phases of the Kutztown farm study and in the economic evaluation.

Mr. BROWN. Mr. Roberts.

Mr. ROBERTS. Yes, Mr. Chairman.

On page 3 of your statement, Dr. Harris, the bottom of the page, you state, "* * * research findings can be integrated into production systems whether they are organic or conventional, small or commercial, major commodity or specialty crop."

Am I correct in using a layman's term here that your approach is that when we are talking about organic agriculture or conventional that you are trying to make the point this is not an either/or kind of situation but more of a partnership perhaps left up to what makes sense to that individual farmer?

Mr. HARRIS. Yes, sir. I think that is what has been evolving. When the discussions first began, there was more of a polarization. I think we have seen movement toward more of a dialog and looking at the total system in which the individual farmer or rancher will have to make his own decisions to those practices that make sense for that particular situation.

Mr. ROBERTS. On page 7, you indicate: "The bill as written is restrictive, leaving the scientists and onsite research managers, who are located where the research would be conducted, little opportunity to design the studies in ways to produce more meaningful results * * *" Then you go on and you indicate the amount of diversity that we have in agriculture today.

And then you go on and say something that I certainly agree with, on page 8, that the application of whatever kind of farming is involved here is up to the individual producer.

I never thought anybody in Washington would actually say that, but I would hope that this would be the case, and that what makes sense to him in terms of his economic situation is the final key.

Would you care to amplify a little bit on the bill as written in terms of being restrictive? Then I will ask this question—hopefully you will have time to respond—if, in fact, it is restrictive and not based on, say, scientific data that is going to work on behalf of the individual producers, would you be willing to work with the subcommittee to come up with something that would not be restrictive?

Mr. HARRIS. In terms of the details of the restrictiveness of the bill, I would like to turn to Dr. Smith. He has worked very closely with this and I think he is prepared to comment on that issue.

Mr. SMITH. The bill specifies the number of farms to be subjected to the transition treatments as well as to specify that certain numbers will be reserved for livestock-based farms and others for grain-based farms and vegetable crops and fruit crops. In addition to this, it specifies a number of the restrictions that would be put on the kinds of treatments that would be imposed, for example, it says imposition of nonchemical practices—which could lead to misinformation and could be very difficult to impose in all cases. It specifies a large number of observations to be made, measurements to be made, in establishing the base year data.

I believe we have difficulty sitting here to determine the number and kind of observations that would be needed to establish a solid data base for conditions that would be studied as variables that would exist in different parts of the country. It is examples like this that present a problem in having what we would like as some flexibility to make the information more applicable once it were obtained. I realize it does not say you cannot make more measurements than what are indicated.

Mr. ROBERTS. I have a personal prejudice, to be quite frank with you, and it seems to me that in hearings before this subcommittee, whether we have been talking about no till or organic farming or integrated management, we always seem to get into the business of either/or polarization. I know in the hearings we just had in Berkeley, the chairman made a point to the witnesses that we are going to have to get these producer groups more interested in this kind of movement on a gradual basis as we go forward together and in behalf of the producer.

I know when he is going through a very, very difficult time, if you set up a model farm or an experiment or whatever, I think the producer is sort of used as an underwriter by the Federal Government. And that is fine for Joe over here. But during my time of economic hardship, I just simply cannot afford to do this, and you find a lot of resistance.

I think perhaps a better way to go is the more flexible approach, an integrated approach, because most farmers are in agreement with the stated goals of the things we have been talking about.

With that editorial, Mr. Chairman, I have no more questions.

Mr. BROWN. Thank you.

Mr. Penny.

Mr. PENNY. I have no questions.

Mr. BROWN. Mr. Gunderson.

Mr. GUNDERSON. Thank you, Mr. Chairman.

I must admit some practical prejudice listening to your testimony when you brought up the Lancaster, Wis. experiment in the rotation of crops. That happens to be in my district.

I thought for the record we would all benefit if you would expand upon that for a bit as to what has been going on there, your results and the projected research that you see down the road in that area.

Mr. HARRIS. I would like to have Dr. Smith respond.

Mr. SMITH. As a matter of fact, I was on the Lancaster farm last week at a meeting of the North Central Regional Research Committee, it No. 157. That is a research group made up of scientists from Wisconsin, Iowa, Minnesota, Illinois, and Indiana who are working with primary focus on the Lancaster research center, because it represents soils and topography and general management systems that are very characteristic of large areas of each one of those States.

They dedicate certain of their scientists' time to work on that station and to work on research in their own States that would apply. These crop rotations I am talking about were set up in the sixties and, since that time, they have had variables of fertilizer including a rate of zero, they also include legumes in the rotation for different lengths of time, and different crop sequences; for example, corn following soybeans, corn following alfalfa. The data that have been accumulated over a period of years are extremely interesting.

If one utilizes the corn yield information in the first year following a legume, the yield from zero nitrogen fertilizer—this is following a legume—is within 4 to 14 bushels of the highest yield that they obtained with higher rates of fertilization.

These experiments are providing a good basis for scientists to take a look at some of the soil changes that have occurred, and in each year there are more activities designed to take advantage of that. This also includes looking at the livestock component. There are pasture experiments, grazing experiments; they are all looking at the total picture.

It is not, though, I would hasten to add, being looked at as a total farm enterprise. It is being looked at to obtain data on the different segments that hopefully can be put into a model which will describe a management system that various people could adopt to their own situation.

Mr. BROWN. Would you yield?

Mr. GUNDERSON. Yes.

Mr. BROWN. I agree with them as to the interest or the importance of this particular type of research, and I would like to inquire of Dr. Smith if there might be a current report on that research which we could include in the subcommittee record of this hearing?

Mr. SMITH. Yes; I could provide that for you.

Mr. BROWN. We would appreciate it if you would, and it will be included in the record as a part of the hearing.

[The information follows:]

Response to Congressman Brown's request for a current report of progress on the crop sequence/rotation research at Lancaster, Wisconsin:

The attached report was prepared for a research meeting so does not contain as much information for the lay reader. Some additional information is included here, and further interpretation will be provided if requested.

The influence of different sequences of crops in long-term rotations on crop yield and quality, and on changes in the productivity of nonglaciated prairie soils, is being researched at the Wisconsin Agricultural Experiment Station at Lancaster with participation of scientists from Wisconsin, Illinois, Iowa, Indiana and Minnesota. Results after 16 years show the substitution options between nitrogen (N) fertilizer and Rhizobium-produced N by legumes. This information is directly applicable to farming systems that use legumes and livestock manure as N sources rather than commercially manufactured fertilizer. The influence of low rates of N fertilizer is measured when it is applied to corn, and the long-term affects on soil properties are expressed and are being evaluated.

Comparisons can be made between growing corn each year and interrupting that sequence with legume meadow, with oats, or with soybeans. For a specific example, in 1982, corn after one year of legumes yielded 148 bu. per acre which was equivalent to continuous corn fertilized at the rate of 100 lb. N per acre; however, N fertilizer applied to first-year corn returned an additional $6 in corn for each $1 invested in N. Two years of legumes plus N from manure provided enough N for a corn yield of 160 bu. per acre, followed, however, by a drop of 40 bu. per acre for second year corn unless N fertilizer was added. These experiments are providing useful soil management information for grain and hay production problems in crop rotation systems.

Many experiments similar to this one are being conducted at experiment stations across the country, with some having been underway for many decades. Many features of these are essentially the same as ones labeled "transition experiments" by some, whereby "conventional" systems are being changed to "organic". Soil and crop scientists recognize and teach the merits of crop rotations and the effectiveness of nitrogen from legumes and manure. A major problem is that essentially all of the manure and waste is already being used, and with current technology the production of legumes for significant nitrogen production means hay, and that necessitates a livestock operation. Through research we hope to develop technologies to produce N more efficiently by plant/soil associations and by-pass the hay crop for those who do not need it.

[The report, 1977–82 Crop Sequence experiment progress report (Illinois, Iowa, Minnesota, and Wisconsin) (Six years of a modified crop sequence study based upon a previous 10 year crop sequence study conducted 1967–76) is held in the committee files.]

Mr. GUNDERSON. If I recall, last year—I can be corrected—the organic farming bill that was before this subcommittee really called for a reallocation of funds within the present authorization or appropriation for the Department. The bill before us this year calls for new funding of $2.1 million annually.

Does the Department have a preference of one type of funding versus the other, or not? Have you not discussed that issue? Last year's bill was defeated. That was only a reallocation of funds. This year, we have a bill that is calling not for reallocation of funds but new dollars. I am not sure that stands a better chance of success or worse chance of success.

Any comments on that?

Mr. HARRIS. The research budgets for the Department are considered as a whole as they go before the Secretary and OMB. So I am not sure in the final analysis if it makes much difference or not.

There is some competition regardless if it is one authority or several authorities.

Mr. GUNDERSON. Probably the one problem that I think many people see when they look at the testimony that you have given, the present Department operation, whether you be for it or against the concept of organic farming, is that it is rather disbursed, it is all over the board, and your testimony verifies that.

Is there any kind of coordinating mechanism or person or agency within the Department to bring together all of the various things that are done in the area of organic farming? I am not ready to endorse it or condemn it myself, but I do see a rather diverse set of responsibilities, listening to your testimony and the examples you give.

How does the average farmer in my district have any idea where to turn in the Department to get some kind of assistance?

Mr. HARRIS. We do have a focal point in the Department where all requests for information on organic farming are sent. Dr. Charles Smith is the coordinator for USDA on organic farming. He has representatives from the other research and education agencies as a committee that work with him to provide this kind of coordination in carrying out the program.

Mr. GUNDERSON. Thank you, Mr. Chairman.

Mr. BROWN. Mr. Evans.

Mr. EVANS of Iowa. No questions.

Mr. BROWN. Mr. Franklin.

Mr. FRANKLIN. No questions.

Mr. BROWN. I am going to call on Mr. Weaver and ask him if he would care to address any questions to the witnesses.

Mr. WEAVER. Mr. Chairman, I appreciate that privilege very much, and I thank the committee. If they would give me a minute or two, I would like that very much.

Mr. BROWN. Take 5.

Mr. WEAVER. The questions of the gentleman from Kansas, Mr. Roberts, I think were particularly interesting, as well as Mr. Gunderson's. It is clear that we are agreed on some things—integration of techniques is essential no question about it. We must study whatever is cost effective; that is, whatever produces the best product most economically. That is all we are after. It is not an either/or thing any more, and it shouldn't be. We have to rely on all forms of agricultural production.

But I have to tell our witness that we don't grow crops in a computer; we grow them on a farm. And this bill sets up case studies.

Now, most farmers, the ones I knew as a boy in Iowa and South Dakota and in Missouri, were "show me" people; they wanted to see it done. That is what this bill does. It sees it done.

Mr. BROWN. What is your question, Mr. Weaver?

Mr. WEAVER. The question is this: the organic farming research that our witnesses talked about here are being done in a piecemeal fashion, which is bad enough. But doesn't your Agricultural Research Service program plan, 1984 to 1990 say that you are cutting back on integration of alternative systems from $7.7 million, to $1.7 million, a 78-percent reduction?

Mr. HARRIS. This is a part of the Agricultural Research Service plan. I would like to refer that to Mr. Knipling.

Mr. KNIPLING. Yes, Mr. Weaver.

I might give a little background about the program plan. I think those particular situations you cited may be somewhat misleading and out of context. The Agricultural Research Service is in fact giv ng significantly increased emphasis to systems-type research. The plan calls for an increase of $9 million for integrated systems research. In fact, we have for the first time identified systems as a component of the research program of equal status and stature along with soil science, plant science, animal science and so forth.

The concept, already stated by Dr. Harris is that we work on systems across a broad spectrum, a continuum, and not on a specific type of farming system or specific alternative, per se. We are not projecting resources into organic farming——

Mr. WEAVER. You are cutting the 6.2, alternative systems, category by $6 million, a 78-percent reduction; is that correct?

Mr. KNIPLING. There was no funding for the organic farming system category per se, in the past, and ARS has not projected any in the future, for organic farming systems per se.

Mr. WEAVER. UAB has recommended you do that, but you are not; is that correct?

Let me ask you one other question. Did you take Dr. Youngberg's place? Mr. Gunderson asked if there was somebody who was the focal point of organic farming activities at USDA. If you remember we did have somebody there until September 1982. Dr. Youngberg was the person. He was the only person in the Department of Agriculture and he was only on half time when he was fired or let go.

Now, have you been put in to take Dr. Youngberg's place, and this is your sole responsibility, or do you have other duties, sir? Doctor, is it you or Dr. Smith?

Mr. KNIPLING. That is not my responsibility, no.

Mr. WEAVER. Is Dr. Smith taking——

Mr. KNIPLING. Dr. Smith is the lead contact person for the Department, yes.

Mr. HARRIS. The responsibilities that Dr. Youngberg had carried out for the Department before are assigned to Dr. Charles Smith. He is the coordinator. But working with him, we have representatives from ARS and the Extension Service and the National Agricultural Library. They are providing that.

Mr. WEAVER. Does Dr. Smith do anything but be the focal point?

Mr. HARRIS. Yes, sir; he does more than that.

Mr. WEAVER. What would those things be?

Mr. HARRIS. He carries out the program responsibilities for soil science in CSRS.

Mr. WEAVER. He has a few other duties?

Mr. HARRIS. Yes, sir.

Mr. WEAVER. About how much of his time is taken up?

Mr. HARRIS. Twenty percent of his time is formally assigned to organic farming.

Mr. WEAVER. Excellent.

Mr. HARRIS. Actually, it turns out to be more than that.

Mr. WEAVER. I will conclude my questions, Mr. Chairman, by citing what I think is most penetrating testimony for the need for this bill. It is contained on the botton line of page 5 of Dr. Harris's testimony, and it demonstrates the extreme need for this particular bill. It reveals that a course in this area of emphasis, biological farming, was offered in the agronomy department at Iowa State University last year, and did not have enough registrants to permit it to be taught. In other words, the whole thrust of our farm culture for the young people coming into farming today is toward capital, and energy intensive practices. But these young people are coming into farming at a time when energy is becoming more expensive—20 years from now we may not even have the oil to produce our food. It is unfortunate that these people who come in the Iowa State University are not even intrigued enough to sign up for this course.

I think we need to bolster the concepts set forth in these case studies, and this bill would do that.

Thank you.

Mr. BROWN. Thank you, Mr. Weaver.

Dr. Harris, there is a strong suspicion among some people that despite the good work which is being done in the Department, which is applicable to integrated farming systems, that there is a strongly held desire not to focus on the concept of organic or unconventional farming, because of perhaps industry objections or other things of that sort.

I tend to share that view, as a matter of fact, although I don't get quite as vigorous in fighting it as I might, as Mr. Weaver does.

But I would ask you to comment as to whether or not there hasn't been a real diminution in the focus in the Department on the concept of organic farming or unconventional farming without derogating the fact you have continued many programs which are applicable to that.

Can you answer that without getting embarrassed too much?

Mr. HARRIS. I don't think there has been a diminution. We don't have a solid plan that we can point to and say this is our organic farming plan, but we have followed the position that there are many of our programs that do have direct application to the organic farming kinds of interests. And we, I think, are involved in more of a systems approach to the needs of agriculture. And we do have many competing demands on our research programs.

The recommendations from the organic farming report have to be viewed along with the recommendations from many other reports. We have soil and water conservation, new biotechnologies, integrated pest management; there is a whole range of things that we have to look at alongside the recommendations from the organic farming report. And I think we have a commitment to do that. And, as Dr. Knipling pointed out, ARS has put major emphasis on a systems approach to the needs of agriculture.

So I think that these things are consistent with trying to meet the needs that are described in the organic farming arena along with those of other arenas.

Mr. BROWN. I think we can accept that all you have said is true. But you haven't answered my question.

You do not feel that the focus that existed 2 or 3 years ago on organic farming, which resulted in a rather good report—which I commend, and I think most observers commend it—which included a sharply defined focus with some staff at least and a coordinating mechanism that could be easily identified—you don't feel that the elimination of all of these things represents any diminution in, we will say, the visibility of organic farming within the Department?

Mr. HARRIS. The structure has changed as to how we approach this; there is no question about that. We have replaced the coordinating mechanism through alternative means by assigning about 20 percent of each of four scientists time, and it is part of the overall change in the Department of our staffing and organizational structure. So we are attempting to maintain that focus in the Department.

Mr. BROWN. Dr. Smith, are you itching to say something?

Mr. SMITH. A comment I would like to make that I believe relates to your question.

In the last 2 years' time—first off, I might add that prior to being assigned this current responsibility of contact person or coordinating within USDA, I did work with Dr. Youngberg on the previous coordinating committee that was in existence, so I had some awareness of these activities as well as when I was in the North Dakota Soils Department.

In the last 2 years, in various meetings—in the course of my regular job I meet with the heads of crops and soils departments in all parts of the country, and along with regional planning committees in the West. The course of conversation and plans pertaining to research have, in my opinion, dramatically changed in relation to taking a look at what is happening in the biological system in the soil as contrasted with what is happening in the strictly chemical system in the soil. This changed emphasis, I believe, is a positive thing with much greater interest. For example, one of the department heads said that they were going to replace a retired professor with one to work primarily on the influences of crop rotations and legumes on characteristics of the soil and on productivity.

To me, this is a real positive thing. I do not see this as being a decrease. I think the actual out-in-the-country interest is increasing.

Mr. BROWN. Well, Dr. Smith, I appreciate that. I think it is entirely conceivable that you are doing more significant research applicable to organic farming today than you were 3 years ago—and I commend you for it, if you are. And I assume that you are doing it because it is scientifically justifiable.

But you know, as well as I do, there are people in the Department, as well as people in the Congress, that don't like to expose evidence or initiatives that say we should eat less meat or eat less eggs or eat less wheat or use less chemicals or use less energy. And I respect these people, many of whom are good friends of mine.

But I want to know if there is an undue influence from those kinds of people, just as they want to know if there is an undue influence from people like me and Mr. Weaver. I think that is quite reasonable.

Does that elicit any comments? Do you want to pinpoint any of those people over there?

Mr. HARRIS. I think the main point that we are trying to make is that we do want to provide the best alternatives for American farmers and ranchers, and whatever category you want to put the practices under, I think we want to make them available.

Mr. BROWN. Fine.

Ms. MacLean, just one last query. You are not under restrictions over at the Library as to whether you continue to compile bibliographies and packages of material that would meet the requests of any inquiry, are you?

Ms. MacLEAN. I am encouraged to do so.

Mr. BROWN. Thank you.

I thank you all for your testimony. We appreciate it very much.

Our next witness is a panel of Dr. Youngberg and Mr. Thompson, and I invite them to come to the witness table.

I might say that we have Senator Leahy on our list of witnesses. Without objection, Senator Leahy's testimony will be included at the beginning of the hearing, then, as the first witness.

I was going to ask you gentlemen to indulge me to allow him to supersede you if he came in. That won't be necessary.

Dr. Youngberg, you may proceed with your testimony.

STATEMENT OF I. GARTH YOUNGBERG, EXECUTIVE DIRECTOR, INSTITUTE FOR ALTERNATIVE AGRICULTURE

Mr. YOUNGBERG. Mr. Chairman and members of the subcommittee, I am Garth Youngberg, executive director of the Institute for Alternative Agriculture, a private, nonprofit agricultural research and education institute with offices in Greenbelt, Md. The institute seeks to advance, through the development and support of educational programs and scientific investigations, systems of food and fiber production that are economically profitable, resource conserving, environmentally sound, and sustainable in the long term.

The Institute for Alternative Agriculture is governed by a nine-member grassroots board of directors consisting of several top, large-scale, U.S. organic farmers, one alternative agriculture industry representative, a county extension agent, an organic foods wholesaler, and a representative of the State and regional organic producer associations.

I have attached a list of the board members and officers for your information. I have also attached a copy of the institute's statement of philosophy and purpose. Because the institute is relatively new—its organizational board meeting was held on March 2, 1983—I thought this information might be of interest to the subcommittee. The institute is grateful to the subcommittee for the opportunity to testify on the Agricultural Productivity Act of 1983.

Throughout this statement, the words alternative, biological, and organic will be used interchangeably to refer to those low energy, resource conserving, environmentally sound and sustainable systems of farming which were defined in the 1980 USDA Report and Recommendations on Organic Farming. According to that report: "Organic farming is a production system which avoids or largely excludes the use of synthetically compounded fertilizers, pesticides, growth regulators, and livestock feed additives. To the maximum extent feasible, organic farming systems rely upon crop rotations, crop residues, animal manures, legumes, green manures, off-farm organic wastes, mechanical cultivation, mineral-bearing rocks, and aspects of biological pest control to maintain soil productivity and tilth, to supply plant nutrients, and to control insects, weeds, and other pests." We are attracted to this definition, in part, because of its emphasis on the total farm operation as an integrated, interactive system.

Because the general intent of H.R. 2714 is to develop sound educational and research programs in the area of alternative agriculture, the institute is supportive of this proposed legislation. We believe it addresses a number of important needs and concerns which I will discuss briefly.

No. 1, Misinformation and Negative Symbolism: Alternative farming systems continue to be overlooked by most conventional agriculturalists, in part because of the lack of credible information or misinformation on these farming systems. As our statement of purpose indicates, many conventional agricultural scientists and farmers continue to believe that: "* * * it is only hippies, health food faddists, and displaced urbanites who practice alternative agriculture. These well-meaning but misguided individuals are viewed as practicing their primitive, labor-intensive, agricultural crafts on small plots and with minimal success."

A recent cartoon by Lynn Johnston that appeared in the Washington Post on July 21, entitled "For Better or For Worse" illustrates the way in which these negative and mistaken images continue to be reinforced. In the cartoon, an older man was shown explaining various agronomic crops to a child. Near the end of the cartoon, the child inquired about a particularly weedy field. The older man explained that the field was full of weeds because, they're farmin' organic.

We believe that scientifically credible educational and research programs provide one of the most important vehicles for correcting these kinds of unfortunate and misleading stereotypes. In this regard, it is important that at least some of these research and education programs be conducted by so-called establishment scientists and institutions. Clearly, most conventional farmers continue to be heavily influenced by the research and education agendas of the USDA, the land-grant colleges and universities, and the educational and extension services associated with these institutions.

To its credit, H.R. 2714 would make it possible for some of these institutions to be involved in the development of modest programs of research and education on biological farming systems. Such involvement would likely have at least three positive effects.

First, those scientists and educators who would participate in these researches would likely develop a more thorough understanding of, and appreciation for, the potential of alternative farming systems.

Second, it would be reassuring to those conventional farmers who may be searching for these kinds of technologies to know that their local universities and extension services were involved in alternative agricultural research and education activities.

Finally, these kinds of activities would help to begin correcting the erroneous perceptions of alternative agriculture currently held by many agricultural scientists, conventional farmers, consumers, and even cartoonists.

No. 2, Informational Needs: Increasingly, biological farmers who may simply wish to improve their production systems, and conventional farmers who are interested in developing alternative farming systems, are beginning to seek out reliable information on biological farming. For example, roughly one-half of the attendees at the highly successful 1981 and 1982 alternative agriculture field days at the University of Nebraska were conventional farmers. These farmers were interested in learning how legume-based crop rotations, green manure crops, improved manure and crop residue management, recycling technologies, and more diversified farming systems, might help to reduce the rising costs of production, and control soil erosion and the pollution of underground water supplies caused in part by excessive fertilization, pesticide use and monocultural cropping systems.

In the short time that the institute has been in operation, we have received scores of inquiries about these same kinds of technologies and concerns. Farmers are particularly interested in the economic benefits and costs associated with alternative agricultural production technologies.

While a substantial amount of relevant information in this area does exist, it is scattered and incomplete. Much of it also may be dated due to various technological advances. Section 4 of this proposed legislation directly addresses the growing need to make this information available to American farmers whether they be organic or conventional practitioners.

No. 3, Research Opportunities and Needs: Over the past several years, it has become increasingly clear that a growing number of agricultural scientists are motivated to conduct research on alternative farming systems. The following selected review of several recent scientific events and activities illustrates and underscores this trend.

The 1981 annual meeting of the American Society of Agronomy sponsored and organized a full-day symposium entitled "Organic Farming: Current Technology and Its Role in a Sustainable Agriculture." The ASA will publish these papers in a special symposium book this fall.

Within the past 15 months, scientists at Iowa State University have hosted and organized two important conferences related to alternative agriculture. The two following proceedings were published as a result of these conferences: "Midwest Agricultural Interfaces with Fish and Wildlife Resources Workshop," June 1 and 2, 1982; "Management Alternatives for Biological Farming Workshop," February 1, 1983.

At last year's biennial research conference of the International Federation of Organic Agriculture Movements—IFOAM—some 40 research papers on alternative agriculture were delivered. Approximately 15 of these papers were prepared by USDA and land-grant university scientists.

In March 1983, the Swedish Agricultural University was cohost for a 3-day international symposium held to develop a research and education plan on alternative agriculture for the Nordic countries—Sweden, Norway, Denmark, and Finland.

This fall, North Carolina State University will begin offering a regular course entitled "Alternative Agricultural Systems." One of the major topics earlier this summer at Virginia Tech University's annual policy conference was alternative agriculture. This past winter quarter, the University of Minnesota offered, on a trial basis, a credit course entitled "Organic Farming."

The recently published Agricultural Research Service program plan called for the development of "alternative agricultural systems, including those of small scale, that are less dependent upon nonrenewable resources and that are productive, efficient, and sustainable in the long term." The plan went on to explain that small farmers and organic farmers "* * * have some needs that are recognized but are not met through current research programs."

The University of Nebraska's Institute of Agricultural and Natural Resources will soon issue a formal position paper on alternative agricultural research and education priorities.

Clearly, there is no dearth of scientific interest in alternative agriculture. Indeed, the opportunity for assembling top scientists to conduct the research envisaged in this legislation is excellent. In this regard, H.R. 2714 could provide an important catalyst for the development of interdisciplinary systems-oriented research on biological agriculture.

The need for conducting research and education programs in the area of alternative agriculture has been documented in a number of scientific studies and reports. For example: U.S. Department of Agriculture, 1980, "Report and Recommendations on Organic Farming," U.S. Government Printing Office, Washington, D.C.; American Society of Agronomy, 1981, Special Symposium on "Organic Farming: Current Technology and its Role in a Sustainable

Agriculture," In press: Elm Farm Research Centre and International Federation of Organic Agriculture Movements, 1983, "Research Projects in Biological Agriculture in Western Europe and the United States," Elm Farm Research Centre, Report No. 2, Great Britain.

In varying degrees, these and other studies and reports have emphasized the need to: Review and make available scientific literature of relevance to biological agriculture; survey and document successful biological farms; conduct comparative studies of conventional and biological farms; and carry-out research on the conversion of conventional farms to biological systems of production. H.R. 2714 directly addresses these scientifically documented needs.

At least two additional positive aspects of H.R. 2714 deserve special comment. First, this legislation correctly provides for both public and private institutional involvement in the conduct of the prescribed research—section 8. We believe that the participation of a variety of both public and private agricultural research and education institutions will contribute to the need for perspective, objectivity, and legitimacy during the execution and reporting of the proposed research.

Second, the interdisciplinary aspects of the information study—section 4—and the pilot research projects—section 5—are also appropriate and necessary.

Given the agronomic, economic, social, and policy complexities of alternative agriculture, a broad range of disciplines, working together, affords the best hope for understanding and improving biological farming systems.

In closing, Mr. Chairman, we would urge you to push for the adoption of H.R. 2714. This bill could help our Nation's farmers—all farmers—begin to wean themselves away from their heavy dependence upon increasingly expensive fossil fuel-based production inputs. In this sense, this legislation directly addresses many of the needs of a broad cross-section of American agriculture: Lower operating costs, resource conservation, environmental protection and long-term sustainable food production. We urge the subcommittee to continue working for these goals.

[The attachments follow:]

INSTITUTE FOR ALTERNATIVE AGRICULTURE, Inc.
9200 EDMONSTON ROAD SUITE 117
GREENBELT MARYLAND 20770
301/441 8777

Dr. I. Garth Youngberg
Executive Director

Mrs. Sarah C. Byler
Program Assistant

BOARD OF DIRECTORS

Mr. Delmar Akerlund   402/721-0589
Akerlund Farm Biological Enterprises
Route 1, Box 348
Valley, Nebraska 68064

Mr. Joseph Dunsmoor Secretary/Treasurer   301/595-5151
Organic Farms, Inc
10714 Hanna Street
Beltsville, Maryland 20705

Mr. Thomas B. Harding, Jr., President   215/759-5911
Progressive Agri-Systems, Inc.
201 Center Street
Stockertown, Pennsylvania 18083

Mr. William K. Kruesi   802/457-2664
The Extension Service
University of Vermont
Town Hall, 31 The Green
Woodstock, Vermont 05091

Mr. Earl Lawrence, Vice-President   703/483-1697
Route 5, Box 467
Martinsville, Virginia 24112

Mr. Jim Lukens   913/738-3866
Kansas Organic Producers, Inc.
Route 3
Beloit, Kansas 67420

Mrs. Lawrence M. C. Smith   207/865-3336
Wolfe' Neck Farm
Freeport Maine 04032
          and
3460 School House Lane   215/438-0008
Germantown
Philadelphia, Pennsylvania 19144

Ms. Barbara Snyder   503/236-5853
1712 Southeast 33rd
Portland, Oregon 97214

Mr. Richard Thompson   515/432-1560
Route 2, Box 132
Boone, Iowa 50036

CONTRIBUTIONS TO THE INSTITUTE ARE TAX DEDUCTIBLE

INSTITUTE FOR ALTERNATIVE AGRICULTURE, Inc.
9200 EDMONSTON ROAD, SUITE 117
GREENBELT, MARYLAND 20770
301/441-8777

DR | GARTH YOUNGBERG
EXECUTIVE DIRECTOR

STATEMENT OF PHILOSOPHY AND PURPOSE

INTRODUCTION - The Institute for Alternative Agriculture is predicated on the belief that biological/organic/eco farming systems offer positive and feasible production alternatives for addressing this Nation's and the World's major agricultural production and environmental problems. Indeed, virtually every recent objective study of biological/ organic/eco agriculture has reached the conclusion that these alternative farming systems and technologies can help:

- Reduce farm production
    - net-farm income;
- Reduce soil erosion and compaction;
- Conserve energy;
- Minimize agricultural pollution of streams and underground water supplies;
- Avoid dependence on increasingly expensive and uncertain sources of agricultural fertilizers and pesticides;
- Contribute to long-term, sustainable food production;
- Improve food quality and safety;
- Ensure farm worker safety;
- Preserve the family farm; and
- Enhance environmental quality for fish and wildlife

Given the known potential and   success of alternative farming systems, why do most agricultural policy-makers, members of Congress, agricultural scientists, farm interest group leaders, and conventional farmers continue to be opposed to (or at least agnostic about)   agriculture?

The Institute believes that biological/organic/eco farming systems continue to be shunned by conventional agriculturalists primarily because of the lack of credible information, misinformation, and negative symbolism. According to the symbolism, for example, is only "hippies," health food faddists, and displaced urbanites who practice alternative agriculture. These well-meaning but misguided individuals are viewed as practicing their primitive, labor-intensive, agricultural crafts on small plots and with minimal success. Unfortunately, these images are often reinforced by the equally mistaken belief that alternative agriculturalists are guided by folklore and mysticism instead of hard science. Finally, it is widely believed that narrow self-interest and the lack of scientific training render alternative agriculturalists incapable of objectively assessing either the biological/organic/eco production systems which they espouse, or the conventional ones which they oppose, in varying degrees.

THE INSTITUTE'S SCOPE AND FUNCTION - In order to help correct these misperceptions and misunderstandings, the Institute will provide two broad categories of functions and services. First, it will provide a national, policy-level coordination, liaison, and educational function for existing biological/organic/eco producers, conventional farmers who may wish to adopt such practices, and agricultural scientists, policy-makers, industry groups, students, and lay citizens. The Institute strongly believes that it is important for members of the conventional agricultural community to become more objectively familiar with the character and potential of alternative agriculture. Presently, there is an organizational and informational vacuum at the national policy level for those persons and groups wishing to obtain objective analyses of biological/ organic/eco farming systems. While several national organizations share many of the goals and objectives of biological/organic/eco agriculture, there are no existing national organizations whose primary purpose it is to develop and disseminate scientifically credible information on all aspects of alternative agriculture. The Institute will also coordinate its efforts with those of similar organizations in other countries, as well as with the International Federation of Organic Agriculture Movements (IFOAM)

Second, the lack of a credible and extensive program of research and education on biological/ organic/eco farming constitutes one of the most important barriers to the widespread adoption of these alternative systems. For this reason, the Institute hopes to distribute private research funds to qualified agricultural scientists and to demonstrate, through the submission of written proposals, a genuine desire to investigate alternative agricultural systems. Projects embracing the agronomic, economic, social, and policy aspects of these systems will be welcomed. The Institute will function essentially as a clearinghouse for submitted proposals and   make grants available for those research and education projects which merit funding, including graduate student proposals.   believes   providing "seed" money to a relatively large number of researchers is the optimum way to stimulate interest and activity in these areas of research.

Mr. BROWN. Thank you, Dr. Youngberg.

I gather that you have brought a real farmer with you in the person of Mr. Thompson?

Mr. YOUNGBERG. That is correct.

Mr. BROWN. I think we will hear your statement, Mr. Thompson; then question both of you.

STATEMENT OF RICHARD L. THOMPSON, FARMER, BOONE, IOWA

Mr. THOMPSON. Thank you, Chairman Brown.

I have a letter here that I received from you, and I see on the letterhead that this is a Subcommittee on Department Operations, Research, and Foreign Agriculture. I trust that this hearing comes under the second category, under research, and not under the third one; that sometimes I have a feeling we are a little foreign to agriculture. So I trust we are in the second category.

Mr. BROWN. You are basically right. But it also focuses a little bit on Department operations.

Mr. THOMPSON. All right.

Along with my wife Sharon and our youngest son Rex, we operate a 300-acre diversified organic farm. Our crops are corn, soybeans, oats, hay and pasture. Most of these crops are fed to 90 sows and 70 beef cows and their offspring.

Our farm is located in the center of continuous row crop corn and soybean country. Our address is Boone, Iowa, but only 10 miles from Iowa State University. Presently, we operate this farm on a cash flow with no borrowed money.

I have a bachelor's and a master's degree in animal science. I am sure you people understand what B.S. stands for. My wife has a new understanding of what M.S. stands for—I am a manure specialist.

We were conventional farmers for the first 10 years of our farming experience with high applications of NH3, herbicides and insecticides in a continuous corn program from 1968 to the present date. We changed to balanced farming with a 5-year rotation.

Eight years ago, composting livestock wastes was added to the program. Four years ago, we started moving toward an on-farm research with side-by-side comparison plots.

I hope using the word organic doesn't make too many people nervous. Some think organic means nonchemical, but there is so much more in its meaning. Organic, to me, is an inner feeling that affects the way you think and then changes the way you act toward the environment and your fellow man. Perhaps regenerative better explains our feelings.

The problem may be in the land, but the cause is in the heart of man. Until there is a regeneration or change in the hearts of people toward the land, all talk, programs, and what-have-you, it is all of no avail.

I come with no quick answers or any special recipes. I find myself asking more questions each day.

The best way I know to convince you that we need the Productivity Act is to read you parts of some letters we have received. This folder is full of letters like the ones I will read. I will read from a few selected ones.

Dear Mr. Thompson: This spring my young cousin graduated from high school and wants to go into farming full time. I am anxious that he be knowledgeable in natural farming that can apply to him in the coming years. Would you know of any published literature such as textbooks which I could give to him as a graduation gift? My inquiries to the academic world have been unheeded, and I am at a loss as to where I could locate a source of sound advice on this topic. Any suggestion you have would be greatly appreciated. From a doctor in Ohio.

I have a postcard here addressed to Richard and Sharon Thompson, Farmers, Boone, Iowa. It is a wonder I ever got it. Down at the bottom: Have you tried sod, buster, or agricultural serium? Is it worth it? Have you read Wes Jackson's book? Hope you receive this card. Please write and send any information would be appreciated.

Another letter:

I and my three sons farm 840 acres in North Central Kansas where we are blessed with lots of rain or burn up in weeks. Do you have any publications or more articles you have written on your type of farming? I am very interested. The biggest problem I can see is presenting it to our landlords, especially when the one is your father-in-law. Signed, A Farmer from Kansas.

Dear Dick: Would you be so kind as to tell me how I can find information on total cultivation of corn and beans to get away from the use of the herbicides? A farmer from Iowa.

I would be interested to learn anything you have to write concerning your organic farming program. Can you keep your weeds under control without the use of sprays or herbicides at first and now? This is the part of the program that scares me more than anything else. I realize we are nearing the busy season of the year, but I would greatly appreciate your answering my letter as soon as possible, as we, too, are about to get into the fields. Thank you. A confused farmer from Ohio.

I am going to read the end of this letter:

If this letter gets to you, we would appreciate if you could give us some information on your farming practices or information on where we can learn more. Thank you for taking the time to read this and hope to receive a reply soon. Signed, From Dairy Farmers in the State of New York.

Dear Sir: I saw an account of your farming operation on a TV program, "Country Canada." I have since become very interested in organic farming. I would appreciate any information you could give me. I would also appreciate the addresses of universities that are doing research. Saskatchewan, Canada.

Dear Mr. Thompson: Many thanks for your articles you sent. I am considering your ideas and will let you know the outcome. From a grape grower in Italy.

My questions go on to say: What happens to crop yields and quality in a closed farm system? What kind of rotation is necessary when there are no livestock in the program? Why do farmers loosen up the soil in the fall and pack it back down in the spring? How can an organic system fit with the minimum tillage system? Why has the smooth, black, clean fields been the accepted way? Are weeds all bad? Can we use certain weeds or crops to control the weeds that are causing problems? Why do farmers usually think they have to buy something? Is there a connection between high nitrogen soils, high protein foods, and disease?

Research on this farm is being conducted in several acres. One, within the farm as a whole, there are four distinct systems being compared: (a) organic: livestock pasture system, no compost; (b) organic: livestock manure composted and applied; (c) organic: non-livestock; (d) 5-year rotation with chemical fertilizer.

Two, comparing a ridge—strip till planet system to a conventional tillage without using herbicides in either case.

Three, interseeding of legumes at last cultivation of corn and seeding rye and oats in fall for ground cover.

Four, the response of soil amendments in organic system.

Five, livestock waste management: (a) turned compost versus stockpiles manure; (b) different rates and timing of applications; (c) the use of innoculates; (d) another grad student in Plant Path—interested in Ph.D. work in composting.

The results from these tests are being published in the New Farm magazine.

The Agriculture Productivity Act ties production and conservation together. Prior to this time, part of USDA was saying to me, produce, produce, exports and more exports; while another part of USDA was saying to conserve the soil.

So back in 1967, we decided to listen to the voice from within. We felt we should raise the right crops according to our soil type.

The reason for a balanced crop rotation, cover crops, leaving residues on the surface is to stop wind and water erosion. The organic farmer is the best friend the soil conservation people have.

Our farm soil loss is 1 ton per acre on part of the farm and 4 tons per acre on the remaining acres. The neighbors' corn-bean rotation would have an 8- to 10-ton per acre loss. Our soil loss does not include the use of interseeding of cover crops. Looks like we need a new soil loss equation.

By late fall, eight out of the nine fields will be green with cover crops without any Government payment.

Presently, Rick Exner, a graduate student in agronomy from ISU, is doing a Master's Thesis on our farm in the area of cover crops.

This organic farm doesn't need Government support because of its diversity and balance. People have asked if we are in the PIK program. The answer is no because most of the farm is 40-percent seeded down to legumes and grasses, and the remaining part is 60-percent seeded to nonerosion crops. We say we have been in the PIK program for many years without costing the taxpayer.

Now is a good time, with all the surplus grains, for farmers to continue on their own with a sound rotation that matches their soil type and management ability.

I am asking for assistance for on-farm research to answer the many questions stated earlier. Assistance is needed in collecting data, keeping records expenses for testing soil and crops, conducting tours of demonstration plots, writing and publishing test results, mailing, letters and phone calls.

If you haven't got my point, I will sum it up in one word: Help. Thank you very much.

Mr. BROWN. Thank you, Mr. Thompson.

We are going to take a 10-minute recess, and then we will return and ask some questions. We would appreciate it if you could remain during that period.

[Recess taken.]

Mr. BROWN. The subcommittee will come to order.

Mr. Thompson, the Agricultural Extension people haven't offered to put you on their payroll yet, have they?

Mr. THOMPSON. No, sir.

Mr. BROWN. Dr. Youngberg, since you were so closely identified with the organic farming program in the Department of Agriculture before your departure, I would like to ask you to comment on the question that I raised earlier with Dr. Harris as to whether in your perception there has been a diminution in at least the visibility of the organic research and extension program in the Department of Agriculture?

Mr. YOUNGBERG. It is a very hard question to answer in terms of how do other people perceive what is happening in the Department.

As you know, there were very few resources being put into the organic farming program even following the USDA report, but there was a certain sense that I think there was interest and movement, there was a long range plan being developed and there was a response mechanism there that people were certainly using, as I think I mentioned before the subcommittee last year.

We had received something like 2,000 requests for information and there was a tremendous amount of that kind of activity going on and interaction with the so-called organic constituency.

Frankly, I am not aware of how much of that is going on in the Department right now.

I know we are getting an awful lot of letters at the institute that sound very similar to the ones we were getting in the Department, but I really can't speak for how other people perceive what is happening in the Department right now.

Mr. BROWN. It is conceivable that the administration would look with favor upon your answering those letters in accordance with their policy of encouraging private enterprise to play a larger role in some of these areas.

Mr. Thompson, you have presented a very good picture of the organic alternative farming situation as you have experienced it, and obviously you are not moved by purely crass commercial motivations in what you are doing, but have you paid enough attention to accounting to be able to say whether you are going broke any faster than other farmers, as a result of your agricultural practices?

Mr. THOMPSON. There was one statement in what I read that I thought would answer your question, that we do operate on cash flow and not using borrowed money and I don't know what other people are doing. I will leave it there.

Mr. BROWN. You mean you are independently wealthy and you don't have to go to the bank, sir?

Mr. THOMPSON. I didn't quite say it that way.

I said, we are working on cash flow. We have got enough income coming to pay our bills and we are updating our machinery without going to the bank.

Now, I know what the other side is like. Prior to that, when I was trying to expand, buying feeder cattle and feeder pigs, I was a good friend of the bankers. If we hadn't made the change in 1967 in our philosophy, maybe our farm would be for sale now by the bank. I trust that may help answer the question.

Mr. BROWN. That does give a fairly good picture of financial soundness, the fact you are in the position you described.

But it also does not tell me whether you are living in voluntary poverty or whether you are providing yourself a good standard of living off of that cash flow.

Mr. THOMPSON. I try to avoid this kind of situation but I will say this: We have just purchased two new John Deere tractors and they are paid for. Does that help?

Another thing I might say is that by not buying fertilizer in our chemical plots, I am spending $60 an acre in the compost plots; there are some expenses. I do have the manure, so I do have to do something with it.

I am saving $60 an acre in that sort, if that helps in the profit picture.

Mr. BROWN. Well, actually what we need is probably what would be produced by the research provided for in this bill, which is a comparison between your profit and loss, or income and expenses with similar sized farms using other more chemically intensive production methods, and how they would relate to each other.

I won't pursue that with you at this time. I will call on Mr. Weaver.

Mr. WEAVER. Thank you, again, Mr. Chairman.

Dr. Youngberg, I appreciate your fine testimony. It was excellent and very helpful.

Mr. Thompson, I think you pointed right at it when you said it takes a whole new way of thinking of things and I am sure it does. That, in my estimation, is the primary value of this bill.

I hope to enact it into law because I think it can start us on a way of thinking differently about farming that will help us meet the coming grave problems that agriculture will face in the next generation.

I would like to ask you though why you changed? You were a conventional farmer for the first 10 years, then in 1968 you changed. What happened?

Mr. THOMPSON. We always get around to that question.

I know the first 10 years of farming I was trying to build my kingdom, I call it, where one shed wasn't enough and I had to have two and one silo wasn't enough and I had to have another, and buy more cattle and get other land and I call that a disease.

There were problems. It seemed like the cattle were sick all the time and the pigs were sick so I was kind of in a corner in the natural. Going along with that, we were also looking for some answers spiritually in our life and these are going along together and we started learning about the part of God, that the Holy Spirit was going to be the teacher, and so a word came to us in a supernatural way that God was going to teach us how to farm, and here I had two degrees in agriculture and had lived on the farm all my life and I wondered how could this be.

So we made a dramatic switch. We were in two corners and so it seemed like the light started to shine and things started to falling into place and that is how this happened and doors have been opening. This is probably another door into something I don't know anything about.

Mr. WEAVER. Thank you very much.

Mr. BROWN. Mr. Thompson, I don't want to get into your spiritual convictions with you, but I will comment that I noted that in connection with the organic farming operation of the old Amish, that that seems to be based upon their spiritual convictions also. This is the proper way to treat the Earth, and that it complies with their interpretation of what the Lord provided in the Bible, and it can be a very powerful instrument.

However, I know that this administration has a number of born-again Christians in it who don't feel the same way you do. Do you care to comment on that?

Mr. THOMPSON. I will put it this way. I am bothered by some people that we walk in and out of the same church doors that don't see this. This is something the light has to turn on from inside. This is the only way I can answer that. Until you see the light, it just doesn't make sense.

Mr. BROWN. I think that is another evidence of the wisdom of the Founding Fathers who felt we should keep religion out of politics.

I have no further questions, gentlemen.

We appreciate your testimony.

Mr. Thompson, I have an additional statement here that is labeled "Thompson's Regenerative Agriculture Demonstration Research Program." Was that to be a part of your testimony?

Mr. THOMPSON. Yes.

Mr. BROWN. Without objection then, this will be included in the record.

Mr. THOMPSON. Thank you, sir.

[The additional statement appears at the conclusion of the hearing.]

Mr. BROWN. Thank you very much.

Our next witnesses is a panel including Mr. Robert Rodale, president of Regenerative Agriculture Association; Dr. Richard Harwood, research director, Regenerative Agriculture Association, and Dr. J. Patrick Madden from the Department of Agricultural Economics at Pennsylvania State University.

Maybe Dr. Madden can answer that question I asked the first panel.

Dr. Rodale, we are very pleased to have you here and obviously you have had a great deal of experience and we recognize your contribution in this area and look forward to your testimony.

You are running up against the noon hour. If you get as hungry as anybody else, you may deal appropriately with your testimony.

STATEMENT OF ROBERT RODALE, PRESIDENT, REGENERATIVE AGRICULTURE ASSOCIATION

Mr. RODALE. Thank you. I am going to begin my testimony talking about productivity. That is the key word in this act and America is today being forced to deal with the consequences of a farm productivity crisis. Those consequences include overproduction, particularly of feed grains, excessive erosion of soil and silting of waterways, pollution of ground water with fertilizers and pesticide residues, reduction in employment opportunities in farming, and a frightening deterioration in the entire financial structure of agriculture.

A result is that both farm and on-farm Americans are beginning to fear American agriculture rather than see it as a source of national strength.

Nonfarmers now fear the tax burden that support of the present system places on their shoulders. They fear also the draining away of national strength that soil erosion and agriculture-caused pollution symbolize.

Farmers, above all, fear that the source of income and way of life that they love will collapse around them, forcing them off the land.

A normal productivity crisis is characterized by a failure of an industrial system to produce enough, or a need for too great amounts of labor, energy, and raw material inputs.

The current agricultural productivity crisis is different. In fact, many people do not see it as a productivity crisis at all, because the most obvious sign that a problem exists is the fact that production levels are extremely high.

They apparently think, "How can there be a productivity crisis when we are being buried in product?"

But there indeed is an American farm productivity crisis. In simplest terms, it is a failure of our agricultural leadership to conceive and create a system of farming that meets all our needs.

Instead, we have been given by farm researchers, planners and thinkers a system that places a supremely high value on the continuous production of food and fiber, but which almost totally ignores the human and biological destruction caused by that production.

As a result, American farmers today are harvesting twin crops of production and destruction, and, unfortunately, the destruction seems to be winning.

There is another way, though, a better way. There is a way to farm that has no destructive side to it at all. Just the opposite. There is a way to farm that literally eliminates every single disadvantage of the present conventional system, and it does more than that. It also preserves all the advantages that farming in this country can and should have, and it does still more. It creates advantages and values that are totally new to the experience of many American farmers.

In order to understand and put to use this other system, it is necessary to introduce into agriculture two concepts which are sadly lacking or missing entirely from the present system.

Flexibility of production is the first. The science and technology which has been used to create the present system places total value on all-out, high-yield agriculture.

The farmers who use it have two choices. They can either not farm, or go for maximum yields and output.

There is no middle ground production level.

Plants are bred to grow big in a soil rich in high levels of soluble nutrients. Cropping patterns leave no option for cutting back easily, if markets are glutted.

And most important, farmers have been encouraged to hitch themselves to high levels of indebtedness. Too many have bankers looking over their shoulder, urging them to keep the accelerator of their whole farm operation to the floor.

Farmers deserve better. They should have the flexibility of a scientifically based system that gives them the ability to produce at different levels, depending on how they assess market conditions.

Regeneration is the other concept that needs to be introduced more effectively into agriculture.

Farming doesn't have to just destroy soil. Different ways of growing crops can also rebuild and regenerate the land. Water can be purified as well as poisoned. Why not structure farming so it helps purify water instead of polluting it?

The families and communities that form the human dimension of agriculture can be rebuilt, restored, and regenerated as well.

The seldom-spoken but well-understood phrase, "Get big or get out" has been a central message to the people managing the American land.

It is time to reverse that message and put out a new welcome mat to the many who love the land, need work and want to participate in the regeneration of themselves and the basic source of this country's strength.

We need an agriculture that says "Come back in" to millions of our displaced rural people.

Is that kind of agriculture merely a dream? Is it beyond the realm of practical action in today's world?

Not at all. The kind of flexible, regenerative agriculture we have described here actually exists on tens of thousands of American farms. It works. The people practicing it are thriving, and their farms are models of rational productivity. And not only that, their farms are getting better with each passing year.

The soil is improving, the water falling on those farms stays clear, and the food and fiber they produce is of highest quality.

The Agricultural Productivity Act of 1983 calls for the systematic study of this kind of farm. We will present in this testimony evidence from our own study of one such farm, and we strongly support the passage of this legislation, which would establish a minimal number of similar studies.

Further, we will show how regenerative agricultural concepts are also important to agricultural development in the developing countries, where inputs and other resources are often extremely scarce.

Thank you. There is a full statement. Dick will cover the remaining part.

STATEMENT OF RICHARD HARWOOD, RESEARCH DIRECTOR, REGENERATIVE AGRICULTURE ASSOCIATION

Mr. HARWOOD. Thank you. For the past 6 years now we have been studying a single farm, neighboring farm to our research center in Pennsylvania, in the eastern end of the Corn Belt in a study very similar to the ones that are asked for in the present legislation.

I would like to just briefly show what we have learned from those 5 or 6 years of study and indicate what its relevance is to U.S. agriculture in general.

Just briefly, this is a 320-acre farm farmed by our neighborhood; it is an integrated beef and animal operation; it has been essentially organic since 1972. It is not entirely 100 percent organic, but uses a minmal number of chemicals.

Just to indicate the productivity of the farm, over the 5 years that we have studied with intensive crop cuts and very specific data taken from every single one of 100 fields, we find that the average yields are 108 bushels on corn, for instance, 27 percent above the local county averages.

In a dry year which was 1980, when the county's average yields were extremely low, 52 bushels; the study farm averaged 48 percent above, for corn, the county average.

A disproportionate share of that farm is on a shale hillside so it has less than average fertility on soil. It has a very small percentage of the farm being in high fertility.

If we compare it with the best farms in the State, the Pennsylvania Corn Club, where farmers take their very best 5 acres, we can assume they are the best managers we have in the State.

In 1981 the average of those corn club competition fields was 136 bushels per acre. In that year the Kutztown farm averaged 121, which was some 10 percent less. But the interesting thing is that in spite of this shale hillside that farm had less than half the soil erosion of the conventional farms growing primarily corn. Its soil losses even on the shaley hillside was less than 5 tons per acre.

But the most revealing thing is from the cost of production. If we compare the costs, the cash costs of production on the Kutztown farm, again looking at corn as being somewhat typical of many of the crops grown, we find that there is roughly a 75-percent decrease in the cost of fertilizer as compared to those corn club farms.

There is a 30- to 40-percent decrease from average conventional cost, just for fertilizer alone. There is about a 30-percent decrease in the cost of weed control. So we are talking about $84 an acre for growing corn, total cash cost, as compared to $152 average for the Pennsylvania Corn Club, which is almost double the cost.

This is cash outlay now.

So we see a highly efficient farm. We have answered, I think, the questions of productivity. Such an integrated farm can be extremely productive. It can be markedly much more cost efficient. How much can we extrapolate? What can we learn from a scientific basis from that?

We cannot say that the one-third, one-third, one-third of small grains, corn and hay that this farm has should be practiced on every single farm. That is not the answer. That is not really the formula that another farmer would use.

What we have learned though is that through efficient structuring of the farm, proper crop rotations, combined with other practices, we can gain a 50- to 60-percent efficiency in use of any nutrients.

We can also reduce energy inputs by 60 percent. The structuring will be different on different farms.

Well now, if we ask the scientific merits of studying 12 farms as compared to other alternatives, we might look at the Washington University study of a few years ago where 50 pairs of farms were studied with those farms being of essentially a single type.

The case study has a very important role in this whole research matrix. It teaches us what to look for in our broad studies and verification study and teaches how to build the computer model which USDA witnesses were talking about.

For instance, we would have no idea of the relative efficiencies of these farms if we couldn't go out and actually see one.

The kind of regenerative farm Mr. Rodale was talking about were considered to be pie in the sky if it didn't actually exist and so it is scientifically defensible to study even a single farm let alone a dozen such farms.

If those farms are included in a matrix of say broad scale and less intensive survey, to place them in context perhaps, and then to verify that yes, these results are applicable to other farms.

So we think that this is a missing link; it is not fashionable today in scientific research to do an on-the-farm detailed study. In fact, it is not particularly fashionable to learn from farmers, and this may be why there is some inherent resistance in the scientific community to this approach.

But certainly it is a missing link and can contribute a lot to our understanding.

We are learning, for instance, how to biologically structure systems to make them more efficient. I think in my wildest imagination as a scientist, sitting with a $7.5 million research budget here a few years ago at the International Research Center, I couldn't have come up or designed a system that would have the efficiencies of this organic farm that we are looking at.

And it is even more amazing that this farm has been put together without really the benefit of scientific expertise in helping the farmer to do it.

It is one thing to have all component pieces coming from the university, the legumes, rotation, in fact there is not a single component of that farm that you can't find some research data on, but you find absolutely nothing on how to put it together.

And a farmer is just left to assemble these pieces according to his own best judgment and most often those pieces are highly slanted in favor of high input kinds of agriculture.

In fact, farmers who disdain from using these practices are discriminated against by the lending agencies and often held up to ridicule as being old-fashioned or not progressive.

From our experience in the international field, especially, I think this is a forerunner of the Third World nations as to what we are going to be facing in the United States as resources become more scarce and here is a model that just has extreme relevance to Third World application as well as to the future in America.

Two months ago we were asked to present an executive level seminar, a 1-week seminar to the Government of Tanzania. The seminar was presided over by President Nyerere of Tanzania, and at the end of the week there was extreme enthusiasm about the relevance of this kind of approach, the regenerative resource efficiency approach that we have drawn directly from the Pennsylvania farm to the 2-acre farm in Tanzania.

So I guess probably to conclude, I should mention a little bit about the frustrations that we feel. I am convinced as a scientist that there are extreme efficiencies that up until now we just haven't realized in some of these farms that have been put together for whatever reason, whether it was religious motivations, as mentioned by the previous witness, or for whatever reason, they were put together under real resource constraints.

The growers did not want to use, for whatever reason, conventional inputs. They were forced to put together really efficient farming systems.

As we sit here, thinking over those farms, the other Dick Thompsons that we know, the Ben Brubakers with the Kutztown farm, we sort of feel like the neighbor who is watching the neighbor's barn burn. We know where the fire hydrant is, but we can't convince the fire department to check it out.

So, I guess that is part of the frustration, but we think the bill is just excellent; that the studies as they are proposed are scientifically defensible, if they are placed in the context of other kinds of research.

[The prepared statement of Mr. Rodale and Mr. Harwood appears at the conclusion of the hearing.]

Mr. BROWN. Thank you. Dr. Madden, would you like to proceed?

STATEMENT OF J. PATRICK MADDEN, DEPARTMENT OF AGRICULTURAL ECONOMICS, PENNSYLVANIA STATE UNIVERSITY

Mr. MADDEN. Yes, thank you, Mr. Chairman.

I am a professor of agricultural economics at Penn State University and I am deeply involved in two research projects which are quite relevant to the whole matter of agricultural productivity and I am trying to start a third project.

The first of these is studies being done along with Irvin Feller and others at the Institute of Policy Research and Evaluation at Penn State, and in this study we are looking at the workings of the public and private systems by which food and agricultural technologies created, developed, commercialized, and diffused to the various kinds of users on farms and industry.

My other study is an interdisciplinary study of organic farmers or, more correctly, what we have come to call regenerative agriculture.

I would like to add at this point a few diagrams which illustrate the contrast between organic, conventional, and regenerative farming.

The first shows that as far as rhetoric is concerned, that the organic and conventional farming seem to be miles apart, but when you talk with the people involved, you find that their beliefs and values tend to converge substantially and their farming practices are even closer together.

Regenerative agriculture overlaps both organic and conventional and extends beyond adding considerations that are beyond both organic and conventional.

I have a staff paper which will be submitted for the record if you have no objection, which summarizes the progress we have had up to the present time in the exploratory phase of my research on organic regenerative agriculture. This study has been supported in part by the cooperative State research service through the Hatch research project, a Pennsylvania agricultural experiment station, but also rather substantially supported by the Rodela Research Center.

Without that funding, I could not have conducted the survey that did plus the visit to some 44 farms in various places in the United States.

These are summarized in my report.

I would like to also comment that we are starting a new project called a sustainable farming systems study which is also interdisciplinary and includes a few organic or generative farms as part of the study design.

The prospectus of that study is also enclosed, but I was told recently that even if the study is approved as an experiment station project, that we will have to go outside for funding because our budget is so tight that it is impossible at this point in history to start new research efforts without bringing in outside funding. This, I understand rather well.

Our study of the agricultural technology is quite relevant to this act because we are learning how new technologies are created and disseminated.

We are examining the interaction between farmers and extension personnel, researchers at universities and in industry, as well as agribusiness firms and various Federal and State agencies in the creation of technologies which intimately affect agricultural productivity.

From State to State, and from one technology to another, we are finding an extreme diversity in the pattern of the involvement of various players.

You will not be surprised to learn that farmers are extremely inventive, often coming up with innovations that have stumped the experts.

One of the best examples of farmers leading the way is in no-till and other kinds of conservation tillage systems which are proving to be both profitable and very effective in reducing soil erosion.

Two weeks ago, as a part of our field work for the technology study, I attended the 6th Annual Southeast No-Till Systems Conference at Milan, Tenn.

Many no-till systems were demonstrated at this field day and as I walked from one system demonstration to another, I had the opportunity to speak with many of the inventors. Several of them were farmers. They had started out with an idea, and then proceeded with their welders and cutting torches to create a workable prototype which subsequently was commercialized.

Other technologies, such as embryo transfer, for example, have featured a very prominent role by land-grant universities, the work of George Sidel, and his colleagues at Colorado State University have been exemplary in this regard and they have both created and simplified a technology so it is now applicable and easily adapted to conditions throughout this Nation and other countries.

In still other technologies, such as large round hay bailers and center pivot systems, private firms have taken the leadership.

There is tremendous diversity in the role of the players in the overall technology system.

Some of the technologies are easily adaptable to local conditions, such as artificial insemination, but other technologies are really vulnerable to the extreme diversity that we find, diversity to climatic soil, ecological, and economic conditions. As a result of this diversity, many of the technologies must be adapted to local conditions if they are to work ultimately or work at all.

I have noticed in visiting various farms, in our study, that tremendous diversity has been found in all of these conditions. One example is the contrast between two farmers just 5 miles apart, both of them producing tremendous fruits, near Stockton, Calif., one of them is prospering using organic or regenerative methods, while his neighbor just a few miles down the road tells us that he is being forced by the economic reality of insect damage to start spraying again this year after several years of producing organically various fruits and vegetables.

Of the 44 organic regenerative farm operators I interviewed face to face, only a handful of these, and that handful consisted of some industry land wheat farmers in Kansas and Washington, only that handful said that they felt they had once and for all answered to organic or regenerative production. All the other farmers said they are still seeking new and better ways. They are constantly experimenting on their own farms with ways to improve their success.

They are constantly alert to the changing weather and soil conditions and insect populations, both harmful and beneficial types.

They realize that what worked last year may or may not work this year to achieve the same results.

The farms I visited are not a scientific sample in that we selected farms largely from the mailing list of New Farm Magazine, which is a Rodale publication, supplemented by the membership lists of various organic farming organizations.

However, one crucial step in the scientific method is the formulation of research questions and hypothesis. The other phase of my research has been designed for this purpose. In seeking farms which are successful already, and had made the transition into organic production methods, contrasting those with farmers still in the transition process into organic or regenerative methods and then third-time farmers slipping back or negative transition back toward conventional chemical intensive methods, I hoped that I would be able to come up with some research questions fruitful in modeling and in generating research both in our own research program and hopefully the programs of other scientists throughout this country.

I try to avoid using the word organic farming because of the many different things that it means to different people.

The work of Dick Harwood and Bob Rodale is particularly commendable here in that they have really clarified this issue and have substituted the word regenerative for organic.

Simply stated, I view a regenerative farming system as one that produces a bountiful harvest of food not contaminated by possibly harmful chemicals, using farming methods that enhance long-term agricultural productivity while minimizing the erosion depletion or despoiling of natural resources.

My understanding of this contrast is illustrated by this series of diagrams that I have just shown you.

Turning now to the Agricultural Productivity Act, I would like to offer a few personal impressions and observations.

First, I am strongly in favor of the purposes of the act.

Also, I am pleased that the term organic farming does not appear in the act, because the term is laden with emotional content that gets in the way of useful discussions and actions.

It is also highly commendable that you mention modern agricultural technologies, making it explicitly clear that you are not advocating a return to the backbreaking technologies of the 1930's and beyond, which many observers mistakenly equate with organic farming.

The farms I visited were all modern and most were highly productive. The really successful farms were operated by some of the best farmers, the most capable businessmen and women I have ever known. Nor is modern agricultural techology necessarily chemical intensive.

The Lundbergs—2,700 acres near Chico, Calif.—certainly use modern technology in producing some 200 acres of rice organically, everything from laser devices on their tractors, to rectangular-move irrigation systems.

Their neighbor Dick Harter and his son-in-law, Brian Leahy, are producing rice organically on their 900-acre farm just a few miles from the Lundbergs, using methods that are elegant in their simplicity, remarkable in their efficiency, and admirable in their harmony with nature.

I am also pleased to see that the act calls for an information study, which includes both the assembly of known information plus identification of gaps. In this connection, I would call attenion to the need for a close connection between the problems and opportunities encountered by the farmers selected for the pilot study and the identification of gaps, as an agenda for further scientific research and development.

This is not now made explicit in the act.

In our technology study, we have encountered many excellent examples of feedback from the grassroots, from farmers, extension personnel, machinery dealers, and others, back to the sources of the technology in the universities or in industry.

Another strength of the act is that it seeks to legitimize in various Federal agencies and in the land-grant system those farming methods we would call regenerative.

Most of the colleagues I have spoken with within the land-grant system seem to doubt that organic or regenerative methods are biologically or economically feasible.

Case studies, such as those called for in H.R. 2714 can establish the credibility of these methods. Existing ARC and CRS research is highly commendable in terms of providing the building blocks. However, these need to be integrated into an overall farming systems model in which more than just the biological reality of legumes or biological controls of insects or other physical sense considerations are put together in terms of the business as a whole.

This is part of the unfinished agenda.

I am also pleased that you are calling for the creation of data to document the workings of these farms. Grateful testimonials and undocumented success stories do little to convince the nonbelievers both among the research communities and among farmers who are good businessmen, who are highly skeptical about jumping into something that is not tried and proven.

We at Penn State are just beginning to create such a data system, working with four more or less regenerative farms and four conventional farms. We do not have enough research funds to be able to afford to collect all the data you call for in the act, particularly the nutritional quality of the crops and the quality of the water and other natural resources, but we would like very much to extend the scope of the study to include these and other factors.

For example, I would like to see research done to find quick and reliable methods, such as human tissue culture, to test chemicals for toxicity and carcinogenic effects. An interdisciplinary team of research and extension faculty are working on this study, sustainable farming system, as indicated in the enclosed prospectus.

Perhaps the act would be more likely to attain its objectives if it required a farming systems approach.

One important concern I would raise regarding the act is that it calls for a very small sample, 12 conventional farms seeking to make the transition to regenerative farming systems, and another 12 that have been employing such methods for at least 5 years.

We would add the requirement that these farms must be showing a profit large enough to entice the operating family to continue farming; otherwise, it would not be sustainable.

By requiring only 12 of each general type of farm, and with specific categories in each type, you are placing all the eggs in one fragile basket if you will pardon the agricultural pun.

Farming is risky business, as you know. What if two or three or more of the pilot study farms go bankrupt due to drought, extraordinary disease or pest problems, and/or disastrously low prices?

Furthermore, the transitional farms must not be required to go cold turkey, for abrupt termination of chemicals can be disastrous to many types of farms. A phased or gradual transition should be permitted in the legislation.

Hopefully the work called for in the Agricultural Productivity Act will build upon the fine work already being done in a few places, such as the Rodale Research Center in Kutztown, Pa., the private experimental farm of Dick and Sharon Thompson near Boone, Iowa, which I had the privilege of visiting last month.

I can assure you that Dick and Sharon, as a family, are not living in voluntary poverty, as you asked a little while ago. In his humility he did not want to tell you he has a very fine home and quite a modern farm.

Also excellent work is being done in the ecological agriculture program of Steve Gleissman at University of California at Santa Cruz, the field days on organic farms, sponsored by University of Nebraska, and other such efforts.

By tying in with ongoing studies, more efficient use of the program funds may be achieved, and the hazards of very small sample size might be overcome.

Perhaps by using videotaping of the farms at key stages of the season, the educational value of the pilot farms would be enriched, while reducing the farmer's hassle and the risk of damage to crops and livestock due to excessive traffic of visitors. These and other ideas could enhance the program.

The objectives of the act are admirable, well worth pursuing, and attainable. It won't be easy. The activities called for in the act are an important step in the right direction.

Given the extreme diversity of agriculture, inclusion of more pilot farms would be highly desirable, and given the high risk of sample attrition, a large number seems imperative.

Thank you again for the opportunity to testify on the Agricultural Productivity Act of 1983.

Mr. BROWN. Thank you very much, Dr. Madden, we appreciate the statement. Without objection, the material that you referred to, and similar material from Dr. Harwood and Mr. Rodale, will be made a part of our record or held in the files.

[The prepared statement of Mr. Madden appears at the conclusion of the hearing.]

Mr. BROWN. Mr. Weaver, do you have any questions?

Mr. WEAVER. Thank you, Mr. Chairman.

You know, I sit here and I think we spend as much on a new weapon system in 1 day as this entire program would take in 5 years.

In other words, we can experiment with a weapon but with the whole burden of feeding the population of the Earth in our hands today, we are told we can't do this one thing, that it isn't a high enough priority. It makes me wonder.

Dr. Madden, I appreciate all of your testimony, Mr. Rodale, to me your great leadership has been responsible for much of what has gone on in this field and I don't believe I am overstating the case when I say that the well-being of the world is in the hands of this form of agriculture.

We are going to have mass starvation in the years to come if we do not make some changes.

I want to thank you for all your good work and tremendous leadership.

I was curious about one thing in reading your staff papers, Dr. Madden, what is basic H?

Mr. MADDEN. Basic H is a soil amendment.

Mr. WEAVER. I don't know what that means?

Mr. MADDEN. Perhaps I could defer to Dick Harwood, who is an agronomist. The farmers that I spoke with were using—several of them were using basic H and gave glowing testimonials, but I understand that the scientific evidence has not supported——

Mr. WEAVER. Dr. Madden, I read your paper. I asked what is basic H?

Mr. HARWOOD. It is a wetting agent like a detergent, but it gives the soil a different physical property, changes the physical property of the soil supposedly.

Mr. WEAVER. You mean it is a spade?

Mr. HARWOOD. It is a liquid material like soap that you apply.

Mr. WEAVER. You spread it on the soil?

Mr. HARWOOD. Spread on so many pounds per acre.

Mr. WEAVER. Isn't that a chemical?

Mr. HARWOOD. There is a question as to whether it would be certified as organic or not.

Mr. WEAVER. That is interesting.

Mr. HARWOOD. There is a field for research on many of these products. There is a long list of those products that are on the market.

Mr. WEAVER. The other question I have, as you describe your farm next to the Rodale area, you said your costs were down and your productivity was in many ways up, even compared with other good farms. * * * But something had to be up as well, I mean, even though your costs were down, $60 an acre for this, did you have more labor costs?

Mr. HARWOOD. Yes; there was 30 to 40 percent more labor, which in this case was farm family labor.

Mr. WEAVER. Mr. Chairman, I want to thank these three gentlemen for their marvelous work and say that I went to an organic farm in my district a couple weeks, ago, and a 70-year old Swede had been farming organically all his life and he was raising some strawberries. I have a farm in Oregon and the largest strawberry grower in Oregon lives next to me. He is a chemical farmer. His strawberries are good. They had harvested the strawberries from the Swedish organic farmer's field before we arrived. As we were walking across it, I saw one or two strawberries still left so I reached down and picked one up and put it in my mouth and I never had an experience like that for 30 years. The flavor just exploded in my mouth. I hadn't tasted a strawberry for 30 years until I ate that strawberry. I didn't expect it. I started yelling. Everybody else started trying to find one as well. That is what made me think when Mr. Thompson said it was an attitude, or state of mind because it wasn't just the fact this Swedish man didn't use chemicals; it was his care of that farm, his devotion to it that created that. That is what is important and I want to thank you again for your tremendous contributions.

Thank you, Mr. Chairman, you are of course, in my estimation, the leader in the Congress in promoting this entire area; your tremendous leadership and contributions have been great.

Mr. BROWN. Flattery will get you nowhere, Mr. Weaver.

Dr. Madden, I raised the question earlier whether there had been any research on the organic or regenerative farming being done by the Mennonite community in Pennsylvania. Are you aware of any such research?

Mr. MADDEN. A little. First of all, I would like to say that my understanding is that the vast majority of the Pennsylvania Dutch farmers are not using strictly organic methods. We are looking at a few of these. I have done some work in conjunction with the Rodale Research Center, particularly in reviewing context looking at the 300-acre farm which is operated by an Amish/Mennonite farmer and his family.

I am working more closely with another farmer to the east of us by the name of Aaron Zimmerman, who is also of that same religious denomination, and I have visited a farmer in Lancaster County, Elmer Lapp, who is approaching retirement but for many years has used organic methods.

But I understand that these are the exception and that they tell me that the typical neighbors are not using organic methods.

Doing research with Mennonites or Amish people has been very difficult because of their in many cases suspicion of outsiders. I have been quite interested in expanding this kind of research for many years and only recently have had the opportunity to get a little bit of information.

Mr. BROWN. You also indicate that, at least in part, your research is being supported by the Department of Agriculture; is that correct?

Mr. MADDEN. That is correct, both directly and indirectly. My research project is primarily—the work I am doing on organic agriculture or regenerative agriculture is supported by a Hatch research project which, as you know, includes money from both the State and from CSRS. That budget essentially pays for my salary and a little bit of operating funds.

Beyond to get the operating funds for the travel and to hire research assistants, I have to go outside here in the funding Rodale Research Center during the first year, plus more recently money from another contract which I have been able to use, the salaries savings from another contract I have been able to divert into this project as well.

So I am subsidizing the organic agricultural work through the salaries savings from the technology transfer study, which also is funded by the Department of Agriculture.

Mr. BROWN. That is probably illegal to do that, but we won't let anybody know.

Mr. MADDEN. It is legal.

Mr. BROWN. I am very much interested in your references to the technology spinoff aspects of this, the development of new technologies, and at such time as you have committed to writing any of your research in this area or any of your studies, the subcommittee would be interested in receiving that material.

I have another kind of question which any of you can answer. There are two types of questions involved here.

First of all, agriculture as a national institution is no longer just farming; in fact on the farm aspects of the food supply system probably represents less than 20 percent of the cost of the total food chain. The rest of it is in processing, distribution, input, supply and so on.

In one of your statements reference was made to the fact that when you reduced the inputs, the chemical and fertilizers and so forth, that you could provide the same degree of productivity but that there would be an impact on the suppliers. We have noticed this in connection with the PIK program also, the farmers may end up doing just as well, but the tractor dealers and fertilizer people and others lose their markets.

The point I am trying to get to, for our own purpose of policy evaluation, is the degree to which that less than 20 percent of the food chain that is represented by the on-farm activities, is that now being manipulated for the policy benefit of the other 80 percent? In other words, the suppliers of the inputs want to keep you using those inputs and keep production high, the processors and so on have their own interest in maintaining a continuing high level flow through this chain because they all get a piece of the action, they all make a profit on it, and in a sense when you talk about the prospects of diminishing the profit of any part of the chain, you are going to run into political opposition.

Now, what is the answer to that problem?

Mr. RODALE. I had a conversation recently with one of the representatives of one of the large grain trading companies. This man told me——

Mr. BROWN. Who will make a huge profit on surplus grain sales when the farmers are going broke.

Mr. RODALE. He was saying that the production cost of American grain is just too high, that he felt that export markets were going to diminish because there are just too much going into, too many inputs going into production of grain in the United States, and he made a statement to me we are going to have to meet you half way because we simply cannot afford to keep running agriculture this way with this enormous input and high cost and be able to find markets.

So, I feel that certainly it is a difficult period of the economy in agriculture, in all phases of agriculture, and as we know in other phases of the economy too, but, I see that in order to continue the health of the production system, we are going to have to infuse into agriculture the kind of conservation mentality and action that has already gone into automobile, power generation and the household economy.

So, in a sense, particularly I am disturbed that the Department of Agriculture, the Federal Department of Agriculture is so slow in responding to this need. They are the ones that have the greatest freedom to design initial systems and be leaders in conservation, but I think even the agribusiness people who the grain trading people know this has to be done, and here we are in the position of trying to drag the Department of Agriculture into a mentality that the whole society is coming to very quickly.

Mr. BROWN. I wouldn't put the whole blame on the Department of Agriculture. They are subject to some political constraints that affect what they can do. However, the criticism that you have indicated has been made at least peripherally in a recent report from the Office of Technology Assessment which indicates a certain degree of misplaced priorities in the Department's research in the sense that they haven't focused enough research on the postharvest technologies and systems that impact profitability of the farm operation, and I think to the credit of the Department that they are beginning to refocus their research more on the total food chain, including the postharvest technology, off-the-farm technology that are involved in the total process, and I think we would encourage them to continue with that approach.

Now, let me ask one more question that bothers me a great deal. A part of the savings that result from regenerative agriculture are difficult to internalize, they are reflected in lower soil loss rates, in a lesser degree of pollution flowing into the environment, the water table, the surface water supply, air, and so on. These savings have tremendous benefit to the whole society but can't be captured by the farmer.

Is there any way this problem can be addressed or do you recognize that as a problem?

Mr. HARWOOD. It depends on the timeframe. In the short term they are not as quickly returnable to the farmer, but over a period of even 5 to 10 years, that is downward movement of nutrients in the profile and reduce 4 to 600 pounds of potash, and that washed off the field from erosion, is the thing that is responsible for maintaining the balances that you are talking about at such low cost.

If you are going to classify that 75-percent reduction in fertilizer cost over a 5- to 10-year period, you absolutely have to stop soil erosion I think or minimize it. So, the timeframe is crucial, and I don't think it has to be 75 years. In 5 to 10 years I think you will really begin to see the payoff.

Mr. BROWN. Well, this is a problem which has affected American industry also. The managers all trained at the Harvard Business School and were not looking at the need to replenish their basic stock of ideas, capital equipment and, in other words, not taking the long-range investment approach, and this has caused some major industries, like steel and autos, to go through some very trying times.

It is hard to get people to focus on the long run and to make their economical calculations based on long run help rather than short-term gain. It is particularly difficult, I would think, in agriculture where more and more of the decisions are being made by corporate managers rather than by family farmers who may have an interest in living on the farm for 30 or 40 years, but the corporations don't.

Mr. HARWOOD. If I might make another point on this. Our traditional approach has been having, as a result, a fall-out of a system which creates these external costs, soil erosion, the pesticide runoff and what not. We tend to think that the farmer has to spend money in order to correct those problems. That is exactly the case. If he is growing continuous corn. There are several costs to society, external costs, as a result of this continuous monoculture corn.

I think what we are looking at is there is a different structure of farm with a different kind of interprice mix that doesn't create those problems in the first place, so it isn't so much the costs of internal, or the problem of internalizing those costs. For instance, on the Thompson farm, he isn't faced with additional cost to the operation of stopping soil erosion, the erosion control is just part of his farming system, not representing the addition of extra cost.

In this study that we have indicated here, for instance, there is nothing in that farming system that you could point to as a specific cost of internalizing some of these other problems. He has no specific cover crops that are grown just for soil protection, for instance, they are all a part of the farming system.

Mr. BROWN. Well, I am not only talking about internalizing costs, I am talking about internalizing benefits. The costs to society of providing for soil conservation, or pollution control, is substantially reduced by these practices, and yet the farmer doesn't get the benefit of those savings to the society as a whole, which leads to the question in terms of broader agricultural policy, of why we don't encourage these practices through our commodity support programs, for example, which is costing us $20 billion this year and instead of encouraging these practices, they may even be discouraging these practices in some cases. And that is a perversion of public policy it seems to me.

Mr. HARWOOD. You see, another way of reducing the costs to society, it is our estimate, based on the data that we have, that a farmer could set aside from a third to 40 percent of his acreage with no more than a 20-percent reduction in income from those acreages calculated over a 2- to 3-year period.

If we were to take then the cost of the PIK program and the PIK program were to be applied today to an organic agriculture setting, we would estimate that the cost to society would be somewhat less than 20 percent of the cost of today's program.

Mr. BROWN. If you can provide me with a legislative mechanism to accomplish that, I will try and get it in the farm bill when we rewrite it.

I think, gentlemen, in view of the hour, and the fact we are going to start the afternoon session in a few minutes, that we had better excuse you at this point, and if we do need additional help from you, we will ask you in writing and hope that you can continue to cooperate with us.

Thank you very much.

Mr. RODALE. Thank you very much.

[Whereupon, at 1:15 p.m., the subcommittee was recessed to reconvene at 2:10 p.m.]

AFTERNOON SESSION

Mr. BROWN. The subcommittee will come to order.

Most of the members of the subcommittee are at a briefing session in the next room with Ambassador Brock discussing agricultural trade, probably focusing on the impact of the Russian wheat agreement and some other things like that. They probably will come in a little bit later. In order to avoid going on too long this afternoon and to conserve your time, I think we might as well proceed.

So I welcome Mr. Charles Boothby who represents the National Association of Conservation Districts. You may proceed with your statement, Mr. Boothby, and I will try and be as intelligent about responding to it as I can.

STATEMENT OF CHARLES L. BOOTHBY, EXECUTIVE SECRETARY, NATIONAL ASSOCIATION OF CONSERVATION DISTRICTS

Mr. BOOTHBY. Thank you, Mr. Chairman. In representing the National Association of Conservation Districts, I would prescript by saying that we represent about 2,950 soil and water conservation districts and their State associations in all 50 States, Puerto Rico, Virgin Islands, and even here in the District of Columbia. Conservation districts cover virtually all of the agricultural land in the Nation and work with over 2.5 million cooperating landowners.

Our association and our member districts have long been involved in support of those farming practices which maintain the long-term productivity of the land, both in terms of physical capacity and nutrients.

We have supported research which will assist landowners in achieving these goals. We support research which will: develop reduced tillage practices economically feasible for use under a wide range of soil, climate, and crop conditions; evaluate the impact of wind and water erosion on long-term soil productivity and crop yields in relation to environmental quality; evaluate the impact of soil and water conservation management systems on energy requirements for food and fiber production.

Much additional reserach is needed to improve the management, treatment, and cropping practices on agricultural land. Among the many problems needing new or intensified study are: improvement in the knowledge of soil, water, plant, and atmospheric relationships; techniques and methods of improving the moisture-holding capacity of soil; modification and improvement in soil tilth; increased research in tillage and traction machinery. This is urgently needed to cope with the rapid development of new and larger agricultural machinery; the many facets of the use of herbicides and pesticides, including development of pesticide and herbicide chemicals that will be nonpersistent in the environment, relatively harmless to nontarget pests, harmless to man, domestic animals, and wildlife and economical to purchase and apply; new technology to control pests by nonchemical means.

As you may be aware, this association, in cooperation with USDA and the agricultural industry, has established the Conservation Tillage Information Center. The purpose of the center is to help in the exchange of information among varying parts of the country. The center is attempting to find out who is doing what in the field of conservation tillage.

We are finding that there is a growing interest in all of the various forms of conservation tillage and these methods are being adapted to an increasing variety of crops. Interestingly, in many circumstances, we are finding that the amounts of chemicals applied may actually not exceed conventional tillage methods. In some instances, the amount of chemicals applied may be less than under clean cultivation methods.

We have a few comments on H.R. 2714. We strongly support the provisions of section 4 which calls for an inventory of existing information on various topics relating to low-energy systems of agriculture. I am sure that there is a vast amount of information out there which should be catalogued and analyzed. Only through this inventory can we determine the state of the art.

The 5-year research projects on 12 farms geographically and climatically dispersed should provide even more valuable data on the economics and agronomics of organic agriculture. We support these provisions of the bill.

There is an apparent lack of interest in alternative systems of agriculture within the Department of Agriculture. I feel certain that all of the provisions of the bill could be carried out by USDA under existing authorities. It is obvious, however, that it has not been done and the increased emphasis of new legislation is probably necessary to catch the attention of USDA.

I would add parenthetically with my stubby pencil this morning, in response to a comment by a USDA witness, the amount of money called for in this bill is approximately one-thousandth of 1 percent of the amount of money which is projected to be spent in the payment-in-kind program this year.

Mr. Chairman, thank you for the opportunity to present the views of this association.

Mr. BROWN. Thank you, Mr. Boothby.

I had the pleasure of speaking to a meeting of the Conservation Society up in, not your group but the professional conservation group, I guess, up in Hartford on Monday. I was amazed to see what a large and enthusiastic group there was there and the interest that they had in how we could utilize some of our current farm programs to encourage conservation.

I think you probably heard the remarks this morning, I think it was by Mr. Thompson, that he was not in the PIK program, but if the PIK program could be converted so that he and his conserving practices could benefit from it, that it would be a large stimulus to the kind of agricultural practices that he was engaged in.

Do you have any thoughts about the possibility of doing something of that sort?

Mr. BOOTHBY. Mr. Chairman, we have been concerned over the past several years about the lack of conservation consciousness, if you will, in the commodity programs. They tend to work at cross-purposes in terms of conservation on the land.

We are proposing, and I believe that Mr. Jones has introduced a bill which we feel would tend to offset some of these problems in that it gives the landowner some credit for the land which he sets aside in a voluntary conservation program. In other words, as it presently is, the land that he diverts from production for the purpose of installing grass waterways, terraces and other conservation practices, is taken out of his basic acreage in the commodity programs.

We feel that he should be credited in some way for this set-aside which is done voluntarily so that he isn't penalized the next time a commodity program comes around.

Mr. BROWN. Is this problem addressed in Mr. Jones' bill?

Mr. BOOTHBY. Yes, it is.

Mr. BROWN. Does it cover things like the targeted diversion program?

Mr. BOOTHBY. Yes, sir.

Mr. BROWN. There is considerable interest in the Congress in how we could make these kinds of modifications. I think it would appeal to members of a wide range of philosophy with regard to farm programs, all the way from those who are strong adherents of organic farming to those at the other extreme.

Mr. BOOTHBY. Right.

Mr. BROWN. It is so obviously in the best interest of the total agricultural community and the country as a whole.

Mr. BOOTHBY. Absolutely.

Mr. BROWN. I presume that in mentioning this legislation to Mr. Jones and from your statement that you would be in strong support of legislative initiatives of this sort?

Mr. BOOTHBY. Yes, sir, we do. We feel that unless the commodity programs and the conservation programs can work toward the same purpose in terms of keeping some cover on that land, why we are going to be in real trouble.

We will also know here shortly, as a result of the 1982 national resources inventory by the Soil Conservation Service, we will have an update on the 1977 data which should give us a much better handle on where we are and what direction that we are moving.

We have noticed over the last year a survey that we did just recently indicates that over 26 percent of the total cropland in the Nation is now under some form of conservation tillage and this is something which has come about over the last 5 to 6 years, it is really an amazing change in terms of farming practices that we have not seen this kind of adoption of an agricultural practice so quickly before.

Hopefully we can keep this moving, hopefully we can also move to more regenerative types of agriculture to get more grasses and legumes back into the rotation. I think conservation tillage and regenerative agriculture are a part of the same package.

Mr. Brown. Yes, I agree with you completely on that.

You made an interesting statement about the possibility that with conservation tillage you would actually use less chemicals than under conventional systems, and I know very little about it, but that seems to fly in the face of reason. Could you explain to me a little bit about that?

Mr. Boothby. I will attempt to explain by using a few examples.

Granted the mix of agricultural chemicals probably changes under a conservation tillage system over a conventional system. But they found in many areas of the West where cheat grass is a real problem in terms of a weed in wheat, that by not plowing is not moving the residual seed to the surface or near the surface where it can sprout and grow.

Therefore, not having to use the herbicide to control the cheat grass in the wheat plantations and, therefore, they are actually getting a reduction in the amount of pesticides used. There is some increase in some areas of some types of bugs and so forth that seem to multiply in the duff on the surface, but for the most part this is controlled with no increase of agricultural chemicals.

Now, conventional agriculture, if you want to use that term, or high chemical agriculture, clean tillage is not chemical free. There is a tremendous amount of chemicals used in this type of agriculture as well, so except there is a shift in the mix of agricultural chemicals but the total is not greater.

Mr. Brown. Mr. Boothby, you were here this morning.

Mr. Boothby. Yes, for most of the morning.

Mr. Brown. Did you hear the brief discussion we had with the last panel having to do with the fact that organic farming or regenerative farming, whatever we wish to call it, because it does seem to reduce the dollar flow through the system and reduce inputs, does not meet with the favor of certain elements of the overall food chain; the input suppliers is a good example, the chemical companies and maybe others who would be involved. What we have is a play of political forces at work here in terms of structuring the politics of the thing and whether or not this kind of a situation can be alleviated so that there isn't quite as much opposition to regenerative farming.

Your members, the various conservation districts, are probably exposed to this on a day-to-day basis.

Mr. Boothby. That is right.

Mr. Brown. I wonder if you have any constructive suggestions as to how we can reach some understanding of what is in the best interests of the total system so that we all get a fair distribution of the costs and benefits here. It seems sometimes that the farmer ends up getting most of the cost and not enough of the benefits.

Mr. BOOTHBY. I think a lot depends on whether the constituency of the U.S. Department of Agriculture should be the farmer or the agribusiness community.

It has been suggested on several occasions in other forums than this perhaps that the constituency of the Department of Agriculture may in fact not be the farmer out there. So I think in terms of this bill, if in fact the constituency is the folks out there on the land, why this bill makes a lot of sense.

Mr. BROWN. Well, I think it is a little more complicated than that. You know the chemical people and the other farm input suppliers, your friendly equipment dealers and your grain elevator operators and whatever, I am not that familiar with all the details of the system, but they are working on the farmer all the time. The farmer can really come to feel the same set of values that they feel, and if when he does that, then his demands in effect reflect their interests rather than his own.

Mr. BOOTHBY. Well, that is true, and I think we have to look a little bit at history. This was not always the case. It used to be that the farmer looked to his extension agent for the most recent and up-to-date information that he could find in terms of operation of his farm. With the lack of emphasis on production, if you will, by the Department of Agriculture and the universities and more and more on terms of what you might call inbed research with the chemicals industries and others, I think the farmers have gone more and more to industry for the answers.

I think this bill could help to turn that around, but I also cite a parallel in our work with the conservation tillage. We found at first that machinery manufacturers were reluctant to assist in this program because they still had more plows to sell and they had not yet developed the new equipment which was necessary to make conservation tillage operational.

Now that they are getting more and more equipment which is geared to various types of conservation tillage, they are much more supportive of the whole concept of conservation tillage. I think it can be turned around with others as well.

Mr. BROWN. Well, I would think so. I have been trying to get the chemical companies to take an interest in integrated pest management, and they will give at least lip service to this. They recognize the fact that the chemicals are not the only answer to the controlling of pests, and they sometimes have on their staff very well trained entomologists and others prepared to advise the farmer, but they haven't yet seen the same commercial opportunity in providing a knowledge service based upon total management of the pest population.

It is much easier to sell a chemical and tell the farmer how much of it to use, and help him spray it on right and so forth than it is to go through the more complex process of understanding the delicate ecological balance that may exist and how the chemicals can screw it up and so forth.

Mr. BOOTHBY. I think that there you are into a field where there isn't the return, more immediate return to the chemical manufacturer which he can get out of his research money in chemicals. If

we can assist with some public inputs in terms of research, I think
that we can assist them to show them where they can turn a dollar
on integrated pest management.

Mr. BROWN. Well, unfortunately, the growth of Federal and
other regulatory activities has made the research more and more
expensive, the costs of putting a new product into the field have
grown. I have a great deal of sympathy for the chemical companies
in this whole process, although they sometimes don't believe it, but
I still think we have to look at the total picture of what is best for
the farmer and the consumer as well as the chemical company if
we are going to survive here. It is our failure to do this in other
areas that has lost us our competitive role in a number of different
fields.

I wonder if Mr. Jeffords has any questions.

Mr. JEFFORDS. No, Mr. Chairman, I appreciate the witness' testimony. I have nothing further.

Mr. BROWN. Thank you very much, Mr. Boothby.

Mr. BOOTHBY. Thank you.

Mr. BROWN. Our next witness is Mr. William Kruesi, extension
service, University of Vermont, Woodstock, Vt., and if Mr. Jeffords
has anything nice he would like to say about Mr. Kruesi, I will recognize him.

Mr. JEFFORDS. It is good to have you with us. I would like to say
that Mr. Kruesi has done an outstanding job of articulating what is
becoming an important part of Vermont's agriculture. I am aware
of his particular interest in another area of agriculture, the sheep
business in Vermont. It is a pleasure to have you here to discuss
with us your thoughts on how we might do more to help the organic farming industry.

Mr. BROWN. You may proceed.

STATEMENT OF WILLIAM K. KRUESI, COUNTY EXTENSION AGENT-AGRICULTURE, UNIVERSITY OF VERMONT

Mr. KRUESI. Thank you, Mr. Chairman.

I am very happy to be able to testify today. I don't often get an
opportunity as a county extension agent to give my views to groups
such as this, and I feel very lucky to work directly with farmers,
the most wonderful people in the world to work with, and particularly two groups of farmers; one is the small and part-time farmers.

The latest USDA census of agriculture tells us that the number
of part-time farmers in this country is about 64 percent of all farmers. In the New England States, we had a growth of 50 to 120 percent in the number of part-time farmers from 1974 to 1978, and
this is growing by leaps and bounds. At any time we have growth
in an agricultural industry, I think we need to look at that and it
is a reason for some commitment and optimism.

The second group that I am fortunate to work with is full-time
commercial farmers who are interested in alternatives. This is
demonstrated by feature articles in such magazines as the Furrow
by John Deere Corp., Harvest Farming Agriview and the American
Fruit Grower. These are conventional farm periodicals that have

come out very recently with articles about alternative or organic farmers, and this is a big change in direction.

So we have a growth in the number of small, part-time farmers who are innovative, often highly educated, willing to change. You tell them something, and they do it. They are very well educated and they are interested in the latest methods of agriculture and I am supposed to supply them with that information.

Our full-time commercial dairymen in Vermont, many of them also are interested in alternatives, particularly the young dairymen who are so strapped for cash at this time.

The major obstacle, as I see it, is lack of recognition by our public agricultural institutions, the Extension Service, the USDA. We have no coordinating role for this program area which we might call alternative agriculture.

As you know, the county extension agent is very accountable to his State director and also to the Federal Government and the program areas which we address funnel up through the system until they get to the Federal Government, and they are shown as big numbers and they are in dairy, nutrition and crops and soils and fertilizer and this type of thing, but I think that resembles organic agriculture as a system is lost in the shuffle.

I think that is a tragedy as far as agriculture education. We have lost an opportunity there.

Let me give you some specific cases. In our pest control recommendations, it is no surprise that they are heavily slanted toward the application of agricultural chemicals. I can't do much about this as a county agent. This information must be approved from a State specialist or from the Agricultural Research Service as bona fide research that has been found to be, in an objective scientific setting, to be worthwhile to pass on to farmers, and I don't have this information for alternatives.

We have pest control recommendations now in a computer. This takes away my opportunity to be face-to-face with the farmer and discuss prevention, prevention of weed problems, livestock parasites, prevention of insect pests on crops. Now we have turned to the computer for a quick and easy answer, and our extension bulletins are the same way. They are very brief, they deal mostly with the product itself rather than the biology or the cultural control of the pest or the problem confronting the farmer.

Second, we have a widespread abuse in the livestock industry and it has to do with drugs. It is antibiotics, it is sulfa drugs, and it is worming medication. It is well known among my farmers that there are a number of worming medications which are no longer effect ve because of resistance to internal parasites from these drugsi

This is difficult to perceive what kind of economic loss this will cause farmers. It is only a matter of time. Antibiotic treatment for certain kinds of mastitis are no longer effective because we have pathogens which are resistant to these drugs.

This parallels the problems with insecticide resistance that we saw 10 or 15 years ago where in a very simple-minded way we used an agricultural chemical to control the pest and that pest, because it is very easily, it is in a large population, you have genetic mutation, you have resistance in the new insect population; this is occurring in the livestock industry and it is an unseen problem grossly ignored by the veterinary pharmaceutical industry because they are sure their product works, and they would like to sell it.

To many farmers it is a real concern. You see it in the veal industry, in many confinement areas of swine, a big problem in sheep and the beef industries, particularly with worming medications.

Another problem has to do with our perception of utilizing forage and range lands. Forty-five percent of the agricultural land in this country is suitable only for permitting vegetation, that means pasture, forest industry and wildlife. So we have a tremendous resource in pastures and rangelands, and yet we are managing them very poorly.

The conventional wisdom of utilizing these pastures has a great deal to do with your synthetic nitrogen, fertilizer, even growth in plants for the cattle so they will produce more, feed additives so they will have a different fermentation on high roughage rations and things that bespeak of high technology which are really product fixes to a problem which is low production on these pasturelands.

The answer or the alternative which needs to be discussed with farmers has to do with grazing management that is practiced in the United Kingdom, in New Zealand and Australia where on a very low-cost, low-input system, low-capital farmers are able to utilize subdivision fencing and have some intensive rotational grazing, doubling and tripling the carrying capacity on the pastureland with very little cost, no herbicides, no growth in plants or animals and better conservation of that grassland resource.

So we have one way of thinking which tells us to use various products to improve pasture productivity and another way of thinking, which is my way of thinking, that there is a low-cost alternative which management we need to get this out to farmers.

Finally, I am most concerned about the skills of young farmers, those that are 30, 35 perhaps. They come to me, and they have lost the technique for cultivating weeds. They only know how to grow corn with herbicide. They have lost the technique for some preventive health care measures.

Instead they have routine visits from the veterinarian, high veterinarian bills, less and less able to manage around livestock health.

They are served very well by industry. In fact, more so than from a county agent. This bothers me. We have people that employ a service in sales to farmers but have few people educating them about cultural practices and these alternatives we are talking about, nonchemical alternatives.

The young farmer is extremely important to our agricultural industry and unless we have a coordinated effort to offer them alternatives, unless we can recognize organic farming as being possible, useful and explore whether it is indeed useful, the county agent can do nothing but simply say that some people practice organic farming. I can make no objective statement about it. I have model farmers in my area that are organic farmers, and I don't dare to put them on a podium for fear of ridicule.

My direction comes from the State director in Vermont and his direction comes from the Federal Government. It is up to a public institution, to a national institution with an umbrella effect, like the USDA, to give us this mandate that, yes, our clients are using these methods, let's see if they have merit, let's publicize the people that are successful with them, and this I think is what in a very small way the Agricultural Productivity Act of 1983 is asking for.

Thank you very much, and I would be happy to answer any questions that you may have.

[The prepared statement of Mr. Kruesi appears at the conclusion of the hearing.]

Mr. BROWN. Thank you.

Mr. Jeffords.

Mr. JEFFORDS. Bill, that was excellent. I am very pleased with your work in the State. I would like to ask you to give me your evaluation of the integrated pest management approach to pest control; in particular, I am interested in your opinion as to how successful this approach has been. Finally, was this not considered somewhat "radical" in the not too distant past?

Mr. KRUESI. I am glad you asked that question. The integrated pest management is a model of having disciplines, agricultural, scientific disciplines working together to solve a problem, and it has indeed reduced pesticide use in a number of crops. The shortcoming is that we have pieces of agricultural research which offer low-cost, low-energy, low-chemical alternatives to the farmer, but they are not integrated in any way; they are not coordinated in any way.

This was possible when there was a USDA organic farming coordinator, at least we had hopes of that. Now we are simply not putting pieces of that agricultural research into an area which says that this is alternative agriculture and can it survive on its own.

Farmers are interested. They are reading about it in the popular press. They do ask questions. They do see their neighbors across the road that use alternatives, but the outreach isn't there, it is not there from the extension service, not there from USDA.

I think we need a coordinating organization, coordinating role to look at alternatives like the IPM program and a pilot to many other aspects of crop and livestock production. Alternative agriculture, as you know, Jim, is a broad based approach and that is important. We want a broad-based approach. It is not very useful to have two or three pieces of agricultural research that, well, if you really dug through the agricultural journals you could apply those to farmers.

I need someone, an agricultural specialist, to transfuse that information and bring it to me as an alternative, and many times the scientific knowledge that is accumulated, which has a nonchemical approach, is not utilized enough, at least within the extension service. Then it doesn't filter down to the farmers and this research is in biological control of insects and using crop rotations to control weeds, these kinds of things.

I know they are bits of pieces you know; where I find out about them is in the organic farming press; that is too bad. I would like to see that come from our university agricultural experiment stations and from USDA; then I would like it better.

Mr. JEFFORDS. You have partly answered my second question. I know of the innovative practices you have recommended for farms such as, Shelburne Farms. My question was going to be, where is that information coming from? Is the extension service giving it? Are our agricultural colleges up to speed on what is going on or are they a little bit behind?

Mr. KRUESI. Thank you for asking that, Mr. Chairman, Jim. My peers in agricultural education in extension, extension specialists and research scientists, are very timid about talking about alternative agriculture. Yes, it has connotations that drift way back 10 or 15 years ago as being outlandish and farfetched. I am most concerned about what the farmer needs in terms of technology, and there is no reason why factual, objective information does not have to be labeled as organic, but essentially that is what it is, and we need that information at least to provide the farmers who are asking me for it, to provide them with information; it is not for my own need or for the need of other extension agents, it is for the farmers and they are asking us for it and that is why I think we are being slow to help them with it.

Mr. JEFFORDS. I know we have a series of votes coming up, so I would be happy to yield to you so that you may ask some questions before we have to leave.

Mr. BROWN. I think I have a couple of questions.

I am not too familiar with Vermont agriculture, but I have heard that in at least portions of New England, after some generations of declining farm acreages and numbers of people on the farm, that there is now the beginnings of a regrowth of agriculture in this area. Is that true in Vermont?

Mr. KRUESI. That is correct. The growth is primarily in the number of small-scale farms. We have many dairy farms which are no longer economic units, and they are split up and subdivided. The median age of our dairy farmers is high, in the fifties, and I am afraid the young people cannot afford to go into full-time commercial farming. They still desire farm lifestyle, still desire to work the land; they have white- and blue-collar jobs, they have part time, they are working two jobs, often it is not a hobby; they are resettling rural America, these small and part-time farmers.

It is very important for New England because they are keeping the land open, and they are supporting the farm service industries that support the dairy farmers, equipment dealers, feed manufacturers, fertilizer and seed sales people remark that their business is only kept alive by these small and part-time farmers because of the shrinking dairy base and the dairy farmers, I feel, feel good about that trend also.

That used to be somewhat antagonistic, simply cultural societal differences between them, between the newcomer and the person who had roots there, but now dairymen feel very much in support and almost a big brother/big sister kind of role with the part-time farmers, and in a way it is funny, it helped, no matter how bumbling they are in getting started in farm, the dairymen want them to succeed too.

Mr. BROWN. You gave us earlier some percentage on the number of small, part-time farmers, and I didn't believe them because I thought I heard you say that 120 percent of the farm population was small and part-time farmers. Would you clarify that for me?

Mr. KRUESI. Certainly, Mr. Chairman, you find those statistics from Connecticut, the growth in the number of small and part-time farmers from 1974 to 1978, with the gross income of $1,000 or more increased 119 percent.

Mr. BROWN. Oh, yes, the income increased. What percentage of the total farm population, though, is small and part-time farmers?

Mr. KRUESI. I believe it is 64 percent of all farmers. Not small farmers, but they are part time. There are people that work off the farm; some of those farms, as you know, are cash crop farms of sizable acreage.

Mr. BROWN. You are enthusiastically supporting this legislation, as I interpret your remarks.

Mr. KRUESI. Yes, I am. My director of the Extension Service was I think a little bit afraid of my testimony.

Mr. BROWN. I was going to ask you about that.

Mr. KRUESI. We are very defensive in the Extension Service, we guard our reputation and our past accomplishments too much. We are not self-critical. There is nothing I would like better than to see the Extension Service be progressive and help farmers.

Mr. BROWN. Well, if you have any problems with your boss, because of your testimony, just speak to your Congressman, he will take care of it.

Thank you very much.

Mr. JEFFORDS. I would just say that Bill can get away with it because he does such a tremendous job with everything he does in his job. They give him a little latitude in this area that they may not give someone else. I want to express my sincere appreciation. It was very excellent testimony.

Mr. BROWN. We have two more witnesses. I am going to have to call a short recess. We will have two votes which will take about 15 minutes; therefore, the subcommittee will be in recess for about 15 minutes, then we will call Dr. Larry Nelson next and then the last panel.

[Recess taken.]

Mr. BROWN. The subcommittee will come to order.

In connection with Mr. Kruesi's statement just before the recess, he slightly abbreviated his testimony, and without objection, the full text will appear in the record together with several additional items which were attached to his testimony reflecting materials available from the Vermont Extension Service.

Our next witness will be Dr. Larry A. Nelson, who is a professor of statistics at North Carolina University, and representing the division of agriculture of the National Association of State Universities and Land-Grant Colleges.

We are pleased to have you here, Dr. Nelson, and you may proceed with your statement. It will appear in full in the record if you should abbreviate any of it.

STATEMENT OF LARRY A. NELSON, PROFESSOR OF STATISTICS, NORTH CAROLINA STATE UNIVERSITY, REPRESENTING THE DIVISION OF AGRICULTURE, NATIONAL ASSOCIATION OF STATE UNIVERSITIES AND LAND-GRANT COLLEGES

Mr. NELSON. Thank you, Mr. Chairman and members of the subcommittee.

I am here today at the request of the division of agriculture of the National Association of State Universities and Land-Grant Colleges, which is primarily interested in section 5 of H.R. 2714, the section dealing with pilot research studies.

Professionally, my own interest lies in the proper design and conduct of agricultural experiments and in the appropriate analysis and interpretation of data resulting therefrom. I have had extensive experience in designing agricultural experiments during the past 20 years and I teach courses in the statistics department of North Carolina State University relating to agricultural field experiments.

I have an interest in on-farm researcher and the design of these types of experiments, and I have done considerable work in Latin America over the years on designing field experiments.

I will be referring to the studies described in section 5 as an experiment because collectively they do have all of the essential ingredients of an experiment. The issue which the division of agriculture and I wish to raise is that an experiment of the type described in the bill is difficult to design and execute.

There are many factors being varied simultaneously but not in a well-balanced methodical way. A few of these factors are crop rotation, use of crop and animal residues and organic wastes, conservation tillage and biological pest control.

In addition, the bill specifies that farms should be chosen to have the widest possible variations in soil, land, and climactic conditions. We contend that unless careful thought is devoted to the design phase of this experiment, it will be difficult to determine which factors are causing the possible responses obtained either because of the confounding of effects inherent in this design or due to the lack of experiment precision caused by the high degree of variability introduced into the system by the deliberate representation of a wide variety of farms—in other words, a lack of experimental control—because we have tried to broaden the scope of inferences to a wider population in the end.

There are a number of questions which arise from reading section 5 of the bill. For example, No. 1, why doesn't the experiment include a third treatment which will serve as a control?

This treatment would involve the use of chemical fertilizers, pesticides, et cetera, on an as-needed basis, which is the practice currently used by many farmers. Without this treatment, the information from the experiment will be incomplete.

One might say that we have plenty of information on this type of treatment already, but again, an experiment contains treatments which are compared under very controlled conditions and it is very difficult to replicate a season or an environmental condition.

No. 2, could more than one treatment be compared within the same season on the same farm or should an entire farm be used as the experimental unit? The former approach is the traditional one and therefore there are statistical techniques available to this type of research.

In addition, the control of variation is much easier to achieve when treatment comparisons are made within the same season on the same farm. Quantitative techniques for comparing responses of entire farms are not as readily available. I wish they were.

No. 3, if the entire farm is the experimental unit, will 12 farms per treatment be a sufficient number of replications in view of the high farm-to-farm variability? Was the number 12 arrived at through objective techniques? Does this number need to be stated explicitly in the bill?

Keep in mind that we have introduced some of this high farm-to-farm variability into the system in order that we would have a broad base upon which to draw our inferences.

How was the number 12 arrived at? I have people call me and say, how many replications should I use on an experiment. And if I say eight, they would be very happy, but if I try to explain how the number comes about, what the process of decision is, they have problems with that.

Mr. BROWN. Twelve was selected because there are 12 disciples.

Mr. NELSON. That is right. OK, thank you.

No. 4, who will do the actual experimentation? Will the farmer or a trained experimentalist, or will they be working together?

No. 5, because crop rotations are involved, are there any provisions for growing each crop on each farm each year? This is one of the basic principles which has traditionally been incorporated into the design of rotation experiments.

No. 6, isn't 5 years a short period of time in which to evaluate effects involving crop rotations and farming systems which usually take considerably longer periods of time to manifest their effects? Rotation experiments are often run for 12–24 years in order to complete several cycles of the rotations.

Some rotation experiments have been run at universities around the country. We had some that ran for 12 years and we had 3-year cycles. It would be more ideal to have them run 24 years. By the time the 24 years are up, the man who designed the project, the statistician is no longer around, usually.

For the rotations with long periods, say 4 years, only one cycle will be included in the experiment. In this case, each crop will be grown in only one environmental setting.

These are but a few of the questions which need to be considered in planning this complex experiment. I do not profess to know all the answers to these questions.

The point which we wish to make is that we would encourage you to specifically state in the bill that specialists in various phases of agricultural research—including experimental design—will be commissioned by the Secretary of Agriculture to plan and design this experiment using accepted experimental techniques in order that the results will be scientifically valid.

We found this necessary over the years to hit this very early at the planning stage. If we don't consider the planning of the experiment properly, then we will be disappointed when we are sorting through the numbers that run from the experiment.

These specialists should be given considerable flexibility in choosing the approach to use. For example, the group which would be commissioned by the Secretary might determine that the experiment would be more informative if a third treatment were included as suggested before. Or it may decide that the number of farms per treatment should be different from 12 in order to achieve the goals of this experiment—maybe 13, maybe less than 12. Or perhaps it may find it necessary to assign the treatments to pairs or sets of three farms which are chosen to be very similar. Such a grouping—called pairing for two treatments—may result in considerable reduction in experimental variability.

The idea there is to take the pair-to-pair variations in order that tests may be made and we will have a good precise comparison of treatments that are to be compared. This usually results in considerable reduction in experimental variability or what we call in statistics, experimental error.

We would like to see it stated also that there would be a follow through, that those who designed the experiment inasmuch as it is possible would be those who continue to monitor the technical aspects of the agricultural research to assure that it continues to be carried out according to those carefully laid plans that I just discussed.

The reason for adding the above two provisions to the bill is that these points are often overlooked in the early phases of research projects and it is only at that data analysis and interpretational phase that it is discovered that the experiment was not designed properly or that improper experimental techniques were used. In simple experiments conducted on one farm, such oversight may not have such far-reaching effects as in complex experiments such as the one being proposed in the bill.

I might mention parenthetically here that we talked a little bit, the term was mentioned this morning "case studies" and information could be obtained from single farms. I am sure there is a certain amount of truth to this, that we do this in medicine. We do a lot of case study work in medical research but we would like to generalize as much as possible, some way or another, try to average over more than one farm so that we can make a recommendation to more than one farm at a time, the population of farms, and so there is some advantage in networking or bringing a complete series of 12 farms together in some kind of combined analysis of the data.

In conclusion, we contend that all of the operational details and specifications of an experiment cannot and should not be described in a bill of this type. On the other hand, there are many operational details which should be established at the planning stage by agricultural and statistical specialists.

We would encourage you to state in the bill that the Secretary of Agriculture will commission certain agricultural and statistical specialists to design this experiment according to accepted techniques and then that these same specialists continue to monitor the experiment to insure that it is conducted according to the well-laid plans.

Our experience has been that written requirements of this type are needed and are very helpful in reminding all parties involved that we simply cannot afford to take chances on the success of a large complex experiment such as this by failing to utilize the expertise available at this point in time.

Mr. Chairman, this concludes my prepared remarks. Thank you.

Mr. BROWN. Thank you very much, Dr. Nelson. Your remarks are very helpful and will be referred to in connection with our further effort to perfect this bill.

I would comment that with regard to the time frame for the bill, it is authorized for 5 years, but if it should be determined that it would be productive for an additional amount of time, it would not be unheard of to extend an experiment of this sort by just renewing the legislation for another 5 years.

I wanted to ask you one question. The bill has been drafted in a rather broad way so as to involve as many of the actors in the agricultural research scene as possible. It also provides that the Secretary can contract out the management of this experiment.

As I read it, it would be possible even to contract it out to your institution. Would you concur in that interpretation?

Mr. NELSON. Well, I think section 8 dealing with agreements deal with this matter. To me, it is still a bit general and I would like to see that made more specific, that there is a interdisciplinary team that does this planning right from the beginning and then not be so specific as to do the work.

But then I would be, perhaps, a little less specific in section 5 where we are specifying how many farms and how many of each type, because the time might find that 12 or 14 or whatever number.

Mr. BROWN. Well, your comment, as one well-versed in research, is highly pertinent and I think it would be possible to add some language stating that modifications could be made in this scheme upon the advice of a proper consulting committee or something of that sort.

Mr. Evans, do you have any questions for Dr. Nelson?

Mr. EVANS of Iowa. Thank you, Mr. Chairman.

Dr. Nelson, I want to compliment you on your testimony. It gets right at the heart of our next problem, which is how to refine the bill. You have been very specific and that is very helpful. I agree with the chairman. We will pay very close attention to your remarks and your recommendations.

I would like to ask you, as the bill is presently written, would you, as a scientist, say that the program we have set forth would be better described as a demonstration rather than an experiment?

Mr. NELSON. I think there are both kinds of aspects. I think you are aspiring to a research experiment, you would like to conduct a research experiment which we call a comparative experiment. You want to compare these two treatments which would be the conventional and the traditional treatment. Yet there are a lot of demonstrational benefits envisaged by those who are designing it, and so I think we would have to consider it an experiment at this point.

If you want to conduct demonstrations, that is more a one to one, one farm doing one thing and the neighbor farm doing the other. It is hard to demonstrate to other people quantitatively. In other words, we are lacking replication when we do that.

In statistics, the father of modern statistics had three principles—replication, radomization and local control or blocking or pairing, like I talked about before. So the thing that is lacking here on demonstrations is the replication.

Certain people will, even though the means could be hundreds of bushels apart or 50 bushels apart, quantitatively it is quite a difference, then you come up with a question: Well, how precise are those two means? And that is where the replication comes in.

So I still feel it is an experiment the way the bill is written but there will be a lot of benefits coming, plowing new ground, so to speak.

Mr. BROWN. Mr. Weaver.

Mr. WEAVER. Thank you, Mr. Chairman.

I just want to also compliment Dr. Nelson on very helpful testimony. I thank you. Your contributions certainly will be considered very carefully when we mark up the bill.

Mr. NELSON. Thank you, sir.

Mr. BROWN. Thank you very much, Dr. Nelson, for your very helpful testimony.

Our last witnesses this afternoon are Mr. Joseph Dunsmoor, Organic Farms, Inc., of Beltsville, Md., and Thomas Harding, Progressive Agri-Systems, Stockertown, Pa.

If both of you gentlemen would come up.

Mr. Dunsmoor, we are pleased to have you here. It is good to know that we have somebody actively engaged in this type of farming in the near vicinity and we will be pleased to hear your presentation.

The full text will be included in the record and you may digress from it in any way that you wish.

STATEMENT OF JOSEPH E. DUNSMOOR, PRESIDENT, ORGANIC FARMS, INC.

Mr. DUNSMOOR. Thank you, Mr. Chairman and members of the subcommittee.

I always like being last; that way I don't have to go over anything that anybody else has already gone over.

I would like to read my statement and then I would like to give the floor to Mr. Harding, and then answer any questions.

I will touch upon the issue of productivity, but my key concerns are with the other purposes.

Organic Farms, Inc., is a full-line wholesale distributor and broker for organically grown produce and commodities serving the east coast. We have, because of our position as a buyer of organically grown food, much interaction with the organic farmers over the years. It is this interaction with the farmers across the United States which allows me to experience the productivity of the organic farming systems firsthand.

The system of organic agriculture follows many different philosophies, yet these philosophies merge into one basic system which incorporates soil and fertility as the key. Tilth, biological activity, macro- and micro-nutrients and farming techniques are the basis of a fertile soil. It is a fertile balanced soil which produces healthy plants and these healthy vigorous plants which produce health in animals and humans.

Crop yields are not the only factor regarding productivity. Nutrition of crops—protein, vitamins, and micro-nutrient content—storage life and shrink factor are all keys to the bottom line profit of organic farmers.

The farmer is the steward of his land and we are the stewards of the Earth. Ours is to leave the Earth not only as good as, but in a better condition than we found it. We have among our resources the capacity to do this but America has chosen in this generation to follow the philosophy of the petro-chemical agriculture, and I need not list the facts of what this so-called modern agriculture is doing to our environment.

We are here as mature men and women looking for a way out of our agricultural rut. A portion of our lives behind us, what will be the legacy of what we leave behind for our children and grandchildren? Will there be a generation of pollution, inbalance in the soil and environment, contamination? Will it be their responsibility to clean up the mess that we have made or will we have the foresight now to do something?

You men of Congress are in a position to legislate change—to create for research a fertile soil, a healthy plant, a balanced environment. May I remind you that this is a beginning of a new technology building upon the system which God created in nature? Fertile soil, in the organic sense of the word, is a creation which America has never experienced before.

We have the technology in front of us; I pray that we have the sense to use it.

Mr. BROWN. Mr. Harding.

STATEMENT OF THOMAS HARDING, PROGRESSIVE AGRI-SYSTEMS

Mr. HARDING. Thank you, Mr. Chairman and members of the subcommittee.

Progressive Agri-Systems has for the past several years been aggressively involved in what was called alternative agriculture and organic farming and somewhat involved in via dynamic techniques and a number of other things, primarily as an agriculture consulting firm but with some product distribution, and currently are involved in the importation and exportation of all natural botanical pest controls.

One of the things that brought us into the field of agriculture consulting, particularly alternative agricultural consulting, was the need for this kind of a service and the great need for information in this particular field.

We are farmers first. We still farm in Pennsylvania. We are deeply involved with farmers today. We are involved in soil, in crop management systems on consulting as well as on a product distribution basis. One of the things that we have tried to do as we employ soil management systems under the alternatives, at least the methodology of alternatives, as we try to find information that will be the most up to date, the most appropriate technology, and some innovative disciplines, and some execution of some very sound practices, as we pursue this endeavor, we found that it is a very tough road to hold.

One of the reasons for that is that most of the people that we are working with are not, as many people would think in this room, organic farmers per se, but they are conventional farmers seeking alternatives and seeking a very desperate change in the current methodologies that they are using.

But when you start to integrate the system, which is probably where we are getting closer to each day, you have a multitude of disciplines to choose from. With that you have to be more exact in the information that you are providing for these people.

The soil is a very complex structure. The crop system is a very complex group of structures, and what we have tried to do is to go to various places for this information. It has not been available, so what we have done is we have started to develop our own information.

The work that the people have done, people like Mr. Dunsmoor and many other people in this room, including Mr. Kruesi, needless to say, has been very helpful.

We are not only involved in soil management but we are also involved in livestock management programs. We don't employ systems that are archaic. We employ systems that are very innovative.

One of the concepts that we are working with now in livestock management programs is that of microbiotics, which is a microgenetic process. One of the largest companies in this country has recognized the need for this area to be advanced. It has been an incredible step forward in recognizing the need for change and the way we are handling the antibiotics within the system of livestock management.

I wanted to make a comment about the term of this particular research and this particular Farm Productivity Act.

As we have started to, through our transitional programs, convert the conventional farm system or the farmer to a more or less energy-intensive system and hopefully to a more organically inclined system, we found that we have realized very quickly somewhere around 2 or 3 years into the system a noticeable change within the soil, a noticeable change within the crop system, and a noticeable change in the debt, particularly if he applies his principles out for him.

I think that 3 to 5 years, particularly the outside of that 5 years, is more than adequate to realize some significant scientific data for us to really fully evaluate. What I am asking for is that we truly give this an opportunity.

We are not asking to advance ourselves out and beyond and have a pendulant effect as we have seen so many times before. We are really saying, let us have a fair opportunity for evaluation. Give us the opportunity to employ this badly needed research. Give us the opportunity to provide to the people that we are serving, all of us here, that is the farmer, the information that he or she needs to choose the alternatives that they so desire to do.

What we most of all have is an incredible responsibility to save the agricultural system from what is obviously going to be a very bad situation in the next several years. We have another responsibility and that is to the rest of the world that looks toward us and at us for direction.

I think we had better fully understand that responsibility in choosing all of the necessary research criteria which I think we can design at some other time after this bill is passed, I hope. I think we have to be very concerned about that responsibility, and what it means to mankind as a whole.

I want to go one step further into what I have recognized in the USDA research programs as they are sort of slanted in many cases. Many times there are cuts in funds and the people have no choice but to go outside to large agribusiness and sometimes to small agribusiness like ourselves for this additional funding.

What we really need in this agriculture research portion of the bill is unbiased, very serious research. It is very critical to it. We need it to remain within the public domain, if you will. It has to be public directed research if it is going to have the influence on the farmer that it must have in order for him to seek new and more positive directions.

I don't think that would occur if we left it totally to the private enterprise system and I, being one of those, might be somewhat concerned about that if I were sitting on the other side of this table. But I am not because I entrust, as the farmer is entrusted and people with wisdom like yourself, Mr. Chairman and the subcommittee and the Congress of the United States, that you are going to give us this opportunity to provide the kind of information that is badly needed to change direction and to change direction for the best and for the right of the farmer.

One of the things that is really important is that he gets away from this debt-ridden situation that he now sits in. One of the things I have recognized as I have gone around is that the average organic farmer and his debt-to-equity ratio is far better off than the average industrial agriculturalist. And that is a rather significant indicator that maybe something else besides the methods that we have been employing for the past several years might just be a better way.

I think this bill and the necessary research that it encompasses will give us that opportunity for that fair and equitable evaluation.

I am involved in, as I said earlier, in the importation and the exportation of natural pest controls, botanicals. Right now, of course, I am caught in the trap of the pending lawsuit of Montsanto and EPA, which is another reason why public research must be an important part. But let me tell you, one of the things that has really impressed me as I have got involved in this natural pest control business is the incredible interest in the developing world and the rest of the world in what we do here in the United States, as I said earlier.

The requests have come from all over the world. The requests have come from not less than six extension services throughout this country who are seriously interested in what botanicals can do in dealing with the pest management situation that we have. That is a very positive step on their part and I am very pleased and will work with them in any way that I can.

I want to tell you the big thing that came out of it as I was sitting in a meeting several weeks ago was when the county extension group was together and the State entomologist stood up and talked many, many times about how important the new pyrethroid were and the wonderful agrichemicals were and he went on for about 1½ hours on how we just got the tomato crops and corn crops improved and how wonderful these new synthetics were.

I sat there with several of the growers that I work with who are full-time farmers concerned about income, all of them knowing that what he is saying is not true. I finally had all I could take and I stood up at the end and I said, "Sir, I would like for you to address the element of resistance." And he said, "Oh, my God," he said, "it is a real problem."

Now, if I had not asked that question, he would have never addressed that issue. What he finally said after a little bit more pressure is that we are finding that just in one and two and three generations with certain pesticides out there that we have resistance buildup and that we have to rotate our pesticides. At least we have learned how to rotate something.

He finally said to me, "I would like to try and see what we can do with some of these botanical pesticides," and immediately made sure he had some that he could take back home. But the important message is there.

Sometimes as we start to look at this research, when it is not truly public research, full funded by the public, it sort of gets slanted in the dissemination process. I think that is a tragedy, not because I am involved in natural pesticides—I am doing it out of necessity because no one else would do it, I suppose—but because I care about the information that is being given to these farmers and the tremendous effect it has on their net income opportunities. I think that is a tremendous responsibility to me as a consultant, you as a congressional body and we as people in the United States. It is an ultimate responsibility that we must meet and that is to do the best for all.

What I would like to say in closing is I would like to invite all the members of the subcommittee, and certainly the Secretary of Agriculture and you, Mr. Chairman, who I know visits many farms, to tour with me on occasion, some of the organic farmers that I work with and talk to them about net farm income, debt-to-equity ratios and see how they are practicing these methods that are so beautifully outlined in this Farm Productivity Act of 1983.

Earlier someone spoke about a partnership. Well, I truly believe that this is a partnership and that there is a need for a more effective partnership. The partnership that we talked about was we were going to use all the information and cover all the avenues that are available to us. Well, all you have to do is take the Pennsylvania Agronomy Guide and turn to it and every page is covered with chemical herbicides, pesticides, fungicides, mydicides. It does not give us any choice for alternatives. It only says different trade names are available. Only different names for the same chemistry.

What I would like to see is at the bottom of those pages we will submit that the bottom will be good enough in this case was that we had the choice of alternatives.

In closing, further, our last responsibility is education. As an agriculture consultant and a provider of product, I found that my biggest job has been providing education for the transitional programs and to maintain good net income in organic farming.

There is no place to turn. This public financed research and its information research would help us do that and it would give county extension agents like Bill Kruesi the opportunity to disseminate not only the one side of the story but the other side of the story as well.

Mr. Chairman, I beg of you and the members of this subcommittee to use the wisdom that I know that all of you employed so much, to not only carry this bill to the floor of the Congress but to make it an active bill.

Thank you very much.

Mr. BROWN. Thank you, Mr. Harding.

I was impressed by a phrase you use about the need for unbiased, very serious research. I am a very great believer in the importance of such research and I think it will give us the answers to a lot of policy questions which we are grappling with at the present time.

The trouble we run into is getting people to accept that need as a way of approaching the solution of problems. They frequently prefer to follow a course which is in their own short-term best interest rather than seeking long-term knowledge that will allow for better decisions.

Also, in connection with your statement about pest resistance, it does get overlooked. I had the opportunity, along with Mr. Roberts, just 3 weeks ago to conduct a hearing in the Imperial Valley area of California on the problems of the cotton boll weevil and the pink bollworm. The testimony there from some of the most eminent entomologists in the country was that the growing cost of chemicals to control the pink bollworm in this case was going out of sight because of the development of resistance in the bollworm.

Many farmers are going to have to go out of cotton. The profit margin has been dropping so much because of the extra cost of the chemicals, and with regard to the weevil, it turns out that the most cost-effective solution is not chemicals at all but a change in cultural practice. Making sure that there is an adequate amount of time between plowing up one crop and planting the next crop so that there won't be a return of the weevil that has wintered over in old crop.

That is a very commonsense kind of approach, which unfortunately in the drive to keep planting cotton as quickly as possible and making another harvest, tends to get overlooked.

Mr. Evans.

Mr. EVANS of Iowa. Thank you, Mr. Chairman. I do have a question for Mr. Harding.

What is the typical size of the operators you work with? Would you describe them as small-scale operators or medium or large, or is there a wide variation in the groups from which you get expressions of interest and inquiries?

Mr. HARDING. I find it will run from a few acres to as high as 1,600 acres. I will give you my personal experience within the farm systems that we work with. Usually it is a very diversified system, a system that is not reliant upon one specific crop or a money-cropping situation. It could be an integrated dairy herd where most of the income comes from the dairy herd and the other part will be a small fruit or a tree-fruit operation. It ranges from a potato grower in Aroostook County, Maine. to a large rancher in Florida. And I would say by and large they are full-time farmers.

Mr. EVANS of Iowa. Very little, I would assume, and correct me if I am wrong, from the typical Midwest corn and soybean farmer or wheatgrower? Those people are the ones that lag behind in expressing interest, is that right or wrong?

Mr. HARDING. Not really. By and large I would have to agree that if we were to take a poll in that part of the country, particularly in the Great Plains and the Midwest area, it probably is true that by and large they are not interested in organic methods, but I was overwhelmed recently by the number of people coming out of that Great Plains area to a meeting that I attended in Ontario in Canada who were just really interested in getting involved, particularly in a better rotation system, who were interested in getting more quality built into the pricing side of this whole thing. So I think even though they may lag now, pricing will dictate some change there so that they can improve and maintain fertility.

I find it very interesting that some of the foreign countries dealing with our grain purchases are starting to put quality as one of the factors built into their procurement process, and I think when that happens on a much more serious basis throughout the world you are going to see these alternatives selected a lot more frequently.

Mr. EVANS of Iowa. I also have a question for Mr. Dunsmoor. In your line of business as a wholesale distributor, what sort of pricing differentials exist at the present time between organic and nonorganic? Furthermore, if organic farming became more widely accepted, would that differential disappear? Can you comment on this general area of the marketing economics just a bit?

Mr. DUNSMOOR. Well, being the buyer of the produce and commodities we pretty much can dictate what we are willing to pay for it. Because of our commitment to the farmer we are mainly concerned with the farmer and the consumer and we try to make our presence in the middle as least felt as possible. Basically because we do dictate the prices that we will pay, we do pay a higher price for organically grown food than conventionally grown foods.

Mr. EVANS of Iowa. What I am really getting at is what is the consumer's attitude on the selling end? Is there a substantial market out there for this produce at a markup over the normal price or not?

Mr. DUNSMOOR. That is a question I could write about but I will try to give you a real good feeling for it right now. We, on purpose, give the organic farmer more money, and that is because we found that starting an organic system the initial costs are high because you have to get into, say, rock mineral fertilizers and techniques that will cost you a little extra money in the beginning. But say something like rock phosphate you may not have to apply again for 10 or 20 years. But the initial costs are high and because of those initial costs we try to give the farmers a pretty good price when they start out that way to help them pay to set up the organic system.

As far as the consumers are concerned, we market quality, flavor, and nutrition. Now one of the things that we are trying to do as a business is to prove that foods grown on an organic system are higher in nutritive value than conventionally grown foods.

Getting back to what Mr. Harding said about the export market for wheat, for instance, I think Japan set a minimum protein requirement. We find that food grown in our organic system is higher in protein and that there has been a regular protein decrease in grain from the Midwest just because of the farming practices and what is going on out there and soil quality. So we market flavor and nutrition, and because of that a big part of our market buys the food not as organically grown but because it is higher in nutritive value and more flavor. More flavor is the key of it.

Mr. EVANS of Iowa. Thank you, Mr. Chairman.

Mr. BROWN. Just following that up for a moment. I gather that you are, because of those factors, able to get a higher price from the consumer on these organically grown items?

Mr. DUNSMOOR. We are able to get a higher price. Although we control, I would say, 90 percent of the organically grown produce or control the marketing of about 90 percent of organically grown produce on the east coast, I do not think we sell as much as the Safeway supermarket sells, and I have to deliver the whole east coast to do that. So a lot of our market is people who have to have the food because of allergies or sensitivities to pesticides, herbicides, fungicides, miticides, et cetera. Also there is a real concern with families with young children that their children are not the guinea pigs for today's agricultural chemicals, because a lot of them have not ever proved what the long-term effects are and a lot of them are relatively new, especially the systemic insecticides.

One of the things that we are doing through right now, you have to remember this is a young industry and the education on trace mineral nutrition and trace pesticide residue and contamination of the environment, et cetera, et cetera is fairly new and the information is just coming out. We have to get these organic farms going and we have to keep these organic farmers alive. So I have made a conscious effort to make sure that they do stay alive as much as our organization can to support them through giving them extra money for their product. But the long-term effect is that through organic systems, after their initial fertilization costs, in long-term systems that their production costs will be lower than the conventional production costs so they will get their bonuses just by competing on the commercial market and having lower production costs. But initially we have to get the ball rolling, and premium prices is one way that we have been able to do that.

Mr. BROWN. You have mentioned one quality difference, the protein content of wheat, which is fairly standard ways to measure, but do we have the analytical capability today and the standards as to quality, nutrition, healthfulness and so on so as to be able to make meaningful distinctions between organically grown foods and the nonorganically grown foods, or are we in need of additional research to establish those quality differences if they do exist?

Mr. DUNSMOOR. That is a very good question, a question I have put a lot of energy and effort into. One factor is trace mineral nutritions and micronutrients. That is something that not very much energy has been put into, but we all know the need of, in Iowa, iodine in the diet, iron, magnesium, different trace minerals in the diet and how they affect the organism. To do a good study on that you would have to define what an organic system is, and even in this room today I got a lot of different interpretations of organic system.

Organic system is not only applying manure. It is not only crop rotation. It is not only anything. It is a lot of things. And unless you have a defined organic system you cannot measure the organically grown food. I think the definition most people have of organic agriculture is organic by neglect. If you measure organic-by-neglect food against conventionally grown food you would find no difference, or the organically grown food by neglect would be lower in nutrients, but we do not define organic by neglect as an organic system. So, if you define an organic system and measure the nutritive quality of that food against a conventional system I think you would be very much surprised at the results of that.

I know Rutgers did a study on that, on trace mineral nutrition, and came out that in iron content alone you would have to eat 2,000 pounds of commercial tomatoes to equal the iron content of 1 pound of organic tomatoes. So I would really love to see Government do research on the nutritive quality of organically grown foods. I have a feeling that we will not see that and my organization, Organic Farms, is prepared to do that ourselves.

Mr. BROWN. Thank you.

Mr. Volkmer.

Mr. VOLKMER. Does the type of soil pretty well determine whether or not you can grow tomatoes organically?

Mr. DUNSMOOR. Pardon me?

Mr. VOLKMER. The type of soil?

Mr. DUNSMOOR. No, because you have hydroponics these days and they are not using any soil at all. You would be surprised to see that in America you have different zones and you see a lot of agriculture out in the desert and you see a lot of agriculture up in the North. Every place is suited for something, be it if it only was to raise crops that were to be used for energy or something like that, but there are definitely soils that have a lot more potential, let us say in their virgin form have more potential or have more fertility, but you will not find any virgin soil that will be 100-percent complete.

Mr. VOLKMER. If I may interject, a lot of our soils that we have now in this country have been pretty well depleted, with nothing except the chemicals being put back on them. Now if we just start growing without the chemicals, without the pesticides and without the herbicides and just use rotation, what are you going to end up with?

Mr. DUNSMOOR. You cannot do that. You cannot just apply one thing, and rotation is very good. And humus in the soil is very important, but that is not an organic system.

I would like to make an analogy here. This is going to fall into my spiritual beliefs. I hope you all do not mind that, but I have this feeling from scripture that the Earth was created perfect and that we have, through a process of erosion, and the main culprit of erosion is rain. Rainfalls are soft water. Soft water when it hits the Earth locks up minerals, and from when the rain falls and hits the Earth then it runs into streams, the streams into rivers, and the rivers ultimately into the sea. So what we have is the sea is a cesspool of all the minerals that were one time in the Earth. Any part of Earth on this planet Earth has been eroded away of essential minerals and you cannot bring back to the Earth in a closed system these minerals unless you use the resources of the sea to bring them back to the Earth, and unless you could transmutate minerals, but that is proven scientifically impossible. So you cannot transmutate minerals, so then you have to incorporate the minerals from the sea back into the Earth.

Agriculture, with the use of rotation, proper organic technique, biological activity, and trace minerals, sea mineral deposits is a renewable resource, but you cannot limit your organic system to just one factor such as crop rotation or any of those systems. They are all viable, but together they make a system, not any one separately.

Mr. HARDING. Mr. Chairman, may I comment?

Mr. VOLKMER. Yes.

Mr. HARDING. I do not think we are advocating here a cold-turkey approach to organic farming. Certainly I am not and I have not heard anyone in this room that is in favor of organic farming, that is that kind of support. What I think we are advocating here is a fair and equitable evaluation of the systems, all of the systems out there and this bill will allow us to do that. My opinion is that if we can start to move in a 3- to 5-year period incorporating not only crop rotation but green cover crops, plowdown manures, incorporating good fertility inputs, and many of them may have to come in initially off-farm and not be provided on-farm, use all of the microsystem's potential resources on that system for that specific variety that is best grown there of particular crops, yes, I think we can make a conversion to a reasonable organic state and a reasonable, sensible, logical step-by-step process. It will only take the initiative to do the planning and make the step forward.

Mr. VOLKMER. Thank you, Mr. Chairman.

Mr. BROWN. Mr. Weaver.

Mr. WEAVER. Thank you, Mr. Chairman. I just want to compliment you on your good work and thank you very much for coming and giving the subcommittee the benefit of your knowledge. You have been very helpful and it will very much help us enact this bill. Thank you very much, both of you.

Mr. BROWN. Thank you very much, gentlemen.

Without objection, the testimony submitted by Mr. W. R. Dunlop and J. B. Forste, Bio Gro Systems, Inc., will be included in the record at the end of the day.

That will conclude our testimony for today, and the subcommittee will be adjourned until the call of the Chair.

[Whereupon, at 4 p.m., the subcommittee adjourned subject to the call of the Chair.]

[Material submitted for inclusion in the record follows:]

```
THOMPSON'S

REGENERATIVE

AGRICULTURE

DEMONSTRATION

RESEARCH

FARM
```

For the last six years we have
traveled and shared the need for
changes in agriculturas. Problems
may be in agriculture or in the
land, but the cause of these
problems is in the heart of man.
If we are really going to be serious
about agriculture and the problems
of erosion, pollution, high input
costs, etc., one must realize the

change must come from within.

E. F. Schumacher, the noted economist, said; "The material scheme is not
working. The change must come from within and not from without." Robert Rodale
said, "The dirt that is polluting our rivers, our air, our food, is produced
in our thoughts, our ambitions, and in our desire to live a life of ease.
Pollution is a state of mind. Man's thinking has to be changed. You can't
legislate purity while people are still thinking pollution." The new head of
Soil Conservation, Meyers, said in Des Moines, Iowa "the solution to the erosion
problems is a changeof attitude of the farmers."

In the past years we could not decide on a name for this demonstration -
research farm. The word organic has had many problems in the past. Robert
Rodale's Regenerative Agriculture term best fit what we had been saying during
the past years. We believe in regeneration from within and the only real
changes that will come to agriculture will be a within commitment by the farmer.
People have told us the theory sounds good, but people's changes are dictated
by economics or by their pocketbook. Sharon's response was, "How long last-

ing will the change be that is motivated-by economics?" Economic pressures are
forcing farmers into a diversified rotation (idle acres - P.I.K. program). What
will happen when economic pressures are gone? The all row-crop, fence row to
fence row rotation willbe back. Government programs come and go. Was there
any real change? Real changes come only by commitment.

Our role in the ecological field has been in investigation and experimentation. The research on this farm has been designed to try to answer questions,
such as: What kind of rotation is needed when chemicals are limited or elimin-
ated? What happens to crop yields and quality in a closed farm system? What
is the best method for handling livestock and human waste? Why do farmers
loosen up the soil in the fall and pack it back down in the spring? How can
an organic system fit with a minimum tillage system? Why has the smooth, black,
clean fields been the accepted way? Are weeds all bad? Can we use certain
weeds or crops to control the weeds that are causing problems? Why do farmers
usually think they have to buy something? Is there a connection between high
nitrogen soils, high protein foods, and disease?

Research on this farm is being conducted in 4 areas.

1 - Within the farm as a whole, there are four distinct systems being compared.

    a. organic - livestock pasture system - no compost.

    b. organic - livestock - compost.

    c. organic - non livestock.

    d. 5 year rotation with chemical fertilizer.

2 - Comparing a ridge-strip till plant system to a conventional tillage without using herbicides in either situation.

3 - Interseeding of covers at last cultivation of corn and seeding rye after
soybean harvest.

4 - The response of soil amendments in both a organic and chemical systems.

	no	Cover crops						no	Cover crops			cont
		Minimum tillage (ridge-strip till plant)										
Plots →	A	B	C	D	E	F	G	H	I	J	K	L	M
Reps. -	3	3	3	3	3	3	3	3	3	3	3	3	3
Reps. -	2	2	2	2	2	2	2	2	2	2	2	2	2
Reps. -	1	1	1	1	1	1	1	1	1	1	1	1	1

|←——Green Manure——→|←———Green Manure———→|←—Green Manure—|
|←———Compost———→|+Chemical fertilizer|←——Compost——|

Table 1. Design of research fields.

The rotation that is used on these five fields is corn (1), soybeans (2), corn (3), oats (4), hay (5). Once every five years the entire field has the green manure treatment-hay (5). There are 13 plots, A thru M, replicated three times in each of the five fields.

The fields are fertilized twice during the five year rotation, preceding each corn crop (1), (3). The chemical treatment is 100 units of nitrogen,

70 units of phosphorous and 70 units of potassium. Approximately 1400 cu. ft. of compost is applied per acre. The green manure only plots (E and I) represent an organic system without livestock. Plot (E) will receive as many cover crops as possible during the rotation while plot (I) will have no added cover crops. The center of each fertility plot, (O), (G), (K) will be used to test amendments.

A minimum tillage system will be used on most of the field while in row crops. The exact details of this operation will be discussed in a separate paragraph. The (M) plot on the edge of the field will be farmed conventionally. Conventional tillage will consist of using an off-set disk in the fall and several trips with a field cultivator in the spring.

The different tillage programs that have been used during the past years, have proved that the deeper the tillage in the spring and the finer the seedbed; the greater the possibilities for more weed pressure. The deeper tillage brings up broadleaf seeds into the germinating zone and a well pulverized seed bed is an excellent environment for the grasses. Weeds are plants of a disturbed soil.

Herbicides have not been used on this farm since 1967 and this has allowed observation as to what different tillage practices respond with the different weeds. In 3 soybean growing seasons, side by side comparisons have shown that conventional tillage, fall and spring produced more weed pressure in both broad-leafs and grasses. The Buffalo ridge-strip till plant plot was easier to manage weeds than the conventional, even without using herbicides.

Ridging at the last cultivation and then planting in these old rows the next year has been successful for many continuous row crop farmers. The question arises, how to adopt these ridge-strip till plant ideas in a hay rotation and where manure or compost has to be applied. To avoid compaction on heavy soils, compost or manure should be applied in the fall and covered. Compost is applied on the third hay crop (green manure), (5) and on the soybean field (2) after combining. Previously an off-set disk was used to incorporate the compost, but it left the field too smooth and too black.

A Buffalo cultivator with hillers and furrow openers was used for the first time to do the fall tillage in 1982. The compost had been applied and the cultivator followed the old soybean rows so as not to disturb the soybean nitrogen fixing root nodules. After two passes with the cultivator, the ridges were 8 to 10 inches high. One bushel of rye was seeded over the ridges with an endgate seeder. A rotary-hoe was used to incorporate the seed. The rye will give ground cover over the winter and protect the soil from heavy rains in the spring. Corn will be planted on these green rye ridges with a Buffalo (till plant) planter. The 16 inch sweep will cut 2 inches below the surface of the ridge, removing the rye growth off the ridge and covering the growth in the valleys. The rye should be cut off, incorporated, or covered up when 6 to 8 inches in height. The growing rye on the ridges will set precedence over any weed seeds.

This same Buffalo cultivator was then used in the hay field with 8 to 10 inches of hay growth remaining. The compost had been applied and needed to be covered immediately. Since there were no rows to follow and the cultivator did not have a marker, a bar was installed across the front of the tractor. The bar had drop chains to run in the previous furrow. This simple, inexpensive devise did an excellent job of making straight rows even at night. Approximately 10 acres of the hay field was doubled cultivated only, leaving some of the alfalfa sticking out of the top of the ridges. The remainder of this field was double disked with an off-set disk and then double cultivated. Next spring while planting, observations can be made in the differences of regrowth of the alfalfa in these two different tillage systems. Weed populations and their growth will be observed during the year and yield checks will be made at harvest. Depending on the amount of alfalfa regrowth, weed populations, and the yields

between the two tillage systems; it can be determined whether the disking is
necessary.

The soybeans will be planted in last years corn rows. The top of these
ridges, that the planter sweep will cut off, were made last year at the last
cultivation in late June. Some alfalfas and clovers were scattered on the
ridges at the same time in late June. This seed mix was metered through the
insecticide boxes mounted on top of the cultivator and mechanically driven by
the cultivator gauge wheel. These alfalfas and clovers growing on the ridges
protect the soil while a green bio-mass grows for soil improvement and last
but not least, these early growing cover crops suppress weed germination and
growth.

The rotary-hoe will be used on both corn and soybean field to keep the row
area free of weeds. The area between the rows is not a major concern right after
planting. A few 3 to 4 inch weeds in the area between the rows can be an asset
to stop erosion and will furnish a green manure to be incorporated with the
cultivator.

Cover crops, like rye, will be seeded following soybean harvest. An early
to mid-season variety of soybeans should be planted to insure early harvest in
late September or early October. The rye will use the nitrogen to produce protein that would have been lost from a bare soil during late fall and early
spring. Also the rye can use the sun's energy during these months to produce
organic matter to be returned as green manure. The rye also produces phytotoxins
from its roots which inhibit weed development.

A combination of alfalfas and different clovers will be seeded on the ridges
during the last cultivation in each corn field. The question to be answered
here is, which alfalfas and which clovers should be combined in this cover crop
mix? What varieties will stand shading and dry weather? What varieties will

give 6 to 8 inch growth at soybean planting time?

These cover crops will be used on the majority of the fields when in row crops. The no-cover plots (A) and (I) will be used as the control plots to determine any differences in yield, quality of crop, soil fertility and structure.

Amendments, such as Basic H, Micro-gram, Agri soil conditioner, lime will be added to plots (C), (G), (K). Each amendment study will not be replicated in the other fields. Most of the university research on amendments was in conjunction with pesticides and not tested in a biological system. Many of the telephone calls and letters we receive are about ecological products. Farmers have been programed to buy something. Do we always have to spend money to make money?

The following data will be collected from the three replications on each plot.

1. Soil fertility at 0-3 inch depth.
   "   "   " 3-6 "   "
   "   "   " 6-12 "   "
   "   "   " 12-24 " "
   "   "   " 24-36 " "

2. Soil aggregate stability.

3. Soil microbial activity.

4. Earthworm hole and casting count.

5. Leaf tissue test of crops.

6. Feed analysis of the grain or forage.

7. Test weight and moisture of the grain.

8. Yield data.

9. Observe kinds and numbers of weeds.

10. Observe and record water penetration after a rain.

11. Observe tilth of soil while cultivating.

The organic plots on this farm have been non-chemical for 15 years. With this length of time, chemical fertilizer carryover would have vanished, so as not to effect the results in the plots now. With another 5 years, maybe some answers should come forth about obtainable rotations with or without livestock. How much tillage is really necessary when deep rooted legumes are used in the rotation? The nitrogen needs of a farm can be grown on that farm, but how do we get faster mineralization of phosphorous and potassium? Or should we even be thinking about faster mineralization?

Eighty acres of this farm will be in a corn-soybean-oats-meadow-meadow-meadow rotation. This rotation system will receive its only fertility from fresh manure from grazing cattle. A test with soybeans will be designed to determine variety difference in early canopy to hold back weed growth when herbicides are not used. Data collected from this section will be compared against a non-grazing compost system.

Since 1975 the waste from the cattle and hogs have been composted. The manure is loaded into a PTO spreader and unloaded along the edge of the field where it is to be applied later. A 5 ft. by 10 ft. pyramid windrow is formed behind the spreader.

During the first two years, starter bacteria was used to start the windrow to heat up. The windrows were turned by reloading the spreader and making another windrow parallel to the unturned windrow. This method was very time consuming, but produced excellent compost. Turning, by reloading the spreader, is applicable to a small farm operation.

The Easy-Over turner was purchased to lessen the time involved in turning. The two day process of reloading the spreader was changed into a one hour operation with the Easy-Over turner.

Experiments down through the years have shown it profitable to double the rates of compost application. The question was asked whether the turning is necessary. The yield results showed no difference in turned vs. unturned compost, but the odor became a problem from the large pile. Also more weeds were expressed in the unturned plot. Presently all the manure and sludge from a nearby town are being windrowed and turned.

The corn yields have increased by 25 to 30 bu. per acre since the manure was composted and incorporated the same day as applied. The unanswered question is how much of the yield increase come from the process of composting or by proper incorporation when applied to the field?

Livestock farms usually have more weed pressures than non-livestock farms. For the farmer who does not want to use herbicides, composting is an excellent technology to control weeds.

Compost starters have not been used since the early years of composting. The windrows heat up very easily now when the bulk and the moisture is proper in the windrow. The added bacteria were necessary in the beginning, but now seem to be present over the whole farm.

Beauty is in the eye of the beholder — manure may be filth to some people — but to others it has the possibilities of tilth.

How can farmers raise hogs without huge capital outlays for buildings, pumps, pits and tanks that will be rusted out before the depreciation expires? Can't hogs live without being poked full of needles or survive without drugs in every mouthful of feed? Isn't there some kind of balance between using the good aspects of Mother Nature without being subjected to the full brunt of her other side?

A Cargill pork system seemed to come the closest to answering some of the above questions. Our 30 isolit farrowing houses, along with the open front fresh air nursery and finishing units, were built to see if hogs could be raised without vaccinations and drugs in the feed. The use of lactobacillus products for the past 15 years has proved very successful in keeping a good natural balance in the digestive system. Ag. lime is used in the bedding because of its drying qualities and the high ph. A high ph level is an effective way to keep the bad pathogens under control. The most vigorous breeds of swine should be used in this open front design. These kinds of ideas will not eliminate all the problems, but maybe the thoughts are headed in the direction so we can get through the problems.

The 80 crossbred cows and their calves are a necessary part of this farm. The cattle consume the hay and pasture and furnish manure to put fertility back on the fields. 10 years of artificial insemination using different breeds has brought about the following observations. The Angus, Red Angus, Shorthorn, Simmental breeds serve best in a maternal cross while the Charolais, Chianina, Limousin are best used in a terminal cross program.

As viewed from the road, this 300 acre farm is not too different from the normal mid-western farm, but, there is a difference. Here's why. After Dick received his B.S. and M.S. degrees in Agriculture from Iowa State University, we farmed conventionally, chemically for 10 years - using the methods he had been taught. There was high use of fertilizers, insecticides and herbicides as well as a mono-culture practice. The transition to organic, ecological, regenerative agriculture was made 15 years ago, after realizing something had to change.

Dr. Richard Harwood is the director of the Rodale Research Farm at Emmaus, Pa. Recently he and part of his staff spent time here viewing the farm operation. They are helping to modify the research design and to determine what data should be collected. It was decided during their visit, that this farm become a part of the Regenerative Agriculture Association. Through this combination we have access to the best minds in alternative agriculture, and the grant monies needed to finance research done on this farm can be processed through the non-profit Regenerative Agriculture Association.

George DeVault, editor and publisher of The New Farm, the Magazine of Regenerative Agriculture; has invited both of us to be contributing editors to the magazine and thereby gave us the vehicle by which to publish the results of our research.

Dr. Garth Youngberg, the founder of the Institute for Alternative Agriculture, Washington, D.C., has asked Dick to be on his first board of directors to serve in a consulting capacity.

Hopefully through all the test plots and the professional expertise at our disposal; some answers will be found to produce a profitable, non-polluting, sustainable agriculture.

Maybe a sign should be posted at the gate to this farm, reading, WARNING – A visit here may change your life!

Thank you for your time and attention.

Dick Thompson
Sharon Thompson

Dick and Sharon Thompson
Rt 2   Box 132
Boone, Iowa   50036
515-432-1560

AGRICULTURAL PRODUCTIVITY ACT OF 1983

By Robert Rodale and Richard Harwood
Rodale Press, Inc.

America is today being forced to deal with the consequences of a
farm productivity crisis. Those consequences include overproduction,
particularly of feed grains, excessive erosion of soil and silting
of waterways, pollution of ground water with fertilizers and pesticide residues, reduction in employment opportunities in farming,
and a frightening deterioration in the entire financial structure
of agriculture.

A result is that both farm and non-farm Americans are beginning
to fear American agriculture, rather than see it as a source of
national strength. Non-farmers now fear the tax burden that support
of the present system places on their shoulders. They fear also
the draining away of national strength that soil erosion and
agriculture-caused pollution symbolize. Farmers, above all, fear
that the source of income and way of life that they love will
collapse around them, forcing them off the land.

A normal productivity crisis is characterized by a failure of
an industrial system to produce enough, or a need for too great
amounts of labor, energy and raw material inputs. The current
agricultural productivity crisis is different. In fact, many
people do not see it as a productivity crisis at all, because
the most obvious sign that a problem exists is the fact that
production levels are extremely high. They apparently think:
"How can there be a productivity crisis when we are being buried
in product?"

But there indeed is an American farm productivity crisis. In simplest terms, it is a failure of our agricultural leadership to conceive and create a system of farming that meets all our needs. Instead, we have been given by farm researchers, planners and thinkers a system that places a supremely high value on the continuous production of food and fiber, but which almost totally ignores the human and biological destruction caused by that production. As a result, American farmers today are harvesting twin crops of production and destruction. And unfortunately, the destruction seems to be winning.

There is another way, though -- a better way. There is a way to farm that has no destructive side to it at all. Just the opposite! There is a way to farm that literally eliminates every single disadvantage of the present conventional system. And it does more than that. It also preserves all the advantages that farming in this country can and should have. And it does still more. It creates advantages and values that are totally new to the experience of many American farmers.

In order to understand and put to use this other system, it is necessary to introduce into agriculture two concepts which are sadly lacking or missing entirely from the present system.

Flexibility of production is the first. The science and technology which has been used to create the present system places total value on all-out, high-yield agriculture. The farmers who use it have two choices. They can either not farm, or go for maximum yields and output. There is no middle ground production level.

Plants are bred to grow big in a soil rich in high levels of soluble nutrients. Cropping patterns leave no option for cutting back easily, if markets are glutted. And most important, farmers have been encouraged to hitch themselves to high levels of indebtedness. Too many have bankers looking over their shoulder, urging them to keep the accelerator of their whole farm operation to the floor. Farmers deserve better. They should have the flexibility of a scientifically-based system that gives them the ability to produce at different levels, depending on how they assess market conditions.

Regeneration is the other concept that needs to be introduced more effectively into agriculture. Farming doesn't have to just destroy soil. Different ways of growing crops can also rebuild and regenerate the land. Water can be purified as well as poisoned. Why not structure farming so it helps purify water, instead of polluting it?

The families and communities that form the human dimension of agriculture can be rebuilt, restored and regenerated as well. The seldom-spoken but well-understood phrase "Get big or get out" has been a central message to the people managing the American land. It is time to reverse that message and put out a new welcome mat to the many who love the land, need work, and want to participate in the regeneration of themselves and the basic source of this country's strength. We need an agriculture that says "Come back in" to millions of our displaced rural people.

122

Is that kind of agriculture merely a dream? Is it beyond the realm of practical action in today's world?

Not at all! The kind of flexible, regenerative agriculture we have described here actually exists on tens of thousands of American farms. It works. The people practicing it are thriving, and their farms are models of rational productivity. And not only that. Their farms are getting better with each passing year. The soil is improving, the water falling on those farms stays clear, and the food and fiber they produce is of highest quality.

The Agricultural Productivity Act of 1983 calls for the systematic study of this kind of farm. We will present in this testimony evidence from our own study of one such farm. And we strongly support the passage of this legislation, which would establish a minimal number of similar studies.

Further, we will show how regenerative agricultural concepts are also important to agricultural development in the developing countries, where inputs and other resources are often extremely scarce.

I. The Research Balance for Support of Regenerative Agriculture

There is a desperate need for agricultural research that looks at the challenge of productivity from a different and more rational perspective. The best way for conventionally-minded scientists to acquire that perspective is to look beyond the test tube and the laboratory itself to what is in fact happening on many farms that evolved a different system beyond the influence of the common productivity pattern.

A. On-Farm Studies

There is a need for two types of studies of existing farms,
the first being surveys which do a statistical sampling of
regenerative farms in many regions of the country and in
different climatic zones. An example of the survey work
initiated by Patrick Madden of Pennsylvania State University
is crucial as a first step. It is important that we know
where these farms are and understand their structure from
broad-scale surveys.

Secondly, we must have case studies of individual farms
taking a detailed look at the enterprise combinations and interactions between those enterprises. The study which we will
describe of the Kutztown integrated beef farm is an excellent
example of such a study. An in-depth understanding of the
functioning of such farms comes from these case studies. They
do not attempt to randomly or statistically sample large numbers
of farms, but in combination with the broad data of other surveys,
they add considerable understanding on the function of regenerative farms. It is precisely this kind of case study that HR 2714
addresses.

B. Experimental Trials

There are two kinds of experiments that should be conducted
under this category. The first are factorial, controlled experiments, experiment-station based, which measure interactions of
components of whole systems. These may be crop rotation studies

having the proper controls and the proper regenerative farming
practices inserted. While many long-term crop rotation studies
are being done at experiment stations, very few at present have
good organic or regenerative systems included. Many of the
present test technologies such as rotation with legumes or
application of manure have relevance, but they are usually
not tested as component parts of a regenerative system.

The second kind of experiment station trials are the
individual component experiments looking at nutrient flows,
pest management and the like. There are many of these trials
now being done, some having greater relevance to regenerative
agriculture than others.

We are pleased that this legislation is specific in its insis-
tence on case studies. There is a tendency when the pendulum swings
or research funds are at hand, to lump all make and manner of
research trials under research headings of "sustainable" or "regenerative." It is important that the legislation be very specific, dealing
with farms in transition to regenerative or farms which have gone
through the transition. From a superficial look at the requirements
of such systems, many research people will say "we are doing research
which is relevant. We have legume rotation studies." Those studies,
however, did not meet the full requirements of completely regenerative systems. For the most part, they fall short of meeting the
goals and needs of those fully-integrated farms. It is important

that if we are to consider the present regenerative models that we go first to existing farms and then look at farms in transition as HR 2714 directs. In our opinion, the focus of the research cannot be more relevant or better-placed.

The Kutztown 5-year Farm Study

The Rodale Research Center has for five years studied a 320 acre integrated crop and beef finishing operation. We have carefully monitored the nearly 100 fields for soil fertility, nutrient concentration with soil depth, crop yield, and have modeled the farm economics. This farm is characterized as mostly organic with very little non-organic material used on the entire farm. The farmer is not a purist, as he does use some chemical on some of his fields. The amount, however, is minimal.

We are presently completing the major report on this farm which will be available in finished form in a few weeks. We have included some of the yield results in the following tables. Table 1 shows the corn grain yields in bushels per acre from the approximately 100 acres of corn on the farm each year. The Berks County figures are averages from the local county. It can be seen that the average over 5 years was 27% above county yields for the Kutztown farm, averaging 108 bushels. In an extremely dry year when county yields dropped to 50 bushels in 1980 (close to the disaster level), the Kutztown farm yielded 77 bushels, or 48% more than the county average. The land and soil type on the farm are below average in fertility, being mostly shaley hillside fields.

Table 1.

CORN YIELDS (bu/A)

	78	79	80	81	82	mean
Berks County	96	95	52	92	85	85
Kutztown Farm	121	124	77	121	97	108
			+48%			+27%

In spite of the steep slopes and shaliness of the fields, the
erosion levels are considerably less than average. In Table 2,
we've indicated calculations of erosion levels on the farm, using
the Universal Soil Loss Equation. The Kutztown farm averages 4.7
tons/acre loss per year, including two sections of the farm with
excessive slopes. The great majority of the fields with up to
2% slopes average less than 3 tons per acre per year. Calculations
of a comparable farm having exactly the same crop mix, but where
the fields were planted in monoculture rather than in rotation
would average 8.8 tons per acre. Both of these figures are lower
than soil erosion rates for average across Pennsylvania or for
Berks County.

With the reduced soil erosion and reduced need for high levels
of production inputs, the crop production budgets show real advantage
on the Kutztown farm. Soil nutrient levels on the farm as shown in
soil tests have been rising steadily over the past 10 years, in
spite of non-use of conventional fertilizers. A small amount of
chicken manure is brought onto the farm each year, but the farm
generates an excess of nitrogen. In Table 3, we can see that the
variable cash cost of production, excluding labor on the Kutztown
farm was $84. per acre for corn. The hypothetical conventional farm
which we have used for comparison would have exactly the same,
structure, exactly the same enterprise mix in crop acreage, but
would use chemicals instead of organic practices. The cost for
that farm would be $98. per acre, exclusive of labor, a 17% increase.

Table 2.

SOIL LOSS AS CALCULATED FROM THE

UNIVERSAL SOIL LOSS EQUATION

(Mean of 13 sections)

Kutztown Farm   4.66 tons/acre/year

Comparable Farm   8.8 tons/acre
(each section planted to a single crop)

Table 3.

CORN GRAIN BUDGETS

Cash Operating Costs

	Kutztown farm	Hypothetical Conventional	1981 PA Corn Club (121 farms)	Doane's 1983 Illinois Projection
seed	$17	$17	$16	$18
pesticides	0	20	16	24
fertilizers	24	22	80	62
lime	11	11	10	
machine fuel, labor, repairs	32	28	30	32
	—	—	—	—
	$84	$98	$152	$136
labor	5.7 hrs/A		3.5 hours/A	

The 1981 Pennsylvania Corn Club having 121 farmers in the state,
using their best 5 acres with conventional tillage methods,
averaged $152. per acre variable cost of production. The Doane's
estimate for 1983 Illinois production costs are $136. per acre.

For cash inputs, the Kutztown farm costs were thus a little
more than half those of the Pennsylvania Corn Club. In 1981, the
Corn Club yields (in corn club competition) were 136 bushels per
acre. The yields that year on the Kutztown farm were 121 bushels
per acre (about 10% less than the Corn Club yields, but considerably
above the 92 bushel average for the county). The best fields with
good soil on the Kutztown farm in 1981 were close in yields to the
better fields of the Corn Club. The significance, however, is the
40% to 50% reduction in cash input costs. Also of significance
is the fact that the Kutztown farm employed considerably more
labor (5.7 person hours per acre as compared to 3.5 person hours
per acre on Corn Club farms). There was a substitution of
labor for pesticide and fertilizer inputs, with leguminous crops
requiring more labor to grow than the application of fertilizer
or cultivation in turn requiring more labor than herbicide application. With labor costs included, the costs are still significantly
reduced on the Kutztown farm.

It must be remembered, however, that only 1/3 of the acreage on
the Kutztown farm is in corn, with another 1/3 in small grain. The
other 1/3 is made up of hay or soybeans. Having about 1/3 of the

land out of crop production each year would reduce gross income over the entire farm. If that cash income, however, is calculated as net, including the decreased cost of production per acre, the net income from the entire farm is about the same as it would be if the whole farm were planted to conventionally grown corn with higher production costs. By achieving the cost savings of rotation with organically-grown legumes followed by organic cash crop production, the cost savings in the conventional crops make up for the decreased acreage of production of cash grain crops each year. The farmer thus achieves approximately the same net return per acre when calculated over the whole farm as if he were planting the whole farm with corn or other cash grains. This achieves a significant net reduction of cash crop acreage at little or no cost to the farmer or to society. In addition, it provides more job opportunities with a higher percentage of the cost being returned to labor rather than to cash input.

The obvious benefit of such a system is that farmers would be considerably better off, but agricultural support industries would be the short-term losers. More importantly, however, a significant level of production flexibility would be built into the system.

If we look at trends in input costs as indicated in Table 4, we see that during the 5 years of the study, the cost of fertilizer

Table 4.

AGRICULTURAL INPUT PRICE CHANGES 1977-1982

Fertilizer	+41%
Ag Chemicals	+34%
Fuel & Energy	+109%
Machinery	+67%

has increased 41%, agricultural chemicals 34%, fuel and energy,
109%, and machinery, 67%. This system is specifically designed
to minimize the inputs from fertilizer and chemicals. This system
is stable, with gradually increasing levels of soil fertility,
having been farmed in a regenerative mode some ten years.

Sources of cost saving are as listed below:

1. the system is self-reliant in nitrogen.

2. the farm has approximately 1/2 the soil erosion with
considerably less nutrient loss than conventional systems.

3. Weeds are controlled using a rotation effect with limited
crop allelopathy as well as mechanical tillage.

4. There are efficiencies of biological structuring in the
system for

    a. insect control

    b. disease suppression

    c. nutrient cycling in the soil

We have dealt at some length with these efficiencies in other
publications. A part of the cost reduction can be realized by simple
rotations, but the full savings is available only with effective
biological structuring.

The Need for Further Studies of Similar Nature

We are here making the claim that there are significant efficiencies from integration of systems in a regenerative manner which
far exceed many estimates from conventional farm studies. We are
claiming that the adoption of these regenerative farm systems and

their continued development would go a long way toward solving the
problems in American agriculture. We claim that there are many
farms across the country which have similar structure to the
Kutztown farm. There is a desperate need for detailed scientific
case studies of a select number of these farms. We feel that to
continue in ignorance of the efficiencies and possible contribution
of this kind of agriculture is not only non-rational but borders
on negligence. It seems curious indeed that the U.S. government
research establishment would have to be forced under protest into
this kind of research.

Adequacy of the Research Design

We feel that the numbers of farms and types of farms selected
for study in HR 2714 are excellent as a start. There is a need for
study of many more farms in a survey mode as well as broadening
the study to look at many more case histories. There is a need
obviously for much ancillary research in cropping systems on
experiment stations. I see this bill as being open-ended. The
U.S. Department of Agriculture and the experiment stations should
not be confined to the small numbers of farms specified in the
bill. The bill, however, provides for support for this crucial
numbers of farms. If we were in the position of the U.S. Department
of Agriculture, we would be asking for more money, in fact, to study
a larger number of farms, but certainly the numbers recommended are
realistic and the criteria for selection of the farms seems ideal.

Every piece of data which we have collected leads us to believe
that there are surprisingly great efficiencies of production,

especially in the animal-based organic or regenerative systems. The studies by Lockeretz, et. al. (1981), Roberts, et. al. (1979) at Missouri and Patten (1982) at Washington, show results remarkably similar to ours for integrated systems both with and without animals. A critical mass of farmers is involved with regenerative agricultural practices. It is long past time that the state and federal experiment stations and research workers become closely involved with evaluation of such farms. HR 2714 does not mandate that all American farms should adopt regenerative practices. It simply states that a limited number of critical research studies be done to determine the efficiencies and potential problems of the proposed regenerative agriculture model. The misconceived notions of regenerative practices being relevant only to gardening mentioned in the CAST Report (Smith, 1980) could be excused on the basis of lack of information in the past. The growing volume of research data since 1976, however, indicates that such notions should be disregarded along with other misinformation and ignorance of the workings of biological systems. Ignorance to a point seems excusable, but at some point it indicates sheer negligence on the part of those in responsible positions. We are strong in our recommendations that HR 2714 be enacted into law. We see little need to change the wording or substance of the bill other than perhaps some reference to the fact that this research is open-ended and should in fact be more broadly supported by the U.S. Department of Agriculture and the state experiment stations than is mandated by law.

135

Literature Cited

Lockeretz, W., G. Shearer, D. Kohl. 1981. Organic farming in the corn belt. Science. 211:540-546.

Patten, A.G. 1982. Comparison of nitrogen and phosphorus flows on an organic and conventional farm. M.S. thesis, Washington State University, Pullman, WA.

Roberts, K.J., F. Warnken and K.C. Schnecberger. 1979. The economics of organic crop production in the western corn belt. Agricultural economics paper no. 1979-6. Department of Agricultural Economics, University of Missouri.

Smith, J., ed. 1980. Organic and conventional farming compared. Council for Agricultural Science and Technology #84. Ames, Iowa. 32 p.

THE KUTZTOWN FARM REPORT:

A Study of a Low-Input
Crop/Livestock Farm

M. N. Culik
J. C. McAllister
M. C. Palada
S. Rieger

Rodale Research Center
Kutztown, PA
1983

SUMMARY REPORT

The Kutztown Farm study was initiated in 1978 to document the overall productivity of an integrated crop/livestock farm. The study farm was located in east-central Pennsylvania, adjacent to the Rodale Research Center. Approximately 220 acres of the total of 320 cropland acres were owned by the Research Center and rented to the farm family. Crop yield data, soil nutrient analysis, and erosion figures, livestock production records and an economic analysis were included in the investigation and are reported in detail in the full report.

Experience is a key ingredient that has affected the total operation of the Kutztown Farm. The father has farmed his own property since 1949, and intensive crop rotations have always been used to produce the crops. The farmer has gained a knowledge of the soils productive capacities through years of experience, and he is able to recognize any situations that may be present that would limit crop yields. Potential problems with weeds, insects and diseases are avoided by rotating the crops and.knowing when these factors may become yield limiting. The soil's nutrient status and water holding capacity are taken into account before deciding each year's crop selection. By taking into consideration all these factors, efficient use of the available resources is maximized.

The soil nutrient levels on the Kutztown Farm fields have remained at levels sufficient for good crop production, even though no synthetic fertilizers are used on the majority of the land. Residual fertilizer nutrients, animal manures, crop residues and probably mineral weathering contribute to the available nutrient pool. After 10-years of crop production without synthetic fertilizers, there does not appear to be any signs that nutrient deficiencies will show up in the near future. Efficiencies of

nutrient cycling also appear to be related to the cropping sequences used on
the Kutztown Farm. Deep rooted, sod-forming legumes that are able to penetrate
and bring soil nutrients from lower levels are alternated with corn, soybeans,
and small grains. The nitrogen fixation potential of the legume hay crops is
also utilized by the following corn crops after plowdown. Animal manures are
applied to the corn because it is the crop that needs the most nitrogen, and
residual nutrients from the manure are available for the other crops in the
rotations. Small grains are placed in the cropping sequence to make best use
of the residual nitrogen from the legume plowdown and manure application after
several years of corn.

Using the red clover or alfalfa hay crops in the rotation helps to
maintain soil organic matter directly because of the relatively large amounts
of plant material incorporated into the soil, but also due to the fact that the
fields are not tilled for two to four years. This avoidance of tillage reduces
the "rapid rate of decay and dissipation of organic matter" that occurs when
cultivated crops are grown on the land (6). Other soil properties may also be
affected by using legumes in the rotation, including biological and physical
characteristics that are important to soil management. Voss and Shrader (32)
found that the organic matter content in surface soils on continuous corn plots
with no fertilizer nitrogen was lower than on plots that had a corn - oats -
two-year meadow rotation. They also found a higher bulk density on the
continuous corn plots. Others (8 and 17) have documented increased water
infiltration and an increase in the percentage of water-stable aggregates after
using a grass-legume meadow in a crop rotation.

The evidence presented above may be interpreted to mean that there are
other factors in addition to the nitrogen contribution from the use of a legume
hay crop in the rotation. If there is a decrease in the soil bulk density, and

increases in soil organic matter, water stable aggregates and water infiltration when using a legume hay crop in a rotation, then there is a good chance of reducing the energy needs for crop production directly due to less fuel needed for tillage and indirectly because of decreased soil erosion. Mannering (17) found that soil losses from first- and second-year corn after meadow were reduced 47 and 17-percent, respectively, compared to that from continuous corn. The soil erosion that occurs decreases the productivity capacity of the soil by removing soil nutrients as well as the topsoil itself. Nitrogen, phosphorus and potassium removal by soil erosion were reduced 55 to 65-percent when a corn-wheat-clover rotation was used in comparison to continuous corn (6). The fine soil particles are the major portion of that which is eroded, and potassium, in particularly, can be removed in large quantities by soil erosion. The Kutztown Farm soil loss rate, as calculated by using the USLE equation, was about half of that on the hypothetical, comparison farm (4.53 vs. 8.74 tons/acre/year). As Brady (6) states it very clearly: "Removal of nutrients by crops is a necessary part of the production process; that by erosion is not." The sustainability of the Kutztown Farm is enhanced by using contour stripcropping, not only by reducing soil erosion, but also by conserving soil nutrients.

Crop yields, in particular corn, respond to legume hays in a crop rotation, and often for more than the first year after legume plowdown. Research has shown a 10 to 18-percent increase in corn yields after legume plowdown in comparison to continuous corn (16 and 32). Forty-six research years at five sites in Iowa have shown a nine-percent yield increase the second year after meadow plowdown than for continuous corn (32). University soil testing laboratory fertilizer recommendations are being adjusted to take into account the nitrogen contributions from previous legume crops (5, 26, and 32).

Nitrogen fertilizer recommendations (32) are in some cases being reduced by 95%
so that only 0 to 20 pounds are being applied to first year corn following a
two year meadow. The Kutztown Farm corn yields are further evidence that
profitable corn production is possible when a sound crop rotation is used with
legumes and animal manures as the nitrogen sources.

Beef cattle manure and chicken manure are used on the Kutztown Farm crops,
and these provide nutrients as well as organic matter to the soil. The manures
are normally spread on hay fields just prior to plowdown, although because
there is no way to stockpile the manure until needed in the fields, some of it
may be spread on small grain stubble fields, or even before planting soybeans.
The cattle manure is a combination of animal feces, urine and straw which is
taken out from the beef cattle stable several times a year after it has built
up to about a two foot depth. The chicken manure is bought from a local
producer and, again, depending on delivery time, may be spread on corn, small
grains or hay land.

Crop production on the Kutztown Farm is managed through a very complex
sequence of the various crops; alfalfa and red clover hays, small grains
(barley, oats, rye and wheat) and corn and soybeans. All of the crops, except
for about 2/3 of the hays, are used on the farm for livestock feed. Except for
drought years, very little of the feed grains are purchased. The cropping
sequence is not a fixed pattern of one crop after another; instead, field and
soil conditions are taken into account prior to selecting each year's crop.
Factors such as field location (hill vs. bottom), soil pH and nutrient status,
weed, insect and disease conditions, and the economic needs of the farm are
important considerations when choosing the specific crop for each field each
year. In general though, the red clover hays are grown for two years, while
the alfalfa is usually left in for three or four years. Corn always follows

legume hay plowdown, and animal manures are normally spread on the hay fields
just prior to plowdown. Corn is grown on the fields usually for two years, but
is sometimes grown for three years if conditions warrant it. Small grains
and/or soybeans follow corn production, with the cropping sequence eventually
beginning again with a legume hay crop. Wheat or the spring barley/oats are
used as nurse crops when seeding new hay fields.

Weed control in the crops is accomplished primarily by rotating the crops
grown in the fields. The small grain and hay fields usually do not have many
weeds, and those that are present are controlled by cutting. The corn and
soybeans are kept clean by using several different cultivation techniques. A
rotary hoe is used on these crops at least once, and sometimes twice, to
control the early weeds. After this, row cultivation is required once or twice
and if there are many weeds in the rows, then a hill cultivator may be used for
the final cultivation. No effort has been made to study the competitiveness of
the weeds that are present in the Kutztown Farm corn and soybeans. The yield
reductions that may be present due to weed competition would not be severe,
and, in fact, may not economically justify the use of a herbicide in most
years. Should the weather during mid-May through June be wet, then cultivating
becomes difficult, and the weed competition may become severe. In this case,
the use of an herbicide might be justified.

Another way that is used to help with weed control is to delay the corn
planting until the soil temperatures are conducive to rapid germination and
plant growth. By so doing, the competitiveness of the corn plants is increased
and the weeds are easier to control through cultivation. In the Berks County
area, corn is usually planted during the first ten days of May, while the corn
on the Kutztown Farm may be planted from May 5 - 20.

The crop yields that have been documented on the Kutztown Farm generally

are equal to or exceed county or state averages. The exception is winter
barley, which yielded almost 30-percent less than the county average, probably
due to the fact that it is planted too early on the Kutztown Farm, and
overwintering survival is poor. Year-to-year fluctuations in the Kutztown Farm
crop yields relative to those of the county or state are present, with a
particularly noticeable comparative advantage for the Kutztown Farm grain corn
during the dry years of 1980 and 1981. The 1982 season, on the other hand, was
very wet in the early part just after planting, and the grain corn on the
Kutztown Farm only yielded five-percent more than the county average. The
soybean yields have consistently out-yielded the county or state, and this may
be due to the fact that cultivating can be done on a more timely basis with
this crop because of it's late planting date.

The livestock production aspects of the Kutztown Farm have changed during
the five years of the study. Beef cattle production increased 68-percent
during this time, and in 1982, the farm produced 276 head. Hog production, on
the other hand, dropped sharply from 168 head in 1978 to only 55 head in 1982.
Apparently there are disease problems with hog production that cut down on the
profitability and, thus, the production has been somewhat curtailed. Egg
production increased almost 69-percent from 3100 dozen eggs in 1978 to 5235
dozen eggs in 1982. Reasons for the beef cattle and egg production increases
are primarily due to better management of the feeding programs, which increases
the productivity of the farm. Also, as less hogs have been fed through the
years, more feed has been available to produce the other livestock.

The crop production budgets for the Kutztown Farm crops are useful as
indicators of the cost savings associated with a production system that uses a
finely-tuned, crop rotation schedule. These savings are most evident due to
the fact that no fertilizers or pesticides are used on the majority of the

farm acreage. Depending on the crop, these reductions in production expenses ranged from essentially zero in the small grains to almost 30-percent in the soybeans compared to those where fertilizers and pesticides would be used. The cost of production for the Kutztown Farm corn grain or silage averaged 14-percent less than that on a hypothetical, conventional farm. The overall farm cost of production difference amounted to 14-percent less than that on a comparable, conventional farm. All of these figures mentioned above are for total cash operating costs and do not include labor costs.

Reducing crop production operating costs is a major concern of many farmers as prices steadily increase for the inputs needed to grow crops. Nevertheless, respectable crop yields must be maintained, and optimum performance should be the long-range goal of the nation's farmers. The study of the Kutztown Farm revealed that farming can be profitable when none or very little synthetic fertilizers and pesticides are used on an integrated crop/livestock farm. Crop rotations that maximize the biological, chemical and physical efficiencies associated with a finely tuned management approach enabled the Kutztown Farm to produce crops and livestock profitably. By adopting some or all of the techniques used on the Kutztown Farm, in theory or in principle, farmers in the U.S. will be able to pass on the next generation a truly regenerative agriculture.

INTRODUCTION

The agricultural situation in the United States at the present time is at a turning point; production expenses are at such high levels that many farmers face uncertain futures. Included with the expensive production inputs is the cost of borrowing money, which further deteriorates the farm income picture. Is it possible to reduce the input costs, or structure a farm to survive the economic crisis at hand? The intentions of the study reported in this document are to point out methods successfully used on a crop/livestock farm in Pennsylvania to reduce production costs. In doing so, we may provide a sign of hope for today's farmers that successful farming operations are possible in the present and the future.

Since the 1950's, many technogical advances have made farming more productive while at the same time reducing the number of farm workers to about three percent of the population. Crop yields have increased dramatically during this period reflecting the use of improved varieties, better weed, insect and disease control management and higher rates of fertilizer inputs. At a time when the cost of energy was relatively cheap, it made agronomic as well as economic sense to use the available technology. Unfortunately, as the costs of the inputs rose during the 1960's and 1970's, farmers were caught in a struggle between high production costs and low market prices.

A recent U.S. General Accounting office report (30) stated:

> "Most of agriculture's energy demand has been in the petroleum-based fuels. The additional energy inputs since 1950 have helped farm productivity to more than double, while permitting farm labor to be halved. Unfortunately, heavy reliance on fossil fuels is a two-edged sword. Although productivity has increased dramatically, farmers are particularly vulnerable to supply interruptions and increasing fuel costs."

Many farmers in the past adopted specialization as a way of "reducing" costs, not realizing that this would lead to a greater need for more expensive inputs. Land ownership and equipment grew to levels that required lots of credit, and interest rates grew as well. Fertilizer use increased over 200-percent during the 1950-1980 period (Table 1). As more productive crop varieties were released, larger rates of fertilizer applications were advised. Even in the 1980's, with fertilizer costs increasing annually, fertilizer recommendations are often economically unjustifiable (13 and 19). It should be plain to see that when fertilizer materials are bought with borrowed money at high interest rates, and they produce very little economic advantage, the red ink is sure to follow.

Pesticide use has also increased (Table 1) rapidly during the past three decades, even more so than fertilizers. Large monoculture cropping practices have necessitated more pesticides because of their increased damage. Crop rotations have been proven to prevent the build-up of high pest populations in most farming systems. Cropping systems encourage biological diversity, which results in biological stability over the long term.

Total operating expenses in farming have grown from 45-percent to almost 58-percent of the cash receipts during the previous three decades (Table 2). The proportion that fertilizers and pesticides account for have risen at a greater rate than the costs of fuel, oil, and machinery. Needlessly, in many cases, farmers have put their faith in the pesticides and fertilizers, and forgotten the benefits and advantages of a diverse farming operation. Now, the questions are being asked by farmers (9), "Why aren't we making any money?"

The Kutztown Farm Report resulted from a five-year, multi-faceted investigation of a low-input, regenerative, crop/livestock farm in east-central Pennsylvania. Included in the study were the agronomic, livestock and

TABLE 1 . UNITED STATES FARM INPUT CONSUMPTION INDEX, 1950-1980[1].

	1950	1960	1970	1980
Petroleum Fuel and Oils	100	101	89	198
Machinery and Equipment	100	84	126	147
Fertilizers	100	117	167	320
Pesticides	100	131	332	541
Total Production Expenses	100	112	138	191

[1] Data from Economic Indicators of the Farm Sector: Income and Balance Sheet Statistics, 1981, ERS-USDA, Washington, D.C. Adjusted with Consumer Price Index (CPI). Data is dollars spent annually.

TABLE 2 . INPUT COSTS AS PERCENT OF FARM CASH RECEIPTS, 1950-1980.

	1950	1960	1970	1980
Petroleum Fuel and Oils	4.1	4.3	3.4	5.8
Machinery and Equipment	4.9	4.3	5.7	5.1
Fertilizers	3.0	3.7	4.6	6.8
Pesticides	0.6	0.8	1.9	2.4
Total Operating Expenses	44.8	48.8	53.1	57.9

Source: USDA, Washington, D.C.

economic aspects of the farm. The objectives were to: 1) document the crop
yields during the five year study period with respect to weather conditions,
crop rotations, and soil nutrient levels, 2) analyze the soil nutrient levels,
particularly the nitrogen, phosphorus and potassium, during the course of the
study, 3) determine the livestock production levels, and 4) to estimate the
costs of production in relation to those on a hypothetical, comparison farm.

(Balance of the report is held in the committee files.)

148

Testimony presented by:

J. Patrick Madden, Ph.D.
Professor of Agricultural Economics
The Pennsylvania State University
University Park, Pennsylvania 16802

Good morning Congressman Brown and members of the subcommittee. Last
year I testified during your oversight hearings on extension, and I'm pleased
to be invited back to testify regarding the Agricultural Productivity Act of
1983.

As a professor of agricultural economics at Penn State University, I am
deeply involved in two research studies. Both are relevant to agricultural
productivity. Along with Irwin Feller and other colleagues in the Institute
for Policy Research and Evaluation at Penn State, we are in the second year
of a study being done under contract with the Department of Agriculture. The
purpose of that study is to document the workings of the public and private
systems by which food and agricultural technology is created, developed,
commercialized, and diffused to various kinds of users, on farms and in
industry. My other project is an interdisciplinary study of organic farming,
or more correctly, what we have come to call "regenerative". agriculture. It
is now officially in its second year as an Experiment Station project. The
enclosed staff paper number 56, which is a preliminary progress report based
on the first phase of that project, is enclosed for the record. This
research is supported by a CSRS (Hatch) and Experiment Station Project plus
grant and contract monies. This study is being done in cooperation with the
Rodale Research Center, which Bob Rodale mentioned during his June 29
testimony before this subcommittee. In addition, several of us at Penn State
are starting a new "sustainable farming systems" study which includes a
combination of so-called "organic" as well as convention farms. The
prospectus for this new study is also enclosed. If this project is approved,
it cannot be funded with experiment station monies, because of the limited
research allocation from state and federal sources (CSRS). We must get money
from elsewhere if we are to implement the sustainable farming systems study.

Our study of agricultural technology is relevant to this act, because we are learning how new technologies are created and disseminated. We are examining the interaction between farmers, extension personnel, researchers at universities and in industry, as well as agribusiness firms and various federal and state agencies in the creation of technologies which intimately affect agricultural productivity. From state to state, and from one technology to another we are finding an extremely diverse and interesting pattern of involvement by the various players. You will not be surprised to learn that farmers are extremely inventive, often coming up with innovations that have stumped the experts.

One of the best examples of farmers leading the way is in no-till and other conservation tillage systems which are proving to be both profitable and very effective in reducing soil erosion. Two weeks ago, as part of our field work for the technology study, I attended the sixth annual southeastern no-till systems conference and field day, in Milan, Tennessee. A copy of the program is enclosed. Many no-till systems were demonstrated in the experiment station fields. As I walked from one no-till machine demonsration to another, I had the opportunity to speak with several of the inventors. Several of the inventors are farmers, who developed the basic idea and set out with welders and cutting torches to create workable prototypes, which were later commercialized.

In other technologies, such as embyro transfer, land grant universities played a key role. In this case, George Seidel and his colleagues at Colorado State University have taken the lead in creating and simplifying the technology so that hundreds of practitioners are now able to perform embryo transfers all over this nation and in several foreign countries. In still

other technologies, such as the large round key balers and center pivot
irrigation systems, private firms have taken the leadership. Extension has
played a very major role in both the development of several technologies and
in education of farmers regarding the selection and use of technologies
appropriate for their operations.

Some technologies, such as artifical insemination, are not particularly
vulnerable to local conditions, so the technology can be widely adopted with
little or no variation. However, another finding of our study that is
relevant to these hearings is the fact that American agriculture is extremely
diverse as to climatic, soil, ecological, and economic conditions. As a
result of this diversity, many technologies must be adapted to local
conditions if they are to work optimally, if at all. The classic example is
hybred grain sorghum

I have noticed that extreme diversity characterizes the techologies and
the productivity of the farms I have visited during the past two years as
phase one of our study of regenerative agriculture. The diversity is best
illustrated by the two farmers near Stockton, California, one of whom is
prospering because of his use of organic or regenerative methods, while his
neighbor just a few miles down the road told us he has been forced by the
economic reality of insect damage to start spraying again, after several
years producing organically grown apples and other fruits and vegetables. Of
the 44 organic or regenerative farm operators I interviewed face to face,
only a handful (some of the dryland wheat farmers in Kansas and Washington)
said they felt they had the "once-and-for-all" answer. All the others said
they are still seeking new and better ways, constantly alert to changing
weather and soil conditions and insect populations, both harmful and

beneficial types. They realize that what worked last year may have to be
modified this year to achieve the same results.

The farms I visited were selected after careful screening of the 22-page
questionnaires we received from some 357 farmers in seven states, mostly
subscribers to New Farm magazine, as described in our staff paper. Therefore
we do not pretend to have data representing all organic or regenerative farms'
in the nation. However, a crucial step in the scientific method is the
formulation of research questions and hypotheses. The exploratory phase of
my research has been designed for this purpose. All I can offer at this
point in time is impressions drawn from studying the questionnaires, talking
with the farmers, and in only a few dozen cases, walking with them through
their fields.

I prefer to avoid using the word "organic farming," because it means so
many different things top different people. Dick Harwood, Director of Rodale
Research Center, recently presented a paper in Tanzania in which he does an
excellent job of unpacking the meaning of various philosophies or groups
related to "organic farming." His paper is entitled "International Overview
of Regenerative Agriculture."

Simply stated, a regenerative farming system is one that produces
bountiful harvests of foods not contaminated by possibly harmful chemicals,
using farming methods that enhance long term agricultural productivity while
minimizing the erosion, depletion, or despoiling of natural resources. My
understanding of the contrast between conventional, "strictly organic," and
regenerative farming is outlined in the attached chart.

Turning now to the Agricultural Productivity Act, I would like to offer
a few personal impressions and observations. First, I am strongly in favor

of the purposes of the Act. Also, I am pleased that the term "organic farming" does not appear in the Act, because the term is laden with emotional content that gets in the way of useful discussions and action. It is also highly commendable that you mention "modern agricultural technologies," making it explicitly clear that you are not advocating a return of the back-breaking technologies of the 1930's and beyond, which many observers mistakenly equate with organic farming. The farms I visited were all modern and most were highly productive. The really successful farms were operated by some of the best farmers, the most capable businessmen and women I have ever known. Nor is modern agricultural technology necessarily chemical intensive. For example, the excellent work being done by agricultural research service and by universities such as the University of California and Texas A&M on integrated pest management and biological control of insects and other pests is a case in point. The Lundbergs (2,700 acres near Chico, California) certainly use "modern" technology in producing some 200 acres of rice organically, everything from laser devices on their tractors, to rectangular-move irrigation systems. Their neighbor Dick Harter and his son-in-law Brian Leahy are producing rice organically on their 900 acre farm, using methods that are elegant in their simplicity, remarkable in their efficiency, and admirable in their harmony with Nature.

I am also pleased to see that the Act calls for an "Information Study," which includes both the assembly of known information plus identification of gaps. I presume the National Agricultural Library will play a major role in this phase of the work. In this regard, I would call attention to the need for a close connection between the problems and opportunities encountered by the farmers selected for the pilot study and the identification of gaps, as an agenda for further scientific research and development. In our technology

study, we have encountered many excellent examples of feedback from the grass

roots--from farmers, Extension personnel, machinery dealers, and others--back

to the sources of the technology in the universities or in industry.

Another strength of the Act is that it seeks to legitimize in various

federal agencies and in the land grant system those farming methods we would

call regenerative. Most of my colleagues in the land grant system doubt that

organic or regenerative farming methods are biologically or economically

feasible. Case studies such as those called for in H.R. 2714 can establish

the credibility of these methods. Existing ARS & CSRS research provides

useful building blocks, but an integrative approach at the firm level is

essential.

I am also pleased to see that you are calling for collection of data to

document the workings of these farms. We at Penn State are just beginning to

create such a data system, working with four more-or-less regenerative farms

and four conventional farms. We do not have enough research funds to be able

to afford to collect all the data you call for in the Act, particularly the

nutritional quality of the crops and the quality of the water and other

natural resources, but we would like very much to extend the scope of the

study to include these and other factors.

For example, I would like to see research done to find quick and

reliable methods (such as human tissue culture) to test chemicals for

toxicity and carcinogenic effects. Perhaps the Act would be more likely to

attain its objectives if it required a farming systems approach.

One important concern I would raise regarding the Act is that it calls

for a very small sample, twelve conventional farms seeking to make the

transition to regenerative farming systems, and another twelve that have been
employing such methods for at least five years. (We would add the
requirement that these farms must be showing a profit large enough to entice
the operating family to continue farming; otherwise it would not be
sustainable.) By requiring only twelve of each general type of farm, and
with specific categories in each type, you are "placing all the eggs in one
fragile basket," if you will pardon the agricultural pun. Farming is risky
business, as you know. What if two or three or more of the pilot study farms
go bankrupt due to drought, extaordinary disease or pest problems, and/or
disastrously low prices? Furthermore, the transitional farms must not be
required to "go cold turkey," for abrupt termination of chemicals can be
disastrous to many types of farms. A phased or gradual transition should be
permitted in the legislation.

One valid criticism of the Act is that it does not include a comparison
group of farms not in transition, and not already using the alternative
practices. Another is that, because of the small number of farms to be
studied, statistical control of important factors such as soil type,
rotation, and managerial ability may be infeasible.

Hopefully the work called for in the Agricultural Productivity Act will
build upon the fine work already being done in a few places, such as the
Rodale Research Center in Kutztown, PA, the private experimental farm of Dick
and Sharon Thompson near Boone, IA, the Ecological Agriculture Program of
Steve Gleissman at University of California at Santa Cruz , the field days on
"organic farms," sponsored by University of Nebraska, and other such efforts.
By tying in with on-going studies, more efficient use of the program funds
may be achieved, and the hazards of very small sample size might be overcome.

And perhaps by using video taping of the farms at key stages of the season, the educational value of the pilot farms would be enriched, while reducing the farmer's hassel and the risk of damage to crops and livestock due to excessive traffic of visitors. These and other ideas could enhance the program.

The objectives of the Act are admirable, well worth pursuing, and attainable. It won't be easy. The activities called for in the Act are an important step in the right direction. Given the extreme diversity of agriculture, inclusion of more pilot farms would be highly desirable. And given the high risk of sample attrition, a large number seems imperative.

Thank you again for the opportunity to testify regarding the Agricultural Productivity Act of 1983.

Chart 1. Comparison of the Basic Philosophies of Conventional, "Strictly Organic," and Regenerative Farming.

	Conventional	"Strictly Organic"	Regenerative
HEALTH	Minimize risks of chemical residues in foods, soil, water, air.	Very concerned; seeks to consume/produce only chemical-free foods, water. Convinced chemicals cause poor health. Concerned about residues of degradation or breakdown products of agricultural chemicals in soils, water, livestock and people.	Shares the concern. Emphasis on finding a better alternative; avoid risks of using chemicals having unknown impact.
SOIL FERTILITY	Importation of nutrients; often over-use; sometimes toxic impact on ground water. Uses least expensive sources of nutrients (e.g., anhydrous amonia).	Shuns fast-release fertilizer, especially anhydrous amonia—concerned for earthworms soil bacteria. Emphasizes manure (esp composted), legumes, rotations.	Import nutrients only as needed to make transition to self-sufficiency—toward maintenance dosage at min. level needed to retain fertility soil genesis—rotations featuring deep-rooted plants to "mine" nutrients.
WEED CONTROL	Prefers weed-free fields. Herbicides are first line of defense, especially in no-till farming.	Refuses to use herbicides. Cultivates; uses crop rotations; hoe; hand weeding; animals (e.g., geese). Considers weeds a major problem in row crops. Also prefers weed-free fields in row crops.	Uses herbicides only in transition and situations (temporary). methods and (e.g., musk Use weeds as green manure, feed, food.
PEST AND DISEASE CONTROL	Synthetic pesticides; antibiotics; IPM in some cases; views "organic" neighbors as a threat of contamination.	Maintain habitat to support vigorous populations of beneficial predators and their food source; vigorously growing crops; animals housed and raised in such a way as to minimize disease danger.	Same as "organic," except may use antibiotics and other chemicals temporarily, in emergency. Seeks to breed local home-grown predators and pathogens; improved detection methods.

Chart 1. (Cont'd.)

	Conventional	"Strictly Organic"	Regenerative
FARM SIZE	Some say "Get big or get out," but most prefer small to moderate scale family farms. Most have off-farm income. Believes "organic" is ok for gardens but not commercial scale farms; low profits, high risk cited as disadvantages of "organic" farming.	"Small is beautiful." Limit size to the acreage or herd size that can be farmed with good stewardship; management and labor are the major limiting factors.	Seeks to adapt regenerative methods to larger as well as small farms, so as to account for greater share of the market; more comfortable income—permanent occupation with decent level of living. Seeks profitable ways to facilitate the conversion of conventional farms to regenerative.
MARKETING	Sells farm products mostly via conventional markets; increasing use of direct markets (esp. fruit, vegetable, and ornamentals); believes "organic" produce is inferior (worms, etc.)	Most field crops sold in conventional markets; some vegetables and fruit sold in "organic" or "health food outlets. Sometimes receives premium prices; criticizes USDA's "cosmetic" approach to grading.	Seeks to improve markets, grading standards. Seeks to reduce dependency on distant food sources by finding ways to make local regenerative farming systems profitable, sustainable, more extensive. Seeks to encourage local or regional production where economically feasible, rather than total dependence upon distant sources of foods.

Chart 2. Strictly Organic, Conventional, and Regenerative Farming

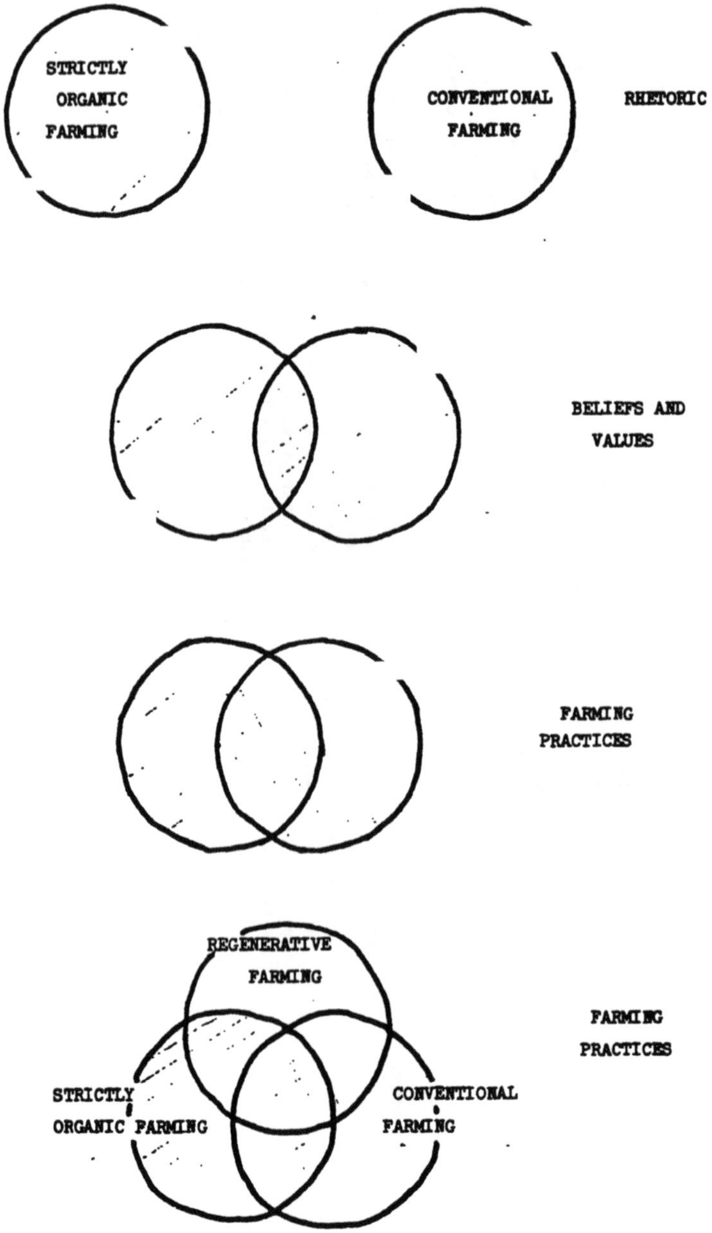

STRICTLY
ORGANIC
FARMING

CONVENTIONAL
FARMING

RHETORIC

BELIEFS AND
VALUES

FARMING
PRACTICES

REGENERATIVE
FARMING

FARMING
PRACTICES

STRICTLY
ORGANIC FARMING

CONVENTIONAL
FARMING

Material Submitted in Support of Testimony by J. Patrick Madden

1. Pennsylvania Agricultural Experiment Station (HATCH) Research Project 2584, "Decision Making Regarding Organized Agricultural Production Practices."

2. J. Patrick Madden, "Case Studies of Farms in Transition Toward a More Regenerative Farming System," Staff Paper 56, May 1983.

3. Prospectus of Proposed Agricultural Experiment Station Project, "Sustainable Farming Systems in Pennsylvania."

4. "Farming Systems Research and Development."

5. Program of "Sixth Annual Southeastern No-Till Systems Conference," Milan, Tennessee. July 20-21, 1983.

6. Richard R. Harwood and J. Patrick Madden, "Research Agenda for the Transition to a Regenerative Food System," 1982.

RESEARCH PROJECT OUTLINE

THE PENNSYLVANIA STATE UNIVERSITY · COLLEGE OF AGRICULTURE
AGRICULTURAL EXPERIMENT STATION · UNIVERSITY PARK, PENNSYLVANIA

PROJECT_____2584

TITLE: Decision Making Regarding Organic Agricultural
              Production Practices

OBJECTIVE: Develop an empirical, multivariate model of decision making
              incorporating the causal interactions and feedbacks among
              various physical, economic, and sociological factors
              affecting farmers using/not using so-called organic farm
management practices and related agricultural production strategies.

PROCEDURE: The manner in which farmers come to decisions about how the
              farm operation is organized is a function of at least three
              broad variable areas: economic factors, physical capabilities
              of the farm, and social/philosophical preferences or goals of
the operator. Systems analysis techniques (5, 8) have been used successfully
to evaluate how new production technology and changing market conditions
impact farmers with different enterprise combinations and resource ratios.
The present research will use the same general techniques recognizing: 1)
that systems analysis has tended to be limited to economic variables, and
2) has not been greatly concerned with so-called organic farming practices.
The present study will direct particular attention at
production modes of so-called sustainable agriculture and will broaden the
analysis of the economic system to include constraints stemming from physical
capabilities and social/philosophical preferences.

              Most farms lie somewhere along a continuum between the
extremes of either "pure organic-ecological" versus conventional farming
practices. The former represent, in some respects, quite different
strategies and farm management practices than those present in most commercial operations yet - as detailed below - they are being viewed increasingly as a potential part of the spectrum of viable alternatives open to all
farmers. The specific organic practices to be examined will be identified
in consultation with agronomists, including organic farming specialists.
Systems analysis techniques will be used to evaluate such alternative
practices and to specify resource situations to which they may be adapted.
Further, specific evaluations will be made by studying the experiences of
organic farm operators and the transitional adopters of such technology.

              For examination of the organic farming alternatives,
geographical areas for the study will be selected, based on prevalence of
predetermined types of farms, as indicated by census data, and availability
of likely organically oriented ones, as indicated by subscription lists of
New Farm magazine and membership in various organic farming organizations.
Letters will be sent to a sample of potential respondents in these study
areas. The letters will explain the purposes of the study and will ask for

certain screening information needed for selection of persons to be
included in the later phases of data collection. Respondents will be
asked to provide their telephone numbers if they are willing to participate in the study. Follow-up phone calls will be made or mail
questionnaires will be sent to a purposive sample of the screening
respondents, to obtain more detailed information, and to assemble a list
of persons willing to have their farming operation visited and be
personally interviewed.

All consenting respondents will be asked detailed questions
regarding farm resources   rop and livestock enterprises produced, conservation and other pract ces fo owed, aspirations and attitudes of the
farmer and other household members and financial information. In collec-
ng data on spirations and ttitudes the prime need is to learn how
farmers who have changed to organic practices came to the decisions and
how they imp emented them, and how these decisions were affected by financial
and physical characteristics of the farm as well as various social and personal attributes of the farm fami y, availability of inputs needed for
organic farming, and access to appropriate markets for the commodities produced.

At the end of the interview (or questionnaire), each respon-
dent will be asked whether he/she would be willing to participate yet further
in more intens ve probing of thei farming experience by the researchers
Farms will be selected for case study based on nformation gathered du ng
the telephone questionnaire interviews and mail ques onna res   In-depth
interviews will be done, especially trying to get additiona financia data
(if possible) so as to ascertain the management pattern of the farm operation
and its generalizability. The in-depth interviews will be taped (with the
permission of the respondents) and later summarized in a series of case
studies.

Findings of the case studies and other interviews will be
integrated into a comprehensive manuscript, including a summary model to
serve as a prototype for follow-up studies to be done later by a possibly
expanded community of researchers and for the creation of conceptual models
to guide the development of sustainable farming systems. The structure of
the descriptive emp rica model will be developed through an interdisciplinary team and in cooperation with the staff of the Organic Gardening
and Farming Research Center in Kutztown, Pennsylvania.

REASONS FOR   Farm organization and reorganization is a never-ending task
UNDERTAKING   because of changes in the technological, economic, institu-
THE WORK: tional, and human environments in which farm operators must
                   operate. Farmers generally lack the economic information
necessary to determine how they should react to these changes to best
achieve their personal and financial goals.

Technological innovations can change both the most economical
method of producing a product and the optimum combination of enterprises for a

162

farm. A specific technology (either "organic" or a new conventional innovation) usually is applicable only to farms with certain combinations of human
and physical resources. The purpose of thi tudy   to evaluate alternative
technologies, including new developments as they occur, and to find: 1) the
farm resource situations to which they are adapted and 2) the changes in
farm organization which should accompany their adoption.

    In the last severa decades American agriculture has evolved
a system of management pract ces heavily involving oil-based chemicals for
fertilization and pest control. For some time criticism of this farm management system has occurred and urgings been given for adopting different ways
of husbanding America's commercia   agricultural production (7, 16). Changing
economic and resource conditions espec a ly escalating oil prices and
accumulated medical sensitivity to toxicity problems, have sparked new interest in such alternatives (19).

    Relatively little is known about the dynamics entering into
farmers' decisions to alter (or not) the microstructure of their operations
when the shift   toward what is often called "organic" methods. Farmers
                                    doption of alternati

technology, if they have full and accurate
of the alternatives on family income uncertainty soil erosion and other
factors. Likewise, adoption of   ternative technology i certa   ocations
may be imited by market conditions, including availability of production
inputs certai kinds of fertilizer or manure for example and access to
markets for farm products Both organic and conventiona technologica
innovations must be compared and evaluated with regard to their feasibility,
impacts on farm income, and acceptability to farm operators as a means of
attaining the financial and personal goals of the farm family.

    Within the mandate of the Land-Grant charter (and consistent
with a democratic society), a fundamental service that social science research
can perform is to chart and try for an understanding of farm practices
adopt on in its fullest meaning. By having the experience of others regarding alternative farming systems made avai able, the given farmer can make

sense of values. Informed decision making requires relevant nformation
inputs, which are not generally or readily available at the present time.

PREVIOUS WORK   The literature on adoption/diffusion is voluminous (20) but
AND PRESENT   much of it may not be directly applied to the case of
OUTLOOK: "organic" methods (4, 14, 15, 18, 19, 22). Past adoption/
                 diffusion work assumes a model where the item(s) at issue
are neutrally or positively oriented to. The conventional evaluation, however, often taken toward "organic" alternatives of agricultural production
in the United States is negative (3, 6, 25). Again, whereas economic

motives of short-term profitability and increased physical yields or labor-saving presumption are among the first-named reasons for taking on conventional technological innovations/practices, less directly economic concerns - such as health improvement or worries over environmental degradation - are apparently foremost to those switching away from present, high chemical/energy use methods to alternative forms (4, 6, 14, 19). Given that (18:57) "environmental innovation is not predicted well by . . . [the] variables commonly used in adoption research," there is a need to examine farm practices adoption anew, with the case of (often) ambiguously valued items.

Work done directly on farmers changing toward so-called organic methods/management practices has shown that the users are not, in terms of farm structure and personal/demographic characteristics, radically different from the majority of farmers following more conventional patterns (9, 14, 19). Such findings are at variance with popular stereotypes and may be surprising in light of the ideologically tinged writing surrounding so-called organic management practices. It is not incomprehendible if one recognizes that the items at issue are not generally exotic behaviors. Often they are merely the reincorporation of principles that were a widespread part of conventional farm practices in the United States before the wave of high energy/chemical technology and are a much larger element in successful European agriculture (2).

Much of the literature to date on "organic" practices has been concerned with economic/agronomic evaluation of such methods (4, 10, 11, 12, 13, 17, 21, 23). The dynamics of a given farmer's opting toward (or rejecting) these types of practices is only beginning to be explored (19, 24). Given that adoption of so-called organic management is not necessarily - or usually - an all or nothing matter (14, 23), then it follows that particular attention needs to focus on the full spectrum of farming experience in the United States and not be concentrated with the extremes of an organic practices continuum (1, 13).

164

LITERATURE CITED:

1. Bealer, Robert C. "Some Concerns About 'Myth and Reality in Organic Farming,'" Newsline, 8:36-39 (1980).

2. Besson, Jean-Marc, and Hardy Vogtmann, eds. Towards a Sustainable Agriculture (Aarau, Switzerland: Verlag Wirz, 1978).

3. CAST, Report No. 84. Organic and Conventional Farming Compared (Ames, Iowa: Council for Agricultural Science and Technology, 1980).

4. Center for Rural Affairs. Barriers to Conversion of Small Farms to Ecological Methods (Walthill, Neb.: National Center for Appropriate Technology, 1980).

5. Churchman, C. W. The Systems Approach (New York: Dell, 1968).

6. Geisler, Charles C., J. Tadlock Cowan, Michael R. Hattern, and Harvey M. Jacobs. "Sustained Land Productivity: Equity Consequences of Technological Alternatives." Report to Office of Technology Assessment. Cornell University, Ithaca, NY (November 1980).

7. Goldstein, Jerry, ed. The New Food Chain: An Organic Link Between Farm and City (Emmaus, Pa.: Rodale Press, 1973).

8. Hallberg, Milt C., and Alden C. Manchester. "Strategy for Development of Systems Analytical Models - A Dairy Experience." J. of the N.E. Ag. Econ. Council, 11:11-22 (1973).

9. Harris, Craig K., Sharon E. Powers, and Frederick H. Buttel. "Myth and Reality in Organic Farming: A Profile of Conventional and Organic Farmers in Michigan," Newsline, 8:33-43 (1980).

10. Klepper, Robert, William Lockeretz Barry Commoner, Michael Gertler, Sarah Fast, Daniel O Leary, and Roger Blobaum. "Economic Performance and Energy Intens venes on Organic and Conventional Farms in the Corn Belt: A Preliminary Comparison," Am. J. of Ag. Econ., 59:1-12 (1977).

11. Lockeretz, William, Georgia Shearer, Robert Klepper, and Susan Sweeney. "Field Crop Production on Organic Farms in the Midwest," J. of Soil and Water Conserv. 33: 30-134 (1978).

12. Lockeretz, William, Georgia Shearer, and Daniel H. Kohl. "Organic Farming in the Corn Belt," Sci., 211:540-547 (1981).

13. Lockeretz, William, Georgia Shearer, Susan Sweeney, George Kuepper, Diane Wanner, and Daniel H. Kohl. "Maize Yields and Soil Nutrient Levels With and Without Pesticides and Standard Commercial Fertilizers," Agron. J., 72:65-72 (1980).

14. Lockeretz, William, and Sarah Wernick. "Commercial Organic Farming in the Corn Belt in Comparison to Conventional Practices," Rur. Soc., 45:708-722 (1980).

15. Madden, J. Patrick and Heather Tischbein Baker. An Agenda for Small Farms Research - A Report on Phase II of the NRC Small Farms Project (Washington, DC: The National Rural Center, 1981).

16. Merrill, Richard, ed. Radical Agriculture (New York: Harper and Row, 1976).

17. Oelhaf, R. C. Organic Agriculture: Economic and Ecological Comparisons With Conventional Methods (New York: Halsted Press, 1978).

18. Pampel, Fred, and John van Es. "Environmental Quality and Issues of Adoption Research," Rur. Soc., 42:57-71 (1977).

19. Powers, Sharon E., and Craig K. Harris. "Adoption of Organic Farming Methods: The Decision-Making Process Among Michigan Farmers" (paper read to the annual meetings of the Rural Sociological Society, Ithaca, New York, August 1980).

20. Rogers, Everett, and Floyd Shoemaker. Communication of Innovations (New York: Free Press, 1971).

21. Shearer, Georgia, Daniel H. Kohl, Diane Wanner, George Kuepper, Susan Sweeney and William Lockeretz. "Crop Production Costs and Returns on Midwestern Organic Farms: 1977 and 1978. Am. J. of Ag. Econ., 63:264-269 (1981).

22. Taylor, David, and William Miller. "The Adoption Process and Environmental Innovations: A Case Study of a Government Project," Rur. Soc., 43:634-648 (1978).

23. USDA Study Team on Organic Farming. Report and Recommendations on Organic Farming (Washington, DC.: Government Printing Office, 1980).

24. Wernick, Sarah, and William Lockeretz. "Motivations and Practices or Organic Farmers," Compost Sci., 18:20-24 (1977).

25. White-Stevens, Robert. "Perspectives on Fertilizer Use, Residue Utilization, and Food Production," in R. C. Loehr, ed., Fertilizer and Agricultural Residues (Ann Arbor, Michigan: Ann Arbor Science Press, 1977).

PROBABLE
DURATION: Five years (1/1/82 to 12/31/86)

FINANCIAL
SUPPORT: Estimated Annual Expenses

              Hatch Funds
                Salaries $70,000

              State Funds
                Maintenance $ 3,500

PERSONNEL: J. Patrick Madden, Robert C. Bealer,
              E. J. Partenheimer, and Carolyn Sachs

ADVISORY
COMMITTEE: Dale Baker, Virgil Crowley, and Tony Stemberger

INSTITUTIONAL
UNITS   Department of Agricultural Economics and Rural Sociology,
INVOLVED: and the PSU Small-Scale Agriculture Center

COOPERATION: Other Departments of the Pennsylvania Agricultural
                Experiment Station, and the Rodale Research Center.

167

Staff Paper #56   May   1983

CASE STUDIES OF FARMS IN TRANSITION

TOWARD A MORE REGENERATIVE FARMING SYSTEM

by

J. Patrick Madden

Staff Papers are circulated without formal review
by the Agricultural Economics and Rural Sociology
Department. Content is the sole responsibility of
the author.

Agricultural Economics and Rural Sociology Department
College of Agriculture
The Pennsylvania State University
University Park, Pennsylvania 16802

168

CASE STUDIES OF FARMS IN TRANSITION
TOWARD A MORE REGENERATIVE FARMING SYSTEM
A Progress Report, May 1983

CASE STUDIES OF FARMS IN TRANSITION

TOWARD A MORE REGENERATIVE FARMING SYSTEM[*]

A Progress Report March 1983

Part I. Background

A. Introduction

This is a progress report on a study entitled, "Decision Making
Regarding Organic Agricultural Production Practices."[1] The motivation for
the study stems from growing public concerns regarding the toxicity and
sustainability of agriculture, plus a lack of knowledge needed to address
these concerns. Increasingly, it seems the public is becoming concerned
about the health implications of toxic chemicals in the environment and in
the foods and water we consume. Some agricultural chemicals such as DDT as
an insecticide, and diethylstilbesterol as a livestock growth stimulant,
have been banned. Recently other chemicals have been suspended because
traces have been found in ground water. Chemicals found in fish and other
goods have raised the flag of alarm among consumer advocates and individual
consumers. While the health implications of these chemicals are not well
understood, and may not become apparent for decades (if ever), the
possibility that the list of banned chemicals may be rapidly extended has
raised the specter of food shortages, where production of certain crops
seems highly dependent upon the use of those chemicals. Other concerns

---

[*] The author gratefully acknowledges the editorial performance of Anastra
Madden in improving the organization and readability of this manuscript.
[1] This is a report of progress for the Pennsylvania Agricultural Experiment
Station Research Project 2584. Funding during 1981-82, plus extensive
staff assistance, were provided by the Rodale Research Center in
Kutztown, Pennsylvania.

regarding the sustainability of the nation's agriculture include soil
erosion, depletion of underground water supplies, and reliance upon foreign
or limited sources of nutrients, such as phosphates.

Lacking is the knowledge of biologically and economically feasible
alternatives to the current state of dependence upon toxic, distant, non-
renewable resources. The purpose of the study is to identify the
oportunities and barriers to a transition from a chemical-intensive farming
system to one that is less toxic and more ecologically and economically
sustainable.

After visiting dozens of farmers in selected states, it has become
clear that, while not all organic farmers are operating at a profit,
several commercial-scale farms are prospering while using cultural
practices that are generally regarded as "organic"—ecologically sound,
sustainable, regenerative, and non-toxic. For purposes of this study I
prefer to avoid characterizing farms as "organic," for several reasons.
First, the word is heavily laden with emotional overtones which cloud
communication. Second, farms are operated with a combination of practices.
Some farmers calling themselves "organic" utilize toxic chemicals and
fertilizers on part of their land, while relying entirely on biological
controls, legumes, and other practices officially approved as "organic" in
other areas of the farms. Likewise, many farmers that would not call their
farms "organic" nonetheless rely on some "organic" practices. There is no
clear line separating "organic" and "conventional" farms; the line is
blurred and the extent of adoption of "organic" practices lies on a
continuum. Words like sustainable, biological, or regenerative seem less
inflammatory. Regenerative is a word that best describes the ideal.

Sometimes, farmers who consider themselves "organic" usually refer to their non-organic counterparts as "commercial" farmers. This is an unfortunate use of the word, since it implies (incorrectly) that organic farming cannot succeed on a commercial scale, and that the only financially successful commercial farms are those on which chemical-intensive practices are used.

Regardless of the words used to describe them, I observed many moderate to very large scale farms that were prospering with abundant yields of high quality crops, sometimes competing in conventional markets, but without regular doses of various petrochemical sprays, and with little if any chemical fertilizers.

I also found many small to moderate-scale organic farms, entirely dependent upon a fragile market for "organic" farm products, and vulnerable to even modest increases in local production of organic foods for health food stores and other selected outlets. But what was surprising is the fact that modern businessmen and women seemed to be prospering financially, using largely or entirely "organic" practices. In many cases, they totally avoided the use of "chemicals," and depended largely on natural or cultural means to control pests and weeds. They use legumes or manure as their source of nitrogen, and deep-rooted green manure crops to "mine" nutrients from deep in tne soil profile, to enhance the productivity of their topsoil. Other farmers were tending in that direction by experimenting with ways to wean their farms from dependence on chemicals and relying increasingly on regenerative farming practices. Some of the farms visited were what we might call "equilibrium" regenerative or organic farms. These farms have made the transition, both the biological and financial conversion, from a chemical-intensive to a more regenerative farming system. I use the word "system" to refer to the entire interconnected set of farming and financial management practices, including equipment and other resources—not just to a single technique or method, such as the use of green manure or the biological control of insects. Nor are we talking merely about "negative organic farming," which consists simply of avoiding the use of certain categories of chemicals and most types of fertilizers (but permitting other types). The term "regenerative" farming system involves a more progressive and active behavior intended to build and enhance soil productivity and enrich the natural balance within the ecological system of the farm and its immediate environment. Regenerative farming systems seek to substitute on-farm sources of nutrients, such as legumes and "mining" of nutrients from deep soil; biological controls are substituted for pesticides and herbicides where possible. As a result, less chemicals are needed to sustain the production and profitability of the farm. At the opposite end of the continuum are the "chemical-intensive" farms, whose operators rely totally upon toxic chemicals and chemical fertilizers in place of natural controls and sources of soil fertility, animal nutrition and health. The extreme advocates of chemical-intensive farming consider the ideal soil as nothing more than a sterile medium in which to prop up the plants. The regenerative ideal views soil as a habitat for millions of living things in a robust ecological balance. Between these polar opposites are hundreds of thousands of farms utilizing a combination of regenerative and chemical-intensive practices.

In addition to those "equilibrium" regenerative farming systems, many combination farms that are in transition were observed. Most were shifting cautiously toward greater use of regenerative practices. Others,

disappointed in their early efforts to "go organic," as they call it, were
intending to switch back to chemicals, for the time being at least. These
farmers said they regret having to increase their use of chemicals, but
they feel they have no choice except bankruptcy.

But when I saw other farms not many miles away that had successfully
shifted to regenerative systems, I could not help wondering why it seems to
work on some and not on other farms. As a researcher, I became intrigued
with the challenge of understanding the causal forces at work. I was
curious about the interacting systems of biological, physical, climatic,
and economic forces that determine the success or failure of various kinds
of farms. A few farmers had tried to "go cold turkey," converting rapidly
to regenerative systems; others intended to remain chemical-intensive,
while still others attempted a gradual transition toward a regenerative
system of farming.

What goes through the mind of a farmer as he contemplates starting the
transition toward a regenerative farming system? What are the ways to ease
the burden of transition? Under what conditions can he or she profitably
make the switch abruptly? When should it be done gradually, and how
gradually? How can the process of transition be accelerated and made less
financially costly? What are the costs and benefits to society of farmers
switching from chemical-intensive to regenerative farming systems? These
and many other questions have motivated and directed the study. We wanted
to know the biological, physical, climatic, and economic realities and
fantasies that either encourage or discourage farmers from using farming
systems that are more sustainable and less toxic to farm residents, to the
environment, and to the consumers.

One of the first questions we had to deal with was how would we select
farms to visit? How could we get a good, cross-section of various farming
systems which would provide insights for planning subsequent phases of the
study? Rodale Press provided a list of subscribers to **The New Farm**
magazine as our initial sampling frame. We augmented this list with the
help of various local and regional organic farming organizations, such as
TILTH in the Pacific Northwest, Kansas Organic Growers, and California
Certified Organic Farmers. We arbitrarily selected seven states for the
study: California (where I resided temporarily while on sabbatic leave
from Penn State), Oregon, Washington, Idaho, Kansas, Pennsylvania, and
Maine, (Table 1). During the site visits, the study spilled over into
other states, as opportunities emerged.

Table 1: Number of Questionnaires Mailed Out and Number Returned

State	Screening (One-Page) Questionnaire		Long-Form (22-Page) Questionnaire	
	Mailed Out	Returned	Mailed Out	Returned
California	877	165	130	83
Idaho	294	67	62	32
Kansas	735	109	98	55
Maine	427	137	69	48
Oregon	303	81	159	58
Pennsylvania	915	207	72	56
Washington	163	39	62	25
Total	3714	805	652	357

So far, we have visited dozens of farmers in California, and a few in
each of the other states except Maine. Dick Harwood accompanied me during
visits to farms in Washington and Oregon. His insights into those farms,
including his suggestions regarding ways to handle the weed and insect
problems and his intimate knowledge of the soils and soil biology have been
a tremendous asset to the study. Patricia Allen of the Small Farms Center,
UC-Davis, served as the local contact person for some of the California
farm visits.

Most of the farms we visited were selected from responses to our mail
survey questionnaire. We also conducted round-table discussions with four
groups of organic farmers, in Oregon, Washington and California, and
attended various conferences which included farmers with an "organic" or
"ecological" persuasion. The following is a brief summary of my
observations and impressions of the farms visited.

(Balance of the report is held in the committee files.)

Prospectus: Farming Systems

Title: Sustainable Farming Systems in Pennsylvania*

Personnel: Carolyn Sachs, Rural Sociology; Patrick Madden, Agricultural Economics;
              Lowell Wilson, Animal Science; James Garthe, Agricultural Engineering;
              Peter Ferretti, Horticulture; and Les Lanyon, Agronomy

Objectives: 1. Develop farm-based strategies for a more sustainable agriculture,
                  including the determination of optimal enterprise mixes appropriate
                  to the various land and human resources of Pennsylvania farmers.

              2. Test and evaluate the applicability and effectiveness of the
                  farming systems research and development model in promoting
                  a sustainable agricultural system as a means of aiding indi-
                  vidual farms and the agricultural community as well.

              3. Develop and evaluate an innovative, cost-effective methodology
                  for replicating the farming systems research and development
                  process on a broad scale.

Approach: 1. A rapid field survey of farmers and Extension personnel
                  conducted by the research team will provide an information
                  base for a selected target county. The field survey will be
                  supplemented with a review of existing marketing data, soil
                  surveys, and census reports. Farming systems will be studied
                  by the team to identify problems and opportunities for increasing
                  production on a whole-farm basis. A research program involving
                  on-site research will be developed. The farming systems team
                  will implement trials and tests.

              2. The farming systems team will analyze the results of their
                  experiments including such factors as production increases or
                  decreases; handling and marketing considerations; and cost/
                  benefit relationships of introduced technologies, cultural
                  practices, and enterprise mixes. The team will also analyze
                  the farming systems approach as a model for agricultural
                  research and development as part of the project evaluation
                  and using a limited survey of other faculty, Extension
                  personnel and farmers.

              3. A literature review, coupled with contacts with Extension
                  personnel, project personnel from other farming systems
                  research projects, and farmers, will be used to develop and
                  test a methodology for replicating the project process itself.

Expected
Duration: Three years

Advisory   Dean Jansma, Agricultural Economics; Shannon Stokes, Rural Sociology;
Committee   Neil Gingrich, Agricultural Economics; and Harold Lockhoff, C.E.D.
Members: Huntingdon County

* See attached page for description of farming systems research

FARMING SYSTEMS RESEARCH AND DEVELOPMENT

As with other approaches to agricultural research and extension,
FSR&D´s purpose is to generate more appropriate technologies for farmers
and, where possible, to improve policies and support services for farm
production, to raise farm families´ welfare and to enhance society´s
goals. But more specifically FSR&D aims at increasing the productivity of
farming systems by generating technologies for particular groups of farmers
and by developing greater insight into which technologies fit where and
why. This latter purpose concerns using scientific methods for generating
hypotheses and then, by deduction, determining which technologies to use in
a particular farm setting. Such an approach contrasts with an empirical
approach that through trial and error arrives at suitable technologies for
the conditions of specific farmers.

DEFINITION OF FSR&D

FSR&D is an approach to agricultural research and development that:
— views the whole farm as a system;
— focuses on (1 the interdependencies between the components
   under the control of members of the farm household and (2) how
   these components interact with the physical biological, and
   socioeconomic factors not under the household´s control.

Farming systems are defined by their physical, biological, and
socioeconomic setting and by the farm families´ goals and other attributes,
access to resources, choices of productive activities (enterprises), and
management practices. The systems approach applied to on-farm research
considers farmers´ systems as a whole, which means:

(1) studying the many facets of the farm household and its setting
    through close and frequent contact with household members on
    their farms;

(2) considering problems and opportunites as they influence the
    whole farm;

(3) setting priorities accordingly;

(4) recognizing the linkages of subsystems within the farming
    system and considering them when dealing with any part of the
    system;

(5) evaluating research and development results in terms of the
    whole farming system and the interests of society.

MILAN NO-TILL FIELD DAY
Wednesday, July 20, 1983

Tours: 7:00 a.m. until 5·00 p.m.

Exhibits: Open all day

Activities: Research Tours, Demonstrations of No-Till Planters & Drills, Weed & Disease Control, and Soil Conservation. Commercial Exhibit & Displays of No-Till & Conservation Machinery, Ag Chemicals, Seeds and Supplies.

SIXTH ANNUAL SOUTHEASTERN NO-TILL SYSTEMS CONFERENCE
Thursday, July 21, 1983

PROGRAM

7 00 - 8 00 a.m. REGISTRATION

PRESIDING—*D M Gossett*, Dean, Agricultural Experiment Station, The University of Tennessee

8:00. . . . . Welcome
Joe Johnson, Executive Vice President, The University of Tennessee

8:10. . . . . The No-Till Situation
Peter Myers, Chief, USDA-Soil Conservation Service, Washington, DC

8.30 . . . . State No-Till Update
8·30 • Alabama—*Ted Whitwell*, Auburn University
8:40 • Florida—*David Wright*, University of Florida
8:50 • Georgia—*Bill Hargrove*, University of Georgia
9 00 • Kentucky—*Ken Wells*, University of Kentucky
9.10 • North Carolina—*Bull Lewis*, North Carolina State University
9.20 • South Carolina—*Jim Palmer*, Clemson University
9 30 • Tennessee—*Elmer Ashburn*, The University of Tennessee

9:50.. . . .. QUESTIONS

10:00. .. . . . . BREAK

PRESIDING—*John Harris*, Soil Conservation Service, Tennessee

10:20. . . . . No-Till Weed Problems & Challenges in Lower South
Phil Banks, University of Georgia

10:35. . . . . No-Till Weed Problems & Challenges in Upper South
Bob Hayes, The University of Tennessee

10:50. . . . . Fertilizer & Lime Problems in Lower South
Joe Touchton, Auburn University

11:05. . . . . . . Fertilizer and Lime Problems in Upper South
Don Tyler, The University of Tennessee

179

11:20   Disease & Nematode Problems in No-Till Soybeans
         Al Chambers, The University of Tennessee

11:45 ... . QUESTIONS

12:00 .... LUNCH

PRESIDING—*George Buntley*, The University of Tennessee

1:00.... .. Mulches, Cover Crops, Crop Residues, N-Fixing Legumes, etc.
           Raymond Gallaher, University of Florida

1:20....... . Innovations in Planting & Spray Equipment
           Fred Tompkins, The University of Tennessee

1:50.......... No-Till Forage Crops—*Ken Evans*, University of Kentucky

2:10.......... Conservation Cropping Systems for Production & Soil Erosion Control in the South—
           George Langdale, USDA-ARS, Georgia

2:30 .... QUESTIONS

2:40 .... BREAK

PRESIDING—*Elmer Ashburn*, The University of Tennessee

3:00.......... It Works on the Farm—*Bill Tanner*, Farmer, Union City, TN

3:15.......... It Works on the Farm—*Neal Worley*, Farmer, Hampshire, TN

3:30.......... No-Till of the Future—*Wilbur Frye*, University of Kentucky

3:50.......... QUESTIONS AND CLOSING COMMENTS

SIXTH ANNUAL SOUTHEASTERN NO-TILL SYSTEMS CONFERENCE
Milan, Tennessee
July 20-21, 1983

Milan No-Till Field Day—Wednesday, July 20, Milan Experiment Station

No-Till Systems Conference, Thursday, July 21, Milan High School

180

RESEARCH AGENDA

FOR THE TRANSITION TO A REGENERATIVE FOOD SYSTEM

By

Richard R. Harwood

Director, Rodale Research Center

J. Patrick Madden

Agricultural Economist, Pennsylvania State University

with the research staff of

The Cornucopia Project of Rodale Press

September 7, 1982

Rodale Research Center
RD 1, Box 323
Kutztown, PA 19530
(215) 683-6383

Rodale Press, Inc., 33 East Minor Street, Emmaus, PA 18049
715-847-5171   Telex 4447338

CONTENTS

Overview

1. Methods to Evaluate the Regenerative or Degenerative Nature of
   Agricultural Systems Must Be Developed

2. Crop Production Research and Development

3. Soil Fertility Research

4. Forest Production

5. Animal Production Systems

6. The Transition from Chemical Intensive to Organic Agriculture

7. Health Implications

8. Education and Research

OVERVIEW

The U.S. is blessed with an extensive and far reaching network of agricultural institutions. These institutions are the best in the world and are largely responsible for the vast productivity of the U.S. agricultural system. But we now are faced with a new set of problems different from those which shaped our existing agricultural research agenda. U.S. agriculture is plagued with a host of problems. American farmers are in deep financial trouble, and getting deeper. During the past decade, farm debt has more than tripled. In 1980, the average farm was more than $60,000 in debt, and paid $6,500 interest. But the earnings from farming averaged only about $8,000. If it were not for off-farm earnings of $15,000 a year, the average farm family would be destitute and bankrupt. Trends indicate things are getting worse, not better. We need another agricultural revolution, but this time we need to figure out how to make agriculture sustainable and ecologically sound — in a word, we need a regenerative agriculture.

Agricultural research should be redirected towards sustaining and regenerating the fragile system which, for centuries, has given us harvests of plenty. The deterioration or depletion of any of our vital agricultural resources can never be set right by a technological fix. Researchers need to look outside their laboratory walls to the economic conditions afflicting the American farmer. Input costs need to be reduced and can be reduced. Regenerative agricultural systems need to be developed — systems that will be profitable to farm families, systems that will still be producing plentiful harvests in the next millennium.

Most agricultural research being done today focuses on specialization

and more efficient use of inputs, and has as its primary goal the production
of high yields. Though human factors and environmental quality are not ignored,
they are clearly given secondary consideration. Reducing the number of people
needed to make the system function has been seen as desirable. Soil erosion
and reduction in water quality (and quantity) are tolerated, even encouraged.

The current system of research has, of course, created many benefits,
but there is now growing concern that it has molded the food production
apparatus into a condition that is both non-sustainable and too vulnerable
to disruption. A more holistic type of food system research, focusing on
benefits to large numbers of people and environmental quality as well as the
high production of commodities, would produce a wider range of benefits for
society.

The following research agenda is a starting point for regenerating our
entire agricultural system. If carried out, we will learn what we need to
know to regenerate America's soils, farms, and farm communities, and thereby
guarantee a sustainable and affordable supply of food for present and future
generations of Americans.

1. METHODS TO EVALUATE THE REGENERATIVE OR DEGENERATIVE NATURE OF
   AGRICULTURAL SYSTEMS MUST BE DEVELOPED.

   A. What is the extent of soil loss/formation? Is there a positive
      balance?

   B. What are the energy expenditures?

   C. What is the effect on nutrient and water resources? Are they
      being depleted?

   D. What is the biocide load on the environment? Is it sustainable?
      Is the environment in and around the agricultural enterprise safe
      for wildlife and humans? Can a water well on the farm be safely
      used for drinking?

2. CROP PRODUCTION RESEARCH AND DEVELOPMENT

   Research for the past several decades has focused on the improvement and production of individual cash crops. Those crops are grown
   as if in isolation without regard to what came before or what follows
   in the same field. A regenerative system must be based on structuring
   of the system to maximize biological interaction. The key as to how this
   can be done lies with crops which are ancillary to the main cash crop
   system. Taking our clues from successful organic cropping systems, we
   see a need for much greater reliance on overseeded, sod interplanted,
   or rotation crops. These are herbaceous perennials.

   A. A shift in research focus is needed.

   B. A wide range of species for overseeding into standing cash crops
      must be developed. In each of the major geographical areas in
      the country, we need to identify species which have prolific
      seed production capabilities which will germinate and grow

under the shade of the cash crop canopy which will grow rapidly
when the crop canopy is removed and which will overwinter. These
preferably will be legume crops but where seeding is late in the
fall, various grass species may be used. These crops must be
screened for relevant dates of seeding to give a wide range of
options depending on when the field is available for overseeding.

C. Methods for overseeding must be developed. In all likelihood,
plant densities, row spacings or even plant types of existing
cash crops should be modified to permit more effective sod
establishment under overseeding.

D. Seed production methods must be developed for these species.

E. Sod crops must be developed for use as an intercrop base in living
mulch systems. In the zero till systems, the prevailing wisdom
is to utilize whatever plant material and cover in the field as
the base for the next crop. Weed control is applied to suppress
the weed cover into which the new crop is planted. It is suggested
that daylength sensitive sods could be used as an interplant base.
In this case the system would be self-regulating with the sod
showing minimal growth during the main growing period of the cash
crop. In other cases, growth regulators may be used to either
hold the sod back or to be used in combination with strip tillage
to form narrow seed beds in the existing sod in which the crop
could be planted. These would be interim types of technologies.

F. Major long term research efforts should focus on the development
of perennial crops for production of cereal grain, carbohydrate
and industrial products. The availability of such crops would

minimize erosion problems and greatly reduce production costs.
The crop which would be renewed initially, perhaps, once in 3 or
4 years with eventual longer term life spans would minimize many
of today's agricultural problems. Crop nutrition would be far
more simple with long term fertility of the sod being paramount.
Weed control problems would be more straightforward. This effort
will require first the screening of tens of thousands of non-
economic perennial crops for production capabilities and potential
use. These must be selected also on the basis of mating system,
genetic makeup and amount of genetic diversity within the species.
Breeding work will have to adapt them to modern cultivation. The
possible industrial uses must be determined. This long term focus
on perennial crops should receive greater and greater focus as we
move toward a regenerative system. This is an especially relevant
area for public research money in its initial stages.

G. Weed control research

1) The effects of rotations and tillage practices on weed shifts
   is a critical area in weed management. It should be based on
   the effects of overseeding and cover crops.

2) Develop new and improved techniques for control of weeds,
   insects, and plant diseases using biological non-chemical
   methods. Methods of pest control using parasites, predator
   insects, nematodes, and other biological methods to eradicate
   or control unwanted species should be further developed.[1]

[1] A. Andres et al. "Biological Control of Weeds," Theory and Practice of
Biological Control, New York: Academic Press, Inc., 1976. See also
L. A. Anders, "The Economics of Biological Control of Weeds," Aquatic
Biology, 3 (1977) 111-123.

Breeding programs should be implemented to develop crop varieties
that are resistant to insect and pathogen attack and that are
more competitive against weeds. This research should receive
continuing and increased emphasis. Improved machinery and rolls
for mechanical weed management are needed. Alleleopathic crops
and plants (those which have an influence or effect on other
living plants) should be investigated as a means of preventing
weed seed germination and growth. Crop rotation systems should
be developed that compete effectively against weeds, supply
symbiotically-fixed nitrogen, increase the soil organic matter
content, and selectively supply nutrients to crops while excluding
weeds.

H. Insect and disease management

The following questions and areas need to be addressed:

1) What are the effects of plant combinations and densities on
pest management?

2) How do soils, plants, and insects interact in a balanced system?

3) What factors permit an insect to locate a host plant and induce
it to feed?

4) Because augmentation of the natural enemies of pests and the
use of microbial pathogens of insects and mites can be ecologically
safe and useful for regenerative farming systems, further research
should be done in this area. Further research is needed that
focuses on a balanced approach for weed control, including combinations of chemical and non-chemical methods, similar to the
concept of Integrated Pest Management (IPM).

5) Plants which have insect-repellent or attracting properties
should be researched for possible use in IFM programs and
organic farming systems.

I. Energy and food system interaction

1) Develop more energy efficient tools and techniques for planting,
cultivating, and harvesting for both intensive and polyculture
farming.

2) Develop more energy efficient food processing, food storing
and food distribution techniques.

J. Research on the holistic nature of crop or animal-integrated farms.
Compared with chemical-intensive farms, integrated farms often have
input cost, lower energy costs and greater stability in adverse
environments because their component systems are integrated as
part of an ecological system. The components of a truly successful
organic farm fit into an overall farm ecology. This means that the
crop x crop, crop x animal, crop x weed and other component interactions are crucial to the system. Weed control in organic
agriculture is impossible without consideration of those interactions. Research is needed to determine how these interactions
vary by:

1) climatic zone

2) farm size

3) type of farm - for example:

a. field crops (with and without animals), dairy-based (with
varying degrees of forage self-sufficiency), vegetable
crops, orchards, vineyards, aquaculture, and various
specialty crops and combinations of enterprises.

3. SOIL FERTILITY RESEARCH

A. Determine the relative efficiency of nutrients cycled into the
cropping system through cover crops rather than applied directly
to the soil in the short term cash crop. The efficient biological
systems used in commercial agriculture today are focused on nutrient
cycling into long term or perennial crops. When these can be used
in rotation with annuals, there is apparently much greater efficiency
of nutrient uptake. This results in less loss through runoff and
leaching.

1) Which cover crops are the most efficient in uptake of nutrients?

2) When should the nutrients be applied? .

3) Which forms are the most effective over the long term in promoting growth of perennial cover crops?

4) Is the use of a cover crop as an intermediate stage in cycling
nutrients to the crop more efficient?

B. What is the role played by soil-borne insect fauna in nutrient flows?

1) How important are earthworms and the various arthropods of the
soil system?

2) What effects do biocides have on this soil borne insect fauna?

C. What materials can be used as nutrient sources which have minimal
disruptive effects on soil microorganisms and insect fauna?

1) Are the concentrated nutrient sources disruptive of these biological
processes?

2) What materials can be used and in what doses?

3) When should they be applied and how?

4) What can most effectively cycle nutrients in the system?

D. What effect do biocides have on nutrient flow within the soil?

E. Develop efficient and safe methods for utilization of municipal
wastes, especially sewage sludge, as sources of plant nutrients
as well as to improve soil productivity. Process technology is
needed for conversion of municipal wastes into organic amendments
that can be used safely and profitably on cropland. Criteria
should be established so that the wastes can be applied to achieve
the desired level of soil improvement. The feasibility and biological implications of enriching these organic materials with
inorganic nutrient sources to increase their fertilizer value
should be investigated. Economically feasible methods for trans-
porting and applying these materials to agricultural land should
be developed. Educational programs are needed to enhance the public
acceptability to these materials.

Further studies on waste should include:

1) Determining the rate of loss (or increase) of soil organic
   matter under different cropping systems and farming practices
   as influenced by the types of fertilizer and/or organic wastes
   utilized.

2) The rate of mineralization of different organic wastes and
   their ability to supply plant nutrients over time.

3) Development of optimum methods for handling waste including:

   a. equipment feasible for a range of farm sizes

   b. detoxification of harmful substances in wastes

   c. determine fate of heavy metals in composts and in soil
      after application of waste

191

d. economic analysis to determine the profitability of alternative
farming systems

F. Develop methods for more efficient recycling of nutrients in organic
wastes for crop production. Improved methods are needed for processing
and managing organic wastes from agricultural and urban sources for
efficient utilization of plant nutrients by crops. Numerical in-
dexes should be developed to predict the nutrient availability of
different organic wastes. The nutrient availability index would
correlate the rate at which nutrients contained in organic wastes
are released to crops for different soil, climatic, and cropping
conditions. Evaluation of the effect of various processing methods
(composting, dehydrating, etc.) on the value of organic waste would
be helpful. Research is also needed to determine how various organic
wastes and residues differ in their ability/to improve soil tilth and
productivity and to maintain or even increase soil organic matter
under differing soil and climatic conditions.

G. Determine the availability over time of phosphorus from rock phosphate
and potassium from low solubility sources when applied to soils that
are farmed organically, that is, research is needed to determine the
effects of the rate and frequency of application of different organic
wastes and residues on the rate of release of P and K from low solubility mineral sources such as rock phosphate applied to different
soils. For example, field application of compost and manure somehow
increases the rate of release and availability of these nutrients
from sources of limited solubility. The interaction of crop management and climatic factors should be investigated.

192

H. Develop refined soil test recommendations for nitrogen, phosphorus, and potassium, based on cropping history, chemical utilization history, soil type, and associated climatic effects. Correlations of soil tests with crop response to applied N, P, and K fertilizers are often unreliable and imprecise. Research is needed to develop refined soil test recommendations for both the buildup and maintenance of N, P, and K for major crops at moderate to high yield levels, and to relate these recommendations to specific soil types. Improved correlations would be of great value to both organic and conventional farmers, and in the latter case would help to prevent over-fertilization. Improved methods to predict nitrogen requirements of crops produced both organically and chemically are also needed. Research findings suggest that some crops exhibit a higher yield response to applications of nitrogen from organic sources than to similar amounts of N from chemical fertilizers.[2] The underlying biological and chemical reasons causing this phenomenon should be thoroughly researched, and the implications for rates of fertilization and the comparative costs and returns from organic and conventional chemical-intensive farming systems should be carefully analyzed.

I. Expand research on biological nitrogen fixation. Research should be expanded on nitrogen fixation by soybeans, alfalfa, clover, and grasses. Special emphasis should be given to nitrogen fixation by nonleguminous crops. Methods of increasing the effectiveness of nonsymbiotic nitrogen fixation in the soil should be investigated. Explore use of

[2] Harwood, Richard R. "Organic Farming Research at the Rodale Research Center." Paper delivered March 29, 1982 at the International Scientific Colloquim on Research Projects on Biological Agriculture, Elm Farm Research Center, Great Britain.

nitrogen-fixing treas. In Senegal, for example, grain yields have been increased 150 percent and contain higher protein quality when interplanted with Acacia trees.

4. FOREST PRODUCTION

A. Develop realistic and ecologically sustainable standards for erosion control, pesticide use, destruction of wildlife habitat, and maintenance of ecological diversity.

B. Provide funds for research and education in small woodlot management and agroforestry as sources of supplemental income to farmers. Explore use of and develop technology for on-farm use of forest products, especially for fodder, fuel, and lumber.

C. Explore more frequent use of trees for multiple purposes -- shade, protection from cold, snow fences, air purifiers, reduction of glare and reflection, wind breaks, channeling wind for windmill systems, as well as to provide food products and firewood.

D. Study the ecological effects on the forest ecosystem of reduced diversity (monoculture forests) and whole tree removal.

E. Increase research and education on forest-atmosphere relationships, including effects of deforestation on local and global carbon dioxide levels, precipitation, air temperature, and wind velocity.

5. ANIMAL PRODUCTION SYSTEMS

A. Animal husbandry research. Develop procedures to reduce use of anti-biotics and chemicals in treatment of cattle. For example, the administration of therapeutic compounds (such as antibiotics and chemicals) is widespread in the U.S. for treating udder infections in cattle. This leads to residues in milk, as well as to the

development of resistant microorganisms. Research is needed to
develop means of utilizing and enhancing the animal's natural
defense mechanism to prevent infections from becoming established.
Also needed is research on the effects of confinement on animal
health, especially pertaining to large animals. For example, what
reductions could be made in antibiotics as a result of regular ex-
posure to outside grazing? Under what conditions could grazing be
profitably introduced into livestock and dairy systems?

B. **Aquaculture and fishing.** Determine the feasibility of introducing
small-scale aquaculture as an alternate method of producing high
quality protein by cost-efficient and ecologically sound methods.
The presently expanding culture of basically two freshwater species
of food fish in the United States, trout and catfish, is rapidly becoming a bioengineering race against depleted water supplies, pollution,
and energy costs. In turn, the cost and subsequently the value of fish
as a protein source increases proportionately. By utilizing some basic
biological concepts and innovative engineering designs, small-scale
fish culture systems can be made both economically and technologically
feasible. To meet these demands, it will be necessary to use available
aquatic resources to their fullest potential. Research is required
which will address the following alternatives:

1) The use of cage culture methods in available farm ponds

2) Optimizing production by ecological methods

   a. appropriate species selection for maximum feed conversion

   b. polycultures of compatible species

   c. fertilization to increase yields

   d. lengthening the growing season with solar structures

3) Development of water reuse systems

    a. filtration techniques

    b. sedimentation designs

    c. aeration efficiency

4) Coordinate methods with agricultural techniques

    a. irrigation with sludge from settling systems

    b. hydroponics using nitrogen-rich water from fish culture

    systems

    c. organic fertilization of water with animal manures

    d. use of garden vegetation to feed certain fish species

5) Documentation for the establishment of marine sanctuaries

    should be continued by the National Oceanic and Atmospheric

    Administration. Areas designated as sanctuaries can serve

    to maintain breeding stocks, as research areas and for public

    education.

6) Improve equipment and fishing techniques to reduce incidental

    catch of non-traditional species. Research the utilization of

    such species for food and other uses. Study the ecological

    implications of harvesting non-traditional species.

7) Conduct marketing research to improve the profitability of

    aquaculture and to ensure its fullest possible utilization as

    a means of providing a safe, reliable and sustainable source

    of food. This research should consider not only trout and

    catfish, but also tilapia and other underutilized species.

8) Undertake research and experimentation with "passive fishing

    techniques" which utilize extensive wire systems and stationary

    anchored nets.

6. THE TRANSITION FROM CHEMICAL INTENSIVE TO REGENERATIVE AGRICULTURE

A. Determine the factors responsible for decreased crop yields during the transition from conventional to organic regenerative farming systems. Many farmers report significant decreases in crop yields during the first three to four years while a rotation is being established following the shift from a conventional (chemical-intensive) to an organic or regenerative farming system. This can be a strong deterrent to those farmers who may wish to make such a change. Part of the problem stems from increased weed infestations and fertility needs, but other unknown factors are also involved. Research is needed to determine the underlying causes of yield reduction and to suggest ways that farmers could make this transition without suffering severe economic loss. Specifically, the following areas deserve intensified research efforts:

1) Transition rotations appropriate for farms of various size (from small to large) under various growing conditions -- soil type, climate, access to markets, available farm labor supply, etc.

2) Comparisons of abrupt transitions with gradual changes.

3) Diversifying -- introducing different crop and livestock enterprises into the farming system.

4) "Cleaning" soil of toxic substances and residues

5) Means of providing economic and technical support for transition

B. The farm family as decision maker

1) What factors contribute to or detract from a "land ethic" on the part of farmers? Our soil conservation programs have been intimately concerned with this land ethic.

2) How do organic or regenerative farming systems differ from conventional agriculture with regard to labor management, energy requirements, and profitability on various sizes and types of farm?

3) Research is needed to determine the potential impact of regenerative farming on the economic viability of small to moderate scale family farms. Many farmers on small farms depend more on labor than capital and can take advantage of the labor-intensive organic farming practices. Many of these farmers have limited funds and could possibly lower their input costs through the use of organic farming practices, such as substituting organic wastes for chemical fertilizers. Research is also needed to develop equipment that is economically feasible for various types and sizes of organic farming systems.

4) Conduct farm management case studies to determine how organic farmers may increase their incomes. Farmers could benefit greatly from research that analyzes the economics of organic farm production systems for various types and sizes of farms. Develop crop budgets for a wide range of crops and livestock on small-scale enterprises to provide a useful farm management tool for farmers. Develop cost figures for various farm "models," including a mix of crops and livestock.

5) Develop simulation or other type models to assess the aggregate socioeconomic and environmental impact of various combinations of conventional and organic agriculture. Research of this nature would be extremely.helpful in providing needed data to examine in

a more rigorous and thorough fashion the aggregate socioeconomic
and ecological impacts of increased use of organic farming in
U.S. agriculture. The "social" benefits and costs of continued
conventional farming versus alternative combinations of conventional and regenerative farming need to be addressed. The whole
issue of how regenerative farming systems would affect the
structure of agriculture would be needed to support a regenerative
farming system also needs to be researched. Research on these
topics would require the construction of an extensive data base.
Currently, little of the data needed for economic modeling and
analysis of organic farming exists.

C. Research on structural changes needed for expansion of regenerative
    agriculture that would make the U.S. food system more sustainable

1) A degree of regional self-reliance is necessary. How can public
   awareness on consumption of local food at the community level and
   at the state level be generated?

2) Develop more effective urban food production and distribution
   systems, including roof-top food production systems. Seek ways
   to make urban food distribution and marketing systems more
   accessible to local and regional food producers. Develop organic,
   energy-efficient greenhouse vegetable production systems for urban
   areas, possibly utilizing waste heat of utilities and industries.

3) Research is needed on ways to alter the present nationwide marketing channels to facilitate more local and regional food production
   and to anticipate the possible impact of those changes. Research
   and development efforts should be mounted to create or strengthen

existing marketing institutions to determine economically-feasible
strategies for sustainable agricultural production in each region.

4) The low rainfall areas that produce rain-fed, cultivated crops
(primarily wheat) have extremely high erosion losses. Present
day agriculture in those areas is clearly non-sustainable. There
seems to be few, if any, solutions to these problems short of a
major structural change. An economic analysis should be done to
look at the conversion of these areas from wheat monoculture to
more sustainable cropping systems including grassland for grazing,
overseeding of winter covercrops, or contour strip cropping of
steep slopes.

5) An economic analysis should be done on the possibilities of de-
centralizing the cattle feeding industry by moving the feedlots
from their present locations to the proximity of the major crop
growing areas.

6) Plans should be drawn for those areas of deficit water use,
particularly those areas irrigating from aquifers that are
being rapidly depleted, to indicate which crops and cropping
systems would be sustainable without depletion of ground water.
What irrigation rates can be used and what crops could be grown
profitably with those amounts of water?

7) A detailed analysis should be done of the current and potential
productivity of the regionally or locally self-reliant food production systems, including backyard gardens, and small family
farms, as well as large commercial farms. What is the true
magnitude of that effort now? What is the feasibility of its

expansion? Some reports have indicated that up to 40 percent
of our national production of some groups of fresh commodities
are from home gardens.

9) What might a more self-sustaining model look like for production
of fresh commodities on a low-cost scale? A major feasibility
study is needed which includes consideration of backyard production, mega-gardens (intermediate scale, part-time or hobby-
enterprise), as well as part- or full-time farms and larger
scale operations in the same region. The analysis should take
account of possible interactions between those various production
sources, and how their feasibility is affected by climatic, soil,
and market conditions.

7. HEALTH

A. How does one draw a connection between family health and the health
of the farm, soil, and animals? What are the connections and what
does one do about establishing or reinforcing them? A series of
studies is needed on the health of families from organic farms as
compared to those on chemical farms -- a study of allergies, cancer,
heart attacks, death rates, etc. Conduct research to investigate
the health safety of food products exposed to and possibly contaminated
with residues of pesticides and other synthetic chemicals in chemical-
intensive farming vs. organic farming systems.

Studies in this area should be actively encouraged by the U.S.
Department of Agriculture. This contemplates increased attention
especially to critical areas of toxicological and chemical-analytical
effort. The public is becoming more concerned about pesticide and

herbicide residues in food and about their current and potential
effects on human health. Strategies should be developed to insure
that they are used safely and effectively. When it becomes politically
necessary to use pesticides, as in the case of the Medfly, measures
should be taken to insure that there are no unnecessary health risks.

B. Develop information on the nutritional contribution of locally-
available and locally-produced and processed foods.

C. Determine the impact of chemical fertilizers and other chemicals on
the nutrient content of foods. For example, research shows vitamin C
content of organically produced vegetables is much higher than that
produced with anhydrous ammonia, while the reverse is true for nitrate
content of plant tissues.

D. Increase research and education on the nutritional values and food
uses of different tree crops.

5. EDUCATION AND RESEARCH

A. Establish education and training programs in agricultural resource
management, horticulture, gardening, etc., to help communities and
individuals to become more food self-reliant and to gain a greater
appreciation of the land.

1) Strengthen and expand the role of the vocational agriculture and
technical institutes for continuing education of commercial farmers,
persons employed in agribusiness, and seasonal workers.

2) Expand the role of cooperative extension in developing and conducting short courses for growers and produce managers to make
local food production and marketing more profitable.

3) Develop consumer education programs to increase consumer awareness
of locally-grown produce.

4) Develop an in-school program about local agriculture.

5) Develop a data base which accurately reflects rural community needs and value systems, as related to creation of a more sustainable agricultural system.

6) Gather information on the nutritional status and food consumption patterns of each state. Regular data collections should be made by state agencies.

B. Develop educational and marketing programs for consumers, growers, and institutions regarding #2 grade produce. Revise grading standards to reflect nutritional status, product end-uses, maturity and eating quality, rather than simply external appearances.

C. Identify and determine feasibility of appropriately-scaled technologies for local production, processing, and marketing of crop and livestock products.

1) Develop regional libraries about on-farm processing, cooperative processing models, custom processing facilities and small-scale processing equipment.

2) USDA and agricultural colleges should encourage greater diversity in farm crops and livestock, where economically feasible, and establish courses on self-sustaining systems of farming.

D. As recommended in the USDA report on organic farming (p. 161), USDA and local grant institutions should develop more information materials for county extension agents and other education to use in providing assistance to organic farmers.

1) Crop enterprise budgets should be developed and updated for a wider range of crops and livestock on small-scale enterprises

to provide a useful farm management tool for farmers. Develop cost figures for various farm "models", including a mix of crops and livestock, and for the transitional phase from chemical-intensive to organic or regenerative farming systems.

E. The role of public institutions in education and research on regenerative food system.

1) A high proportion of public research money is now going into research and high cash-flow technology that is actually the domain of private industry. Public money should focus on those areas not attractive to private industry. For example, the public money going into insecticide physiology studies should be diverted to the search for naturally-occurring compounds that modify insect behavior. Such lines of research, as well as those on IPM are not attractive to industry because of the lack of profit in such technology and materials.

2) The preponderance of herbicide work in U.S. universities is likewise oriented to short-term gains by industry rather than the long term development of integrated weed management strategies that would be in the greater public interest.

3) Federal support for agricultural research and extension in the United States has been declining at the rate of 2 percent per year since the early 1970's. It is interesting to note that the Soviet Union has now edged the United States out of the leadership position in research investments relating to the production and stability of food supplies. And in China, food and agricultural production research is the number one

priority.[3] It is evident that we need to increase funding and reorder priorities so that the outstanding productivity of this nation's agriculture may be sustained and strengthened for generations to come.

.

[3]Sylvan Wittwer, "Agricultural Research: Some Comparisons of the Soviet, Chinese, and the United States Systems. National Forum (the Phi Kappa Phi Journal), Winter 1981, pp. 20-21.

Testimony of

William K. Kruesi,
County Extension Agent-Agriculture

American agribusiness is the most efficient in the world and no competitor
comes close to matching our productivity per worker. The typical United States
farmer reaches a production level that is more than three times that of the
farmers in Western Europe, about five times that of Japan, and six and-a-half
times that of the Soviet Union.

While crop production has doubled since 1950, the farm-work force has declined
from 9.5 million to less than four million farmers. The size of the average farm
has more than doubled since 1940, and with this comes an increased investment in
equipment. The successful full-time farmers are a select group who average over
500 acres and have a $500,000 to $1.5 million investment. Despite their apparent
affluence they do well if they can realize a profit of 3% on their investment.

There is another significant trend in our agricultural industry, i.e. the
swell in numbers of small or part-time farm operators. The latest USDA Census of
Agriculture revealed that 64% of all farmers are part-time, with some of the Northeast states reporting a staggering 50 to 120% increase during 1974-78. Small and
part-time farming is replacing capital-intensive production with less mechanization,
less energy, and greater concervation of resources. The small-scale farmers are
typically younger than their full-time counterparts, are well-educated, and very
innovative. They are resettling rural America with hard work, devotion, and a keen
awareness of environmental quality.

The role of the county extension agent will be renewed by the needs of small and
part-time farmers. Large farms, on the other hand, will be served more often by
private industry consultants and may be totally integrated with agricultural suppliers,
farmers, processors and marketing firms. County agents and other government services will be passed over by large farm operations as their information needs become
more technical, and more "protected" by the parent company. Bioengineered crop
varieties, chemicals, harvesting machinery and market outlets will be so guarded
that no public worker will have the privilege to know about them.

The Agricultural Productivity Act provided support for educating producers
in agricultural methods which conserve energy, soil and water resources. All
too often our private and public agricultural research has focused on product
development rather than cultural practices to improve output. Research and outreach to farmers has become limited to product recommendations for short-term
control of crop and livestock pests and diseases. The microcomputer takes this
process one step further, providing blanket recommendations to the farmer, and
a valuable educational opportunity is lost for the Extension Agent. Instead of
serving the farmer with information on the biology and stages of pest development,
and relating this to the conditions on the farm, we minimize our effort and recommend a set of agricultural products to temporarily correct the situation.

The first obstacle to educating farmers about alternative agricultural techniques is a lack of recognition and support by the Extension Service, Department
of Agriculture, and the farm supply industry. From Extension, there is almost
no technical information which emphasizes cultural and biological control of
insects, pests and diseases. In particular our information needs to deal more
with the nature of the pests and less on the treatment of pest outbreaks.

Prevention is the basic principal of alternative agriculture methods: in plant
disease, insect pests, livestock diseases, parasites, weed control, or soil erosion.
Currently our recommendations are very biased towards the application of agricultural
chemicals -- without a hint as to how these problems could be prevented by timely
cultural practices. Recognition of alternative agricultural methods is easily
accomplished by integrating cultural/sanitation and biological controls into our
pest control recommendations.

On many livestock farms, a problem is developing slowly without anyone taking
notice. The problem is drug resistance, and it parallels the problem of insect
resistance to synthetic pesticides. It is well known in the sheep and swine industry

that many worming medications are no longer effective due to resistance in new generations of gastro-intestinal parasites.

Follow this problem further to the dairy farm, poultry, veal or beef operation where resistance to antibiotics, anthelmintics, sulfa compounds and other drugs is commonplace. It is only a matter of time before various mastitis treatments are recognized as being ineffective. The loss in herd health, farm income and consumer dollars is hard to estimate. I believe alternative (and conventional) agriculture must be informed to a greater extent on preventative health care. Producers have little knowledge of parasite life cycles, disease prevention, and the abuse of veterinary drugs.

In the field, it is not unusual to hear livestock producers and veterinarians say that many of the available vaccines are ineffective, e.g. for the pneumonia or shipping fever complex. Oftentimes when the vaccines fail to work, we can identify poor environmental conditions, nutrition, and undue stresses as complicating factors, yet we continue to rely on the injection, the medication, or the feed additive. In my opinion, the agricultural drug industry is grossly ignoring the alternatives to the use (and abuse) of veterinary medicines.

Alternative agricultural methods are also being developed to improve the productivity of our pasture and range lands. Approximately 45% of the agricultural land in the United States is limited to permanent vegetation for grazing, forestry, or for wildlife. Of the land suitable for cultivation, a significant portion is devoted to forage crops, later to be marketed as milk, meat, or wool. Much of our forage land is too steep to plow, too rocky, or inaccessible. The only way to utilize this crop is with a four-footed grazing animal.

Although our forage resource is enormous, our grazing management is for the most part in the "Dark Ages". Productivity per animal or per unit of land is low, compared to the dairy, beef and sheep farmers of the United Kingdom, New Zealand, and

Australia. Our conventional practices emphasize the use of sophistocated no-till planters, herbicides, nitrogen fertilizer, and growth implants to acheive higher productivity from a grazing system. The alternative lies in greater adoption of intensive, rotational grazing as practiced by the best grassland farmers of Europe and New Zealand. Carrying capacity on permanent pasture can be doubled or tripled with fewer inputs, through better grazing management.

In the Northeast, we are reclaiming poor, overgrown hill pastures with sheep and beef cattle in a low-capital system which used no tillage, no diesel fuel, herbicides or nitrogen fertilizer. The end result has been highly productive stands of blue-grass and white clover which provide exceptional feed at one-fourth of the cost of harvested forage.

Anyone familiar with the dairy industry in the East will recognize that we have lost the techniques for producing milk off pasture. We traded this for push button mechanical feed systems which have added to an unprecedented debt load on our family farms. The technology is ours for the taking, without making the same mistakes that innovative grassland farmers first made overseas, twenty years ago. New technology in fencing, fertilization and other agronomic practices needs to be disseminated to farmers seeking a low cost alternative for pasture renovation.

Little research on these and other alternative agriculture practices is avail-able to Extension workers or to farmers, for them to make objective decisions. Many of our crop and livestock producers have an interest in crop rotations to control weeds, use of legumes for nitrogen, management techniques to reduce parasites, bio-logical pest controls, and other cultural practices that go unresearched for lack of industry support.

The Agricultural Productivity Act would go far in providing research and informa-tion on lower-cost farming practices, thus benefiting the growing number of small scale farms in our country. Small farmers in turn will adopt alternative methods of farming which will sustain agricultural productivity far into the future -- with less pollution, less energy, and less waste. The county agent would do well to help educate the emerging agricultural producers who are willing to learn, and who seek long term answers to the problems of modern agriculture.

William K. Kruesi
County Extension Agent
Town Hall, 31 The Green
Woodstock, Vermont 05091

INFORMATION ON ORGANIC GARDENING AND FARMING

Selected Publications from the UVM Extension Service

Organic Farming Fact Sheets ((\$ .25 each)

#1. Non-Chemical Weed Control in Corn Fields
#2. Non-Chemical Weed Control in Pastures
#3. Natural Organic Insecticides (selection)
#4. Natural Organic Insecticides (application)
#5. Organic Fertilizers
#6. Green Manure Crops
#7. Seaweed Concentrate for Horticultural Crops
#8. Principles of Organic Gardening and Farming

Cover Crop Series (\$ .25 each)

#1. Winter Rye
#2. Buckwheat
#3. Red Clover

Apple Growers Handbook (\$1.00 for complete handbook)

#1 Planting Apple Trees	#10 Grafting and Budding Fruit Trees
#2 Soil Care for Apple Trees	#11 Harvesting and Storage
#3 Buyer's Guide to Sprayers	#12 Cider
#4 Dormant Oil	#13 Marketing
#5 Disease Control	#14 Calendar for Orchardists
#6 Apple Scab	#15 Natural Apple Spray Calendar
#7 Insect Pests	
#8 Pollination	
#9 Fruit Thinning	

"Landscape Notes" newsletter for gardeners. Issued free, bi-monthly. Emphasis is on organic methods. Contact your county agricultural agent to be placed on the mailing list.

Soil Testing Information (free) describes procedure for taking a representative soil sample, and submitting it to the soil testing laboratory at the University of Vermont. Soil Tests are available for Horticultural Crops and Lawns at \$5.00 each; those for Forage & Field Crops sell for \$6.00. A complete micronutrient test is available for iron, manganese, copper, zinc, sodium, and calcium (\$5.).

All publications are postpaid. Make checks payable to the "Windsor County Advisory Board".

Order publications from: County Agricultural Agent, UVM Extension Service, 31 The Green, Woodstock, VT 05091. For further information on organic farming and gardening methods, contact Bill Kruesi, Windsor County Agricultural Agent, Woodstock, VT. Phone (802) 457-2664.

ORGANIC FARMING FACT SHEETS

This series of eight fact sheets, and a series on cover crops
has been made available from the UVM Extension Service since 1981.
In two years we have distributed nearly 3,000 fact sheets to 37
states and Canada, and to nearly 20 Universities (by request) including:

> Cornell University Cooperative Extension Service
> University of Wisconsin - Dept. of Agronomy
> University of Missouri - Dept. of Agronomy
> Iowa State University - Dept. of Agronomy
> Louisiana State University - Cooperative Extension Service
> University of Minnesota - Cooperative Extension Service
> Michigan State University - Dept. of Agricultural Economics
> South Dakota State University - Dept. of Plant Science
> Tennessee - Soil Conservation Service
> University of New Hampshire - Dept. of Animal Science
> University of Delaware - Dept. of Plant Science
> West Virginia State University - Cooperative Extension Service
> Wisconsin - Dept. of Economic and Community Development

William K. Kruesi
8/83

Organic Farming Fact Sheet no. 1

"Weed Control in Corn Fields"

Modern weed control involves every aspect of crop management, including rotations, planting dates, soil fertility and drainage. Weed competition can be reduced to tolerable economic levels by a good cropping system and timely field operations. We need to understand the biology of the weeds and of the crop species, to favor one and not the others.

CONTROL METHODS

Soil Conditions Corn grows best on fertile, well-drained loam soils. The pH should be 6.1 to 6.8, and a level of organic matter above 3%. Using soil tests, optimum levels of plant nutrients can be established as follows:

Magnesium	120+	pounds Mg/acre
Potassium	240+	pounds K_2O/acre
Phosphorus	28+	pounds available P_2O_5/acre
Phosphorus	100+	pounds reserve P_2O_5/acre

Nitrogen, either from previous legume rops, manure soil organic matter or fertilizer should be available from seedling stage through filling out the ear. For a yield of 20 tons of silage or 100 bu. of grain, some 120 pounds of nitrogen is required.

Compacted soil will require tillage to break up tight layers, plus some deep rooting crops such as sweet clover or alfalfa to penetrate hardpan. Straight, winged and parabolic (shank) subsoilers and some chisel plows are effective at breaking up compacted zones.

Wet spots should be drained through tile systems, ditches, diversions, or sub-soiling to favor corn rather than nutsedge smartweed, barnyard grass (Echinochloa crusgalli), rushes, buttercups, docks, sticktight (Bidens Spp.), cockleburs, etc.

Rotation Vigorous, competitive stands of hay crops will have few annual weeds. A dense sod will not allow annual weed seeds to germinate and grow. Some tall growing crops shade out low-growing weeds notable buckwheat, Sudan grass, sweet clover, rape, and winter rye. (Corn fo silage is very effective in smothering annual weeds late in the season if early weed control is practices.) Row crops permit thorough and regular cultivation to control perennial and some annual weeds.

Crested wheatgrass is a quick, tall-growing smother crop used successfully to eliminate perennial sow thistle, Canada thistle and quackgrass Alternating buckwheat with winter rye provides control of spring and summer-germinating weeds. Buckwheat and rye are turned under for green manure, improving tilth and adding organic matter to the soil.

Typical corn rotations for the northeast include (a) corn-corn-legume and grass hay (b) corn-corn-oats/alfalfa (c) corn winter rye as a green manure. A combination of tillage and competitive crops has given good results in the control of all classes of weeds, including deep-rooted perennials.

Cultivation Thorough moldboard plowing can bury many weed problems for the immediate crop of corn. Weeds are easily controlled by a cultivation just as the seedlings emerge. A second cultivation between emergence and the five leaf stage will destroy many spring germinating annuals.

A rotary hoe is ideal for this first cultivation, followed by a row cultivator with sweeps, shovels, or S-tines between emergence and the five leaf stage. (Row cultivators can be used on corn until it reaches 30-36 inches tall.) Cultivation should only be deep enough to kill the young weeds. The middles between crop rows should be loose and cloddy following cultivation.

Fall cultivation after harvest should be practiced to control cool season weeds (wild mustard, dandelion, milkweed seedlings, crabgrass), followed by winter rye or kale.

For weeds past the 6-8 inch stage, use two pairs of disk hillers and one pair of sweeps per row. Weeds along fence rows should be mowed with a rotary or sickle mower before July 15th, to prevent seed dispersal into the corn field.

Delayed planting by 2-3 weeks may enable the farmer to disc or use a spring tooth harrow to kill already-started weeds. Leave a rough seedbed at planting!

Tips for better corn

1. Fertilize and lime according to soil tests, for corn.
2. Use a variety with extra vigor in cold soils, or delay planting two weeks.
3. Adjust your planter properly and don't plant too fast.
4. Band place a starter fertilizer high in phosphorus.
5. Follow corn with a winter rye cover crop. Broadcast rye from the end of August to October 15.
6. Practice two or more timely cultivations.

Questions? Information on soil types, drainage and land reclamation is available from the Soil Conservation Service technician in your county. Additional help on corn varieties, soil tests, and weed identification is available from your county Agricultural Extension Agent.

William K. Kruesi, County Agricultural Agent
UVM Extension Service
Woodstock, Vermont 05091
Telephone: 457-2664

The Extension Service, University of Vermont, and U.S. Department of Agriculture cooperating, offer education for everyone, without regard to race, color, national origin, sex, religion, age, and handicap. The Extension Service is an Equal Opportunity Employer.

Concluding Remarks on the Testimony of

William K. Kruesi
County Extension Agent - Agriculture

According to the latest USDA Census of Agriculture, there is a growing number
of small and part-time farmers, and with this expansion comes a need for small-farm
technical assistance and education. The Extension Service has experienced the demand
for information, books, periodicals, workshops and conferences on small farm topics,
and has devoted a significant amount of time and program effort in this direction.
Small and part-time farmers seem particularly interested in alternative agriculture
methods which conserve energy, soil, and water resources.

Conventional and large-scale producers also seek information on alternative
agriculture practices as demonstrated by several feature articles in The Furrow (published by the John Deere Co.), Harvestore Farming, American Fruit Grower, AgReview,
Forbes, MD, and The New Farm. The agricultural industry has been slow to respond to
the need for objective information on cultural control of weeds, insects, and diseases.
Instead they directed their efforts towards product development, which can be patented,
merchandised, and sold at a profit.

It may be up to public, educational services within the USDA and Land-Grant College
System to provide farmers -- large and small, with factural information on alternative
production methods. Already some programs in the Extension Service have been directed
at educating producers about alternative or organic methods. These include the organic
farm tours sponsored every year by the Department of Agronomy at the University of
Nebraska, and the publication of several resource materials on organic farming methods
by the University of Vermont Extension Service.

With better education on the application of crop rotations for weed control,
biological insect control, the interplanting of legumes to supply nitrogen, and other
alternative practices, the agricultural supply industry will have new opportunities
to develop products and equipment that work under revamped crop and livestock production systems.

The Extension Service is willing to meet the educational needs of alternative
agriculture. What is missing is the research to substantiate these methods, and the
acknowledgement from the USDA that the need exists in all regions of the country.
There are model farmers already using alternative agricultural methods who need to be
recognized. They need to be encouraged to demonstrate their methods to other farmers.
We have enough flexibility in the Extension Service to provide information on alternative agriculture if there is confidence (within the national organizations of the
USDA, Agricultural Research Service and Extension) that these unconventional practices
are indeed being used by our clients.

STATEMENT OF THE AMERICAN FARM BUREAU FEDERATION
TO THE SUBCOMMITTEE
ON DEPARTMENT OPERATIONS, RESEARCH AND FOREIGN AGRICULTURE
OF THE HOUSE COMMITTEE ON AGRICULTURE
WITH REGARD TO H. R. 2714,
TO IMPROVE PRODUCTIVITY OF AMERICAN FARMERS

August 12, 1983

The American Farm Bureau Federation is a general farm organization representing farmers and ranchers in 48 states and Puerto Rico.
Farm Bureau membership exceeds 3.2 million member families.
Agricultural research, extension, productivity and soil conservation
are issues of importance to Farm Bureau members.

We recommend a number of changes in H. R. 2714. In Section 2 (3)
we suggest deleting the phrase "...and raises the spectre of another
dust bowl." Soil erosion is of concern to farmers and the public.
The problem is serious in some areas, and well-managed in others. We
have seen no documentation to support a "Congressional finding" that a
dust bowl is in the future.

We suggest deleting Section 2 (4). The purpose of agricultural
research is to find better production and marketing alternatives.
It is totally inappropriate to declare the current agricultural
structure inadequate or unfounded prior to the conclusion of the
research being supported by the bill. Just the opposite may be found
when studies called for in Section 3 (1) are completed.

We suggest deleting Section 3 (2). Let's conduct the research on
farming methods outlined in the previous subsection, and not
prematurely engage in a farm assistance program. Federal assistance
of an unresearched technology may provide incentives to move farmers
down a dead-end path.

We suggest modification of Section 5 to remove directions on how
USDA should conduct the various recommended research projects. This
section proposes twelve pilot research projects. We believe the
mandate to conduct research is appropriate, but efforts to specify
protocols of research in legislation ought to be resisted. Section
5(a)(2), (b), (c), and (d) should be deleted.

We suggest deleting Section 11 (5), as this definition is not
necessary with the other recommended changes.

Agricultural technologies are widely diversified in this country
and around the world. Surely no single mix of cultural approaches is
"best" for all farms. Continued research on the applicability of
various imputs into the production process is our best assurance of an
economically viable and sustainable agriculture in the United States.
We support all efforts to achieve this objective.

JIM WEAVER
4TH DISTRICT OREGON

COMMITTEES
AGRICULTURE
INTERIOR AND INSULAR AFFAIRS
CHAIRMAN
SUBCOMMITTEE ON
MINING, FOREST MANAGEMENT,
AND
BONNEVILLE POWER ADMINISTRATION
JOE RUTLEDGE
ADMINISTRATIVE ASSISTANT

WASHINGTON OFFICE
LONGWORTH HOUSE OFFICE BUILDING
WASHINGTON DC 20515
(202) 225-6416

DISTRICT OFFICE
FEDERAL BUILDING
211 EAST 7TH AVENUE
EUGENE OREGON 97401
(503) 687-6732

Congress of the United States
House of Representatives
Washington, D.C. 20515

June 24, 1983

Honorable George E. Brown, Jr., Chairman
Subcommittee on Department Operations,
   Research and Foreign Agriculture
1301 Longworth House Office Building
INSIDE MAIL

Dear Mr. Chairman:

We are writing to urge you to schedule a hearing and mark-up on H.R. 2714, the Agricultural Productivity Act, as soon as possible after the July recess.

As you know, agricultural research is one of the cornerstones on which agricultural productivity is based. However, the rapidly changing structure of our farm economy in recent years has altered the needs of our farmers. A close examination of past and present priorities in agricultural research will assist the USDA, Land Grant and other colleges, and private industry in structuring the future course of the research that will address our most pressing agricultural needs. You are to be commended for your foresight and initiative in calling oversight hearings on these issues.

With many of our farmers trapped in a cost-price squeeze, it is essential that agricultural researchers strive to develop integrated farming systems that will help farmers cut their production costs, conserve water and energy, and control erosion. This need was clearly recognized when, in 1980, and again in 1981, the National Agricultural Research and Extension Users' Advisory Board recommended that USDA "significantly redirect current levels of research and extension work to expand and improve the use of economic organic methods" as outlined in the 1980 USDA Report and Recommendations on Organic Farming.

Unfortunately, the Department continues to ignore the Board's recommendations. In a July, 1982 memo entitled "Reducing Farmers Production Costs", Agricultural Research Service (ARS) Acting Administrator Mary Carter reported that "there is no research presently being conducted by ARS that conforms to the concept of holistic research as described in the July 1980 'Organic Farming Report'".

In January 1983, the Agricultural Research Service proposed its 6-year program plan. In the plan, ARS advocates developing farming systems "characterized by less costly methods and by technologies that are safe, sustainable and environmentally sound". The plan further recommends innovative research "to

reduce farm production costs while maintaining a high level of
sustainable productivity through the development of efficient and
diversified crop- and animal-production systems" and "to insure
conservation of our natural resources".

Once again, however, no funding was proposed by ARS to carry
out this research. The plan recommended zero funding for this
type of systems research during fiscal years 1984-90.

We believe that the Agricultural Productivity Act, which we
introduced in April, would help remedy this problem. It would
implement a research and extension program that the Department's
own experts and advisors have been recommending for several
years, and is endorsed by the National Farmers Union, National
Grange, National Farmers Organization, National Association of
Conservation Districts, and many other farm, public interest and
conservation groups.

We believe it would be appropriate to follow your oversight
hearings on agricultural research with a hearing and mark-up on
the Agricultural Productivity Act sometime in July. If the bill,
which has broad support and no announced opposition, is to have
any real chance of passage this year, it is essential that it
move through the Agriculture Committee before the August recess.

We thank you again for your past leadership on this issue,
and look forward to your assistance in moving the bill through
the House.

Sincerely,

BERKLEY BEDELL, M.C.   LANE EVANS, M.C.   JIM WEAVER, M.C.

TOM HARKIN, M.C.   TIMOTHY J. PENNY, M.C.   THOMAS S. FOLEY, M.C.

CHARLIE ROSE, M.C.   JIM JEFFORDS, M.C.   TOM DASCHLE, M.C.

Sludge Disposal • Specializing in Land Application

Bio Gro Systems, Inc. specializes in the design and execution
of land application projects. They have operated over 30 successful
land application projects in 9 states. Bio Gro Systems has permitted
approximately 79,000 agricultural acres and land applied in excess of
200,000 dry tons of sludge during the past four years.

Bio Gro Systems maintains a staff of highly qualified and experienced personnel in the area of land application of sludges. Agronomists, soil scientists, engineers, project supervisors, and corporate
management are responsible for the successful execution of projects.

Bio Gro Systems has a unique capability to design and execute large
application projects. THIS ORGANIZATION RECOGNIZES SLUDGE AS A VALU-
ABLE RESOURCE FOR THE AGRICULTURAL COMMUNITY AND IS COMMITTED TO TRANS-
PORTING AND APPLYING SLUDGES TO AGRICULTURAL LAND IN A BENEFICIAL
MANNER. The organization also has the professional staff available to
maintain a positive working relationship with various agricultural,
civic and political organizations.

Bio Gro Systems, Inc. supports the passage of HR2714 as a measure
to aid American farmers in the search for farming techniques which will
reduce their dependence on the use of high cost, energy intensive and
soil depleating farm technologies. The use of municipal sewage sludge,
animal wastes, and certain industrial wastes in modern cropping systems
fits into this plan very well.

Sludge is the end product of a wastewater treatment system. Wastewater as it enters a treatment plant is more than 99% water; the
function of the treatment system is to collect and stabilize the less
than 1% of solids from that flow. As solids are removed from the
sewage flow, they are treated and stabilized separately by biological
digestion or chemical means. These solids, after being isolated and
stabilized, are collectively known as sludge.

Bio Gro Systems Incorporated
P O Box 209 Annapolis, Maryland 21404 Telephone (301) 263-2237

Sludge may be regarded as a relatively low-analysis fertilizer (usually less than 5% nitrogen on a dry weight basis). It contains 40-60% organic matter and contains both macronutrients (e.g. nitrogen, phosphorus and calcium and micronutrients e.g. zinc, copper, and manganese) which are essential for plant growth. Utilizing 5-15 dry tons per acre, both nitrogen and phosphorus requirements of most crops can be met. Sludge is applied at agronomic rates as a liquid or semi-solid and is easily assimilated into the soil system.

Direct benefits result from sludge application to land. Because of its high organic matter content sludge improves the moisture holding capacity of soils. Improved soil physical properties also result from the addition of sludge. Soiltilth is improved which results in lowered energy costs to the farmer as tillage is made easier. Improved soil structure, due to organic matter additions, results in higher water infiltration rates and a corresponding decrease in soil erosion. As water is prevented from running off the surface, it penetrates the soil and is made available to crops.

Annual U. S. sludge production is expected to exceed 10 million dry tons by 1985. Currently, about 30% of the sludge generated natio-nally is applied to the land. If all the sludge produced in the U. S. were to be applied to cropland at a rate suitable for nitrogen fertili-zation, the estimated proportion of total U. S. cropland required would be about 2% by 1985.

The use of sludge and other wastes for crop production has been shown to be a safe practice through years of research and practice. Unfortunately, much of the information gained through this research has not reached the majority of American farmers. The establishment of the twelve pilot research projects will provide farmers and Extension Service personnel with active, large scale examples to observe and initiate. Information gathered through these projects and from other sources will be a data base for farmers to draw on should they wish to implement any or all of the methods listed in HR2714.

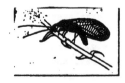

RINCON-VITOVA
INSECTARIES, INCORPORATED
POST OFFICE BOX 95 — OAK VIEW, CALIFORNIA 93022

August 1, 1983

Congressman George Brown
House Agriculture Subcommittee On
Dept. Operations, Research and Foreign Agriculture
U.S. House of Representitives
Washington, D.C. 20515

Attention of Dr. Chuck Benbrook

      Subject: HR #2714 Agricultural Productivity Act

Dear Dr. Benbrook:

I am writing to you not only as a concerned citizen, but as an
owner of an agribusiness concern. Our company grows and markets
beneficial insects as a biological control of agricultural pests.
We have been in business since 1960, supplying not only farmers
and gardners, but agricultural researchers at our nation's
Universities and USDA research facilities.

We are are part of a small but growing industry, probably less
than 5 million dollars in sales annually. However, we feel that
there is a definite movement worldwide to research new techniques
and methods in producing the food and fiber that accounts for
such a substantial portion of the world economy. Our specific
area is in pest management, where in this nation alone, billions
of dollars are spent annually to combat our insect competitors.
However, this is not the only problem that production agriculture
faces. Soil erosion, the dependance on petroleum products that
are increasing in cost. The loss of soil fertility, decreasing
farm profits and the increase of toxic materials in our air,
water and soil are only a few of the difficulties faced by
agriculture.

It is quite obvious that there are several problems to be dealt
with in the coming years if we as a nation are to keep our people
fed and have a surplus of products to export, which is so very
important to our balance of payments.

There are a growing number of people using alternatives to age
old practices in agriculture. Some of these methods are
extremely economical, and easy to adopt to present farming
routines. Still, many medium and large scale farmers are
skeptical about many of these new methods. How do they convert
to these new systems efficiently without disrupting their
production, on which they depend for their livelihood? When do
they turn to for help in this conversion. Here, farmers insist
on SEEING a new method or product used successfully before they
would adopt the technology themselves.

MAIN OFFICE AND SHIPPING DEPARTMENT, VENTURA, CALIFORNIA - PHONE (805) 643-5407
CALIFORNIA PLANTS LOCATED IN RIVERSIDE, VENTURA, OJAI AND SAN FRANCISCO

RINCON-VITOVA
INSECTARIES, INCORPORATED
POST OFFICE BOX 95 — OAK VIEW, CALIFORNIA 93022

It is my feeling that the program outlined in Agricultural
Productivity Act is exactly the vehicle needed to carry our
agricultural system into the future. This country, like many
others, may be on a collision course with widespread agricultural
failure unless the proper steps are taken to research and
disseminate alternative technologies to our present agricultural
production system. I believe the benefits to be had from the
passing of HR #2714 far outweigh the costs of such a program.

Civilization as we know it depends heavily on a sound
agricultural system for its survival. Let's take this important
step to insuring our future as a nation of plenty by supporting
this much needed legislation.

Thank you for your time and consideration of this matter—

Sincerely,

Jake Blehm

July 25, 1983

Chris Geiger

Appropriate Technology Group

c/o 323 Cnestnut St.

Santa Cruz, CA. 95060

(423) 426-6451

Office of Congressman George Frown

House Agricultural Subcommittee

on Dept. Operations, Reearch and Foreign Agriculture

ATTN: Dr. Penbrook

U.S. House of Representatives

Washington, D.C. 20515

Dear Dr. Penbrook:

We are writing out of deep concern for the fate of American agriculture, and ultimately on behalf of our planet's nealth. We urge you to support HR#2714, the Agricultural Productivity Act of 1983, in every way possible; for it is a positive, critical step towards an ecologically, socially, and politically sound agricultural system.

Whereas modern agriculture may appear to have increased its productivity dramatically in the past few decades, there are many subtle forces at work which cannot be ignored, for in the end they will be its undoing. Not least of these is energy: transportation and distribution included, agriculture consumes up to 13% of the nation's total energy budget. The impressive leaps in production have been possible only through astronomical investments

of irreplaceable fossil fuels. Because of its utter dependence on
chemicals, mechanization, and centralized distribution, American
agriculture (the "breadbasket of the world?") has become precari-
ously dependent on unstable global politics. As noted ecologist
F.T.Odum puts it, "we no longer eat potatoes made of earth, sun,
and water, but potatoes made of oil..."

Another devastating trend which has arisen relatively
recently is the destruction and loss of massive quantities of
irreplaceable topsoil. In its natural state, topsoil is dark,
crumbly, rich, and full of life. It holds water and nutrients,
and allows easy growth of crop roots. Modern agriculture has
chronically failed to recognize the dynamic, living nature of
soil. In single-minded, short-sighted drive to maximize production, agribusiness routinely utilizes thousands of tons of pesticides, herbicides, fungicides, and fertilizers. In the long run
these products sterilize soils, creating an inert, dusty growth
media incapable of maintaining its own fertility, and increasingly susceptible to erosion. In most cases, a "chemical tread-
mill" situation is unwittingly created-- the soil becomes
"addicted" to the chemicals. The naturally-occurring organisms
that normally provide control of insect pests, maintain soil fertility, and hold water and nutrients are decimated; requiring
either escalating, higher chemical doses or a painful period of
"withdrawal." The evolution of one foot of topsoil takes hundreds
of years in natural systems; yet we have been losing an average
of 22.2 tons of soil per hectare per year.(K.J. Nicol, 1974)

From the standpoint of national security, we can only be less secure in such a position. In reducing the germ plasm to a few high-producing hybrids, utterly depending on chemicals for all pest and weed control, and relying on far-flung marketing schemes, a highly vulnerable and unstable ecosystem is created. We become progressively less self-reliant, and more dependent on foreign resources. This sense of vulnerability is reflected in increased interventionism and bloated military budgets, and the myriad interconnecting factors build on each other. As it stands, the situation can only grow worse.

Amidst all this doom and gloom, tucked away in obscure valleys here and there, lies hope. People are learning that they can live in harmony, both with themselves and the earth. Despite a system which provides practically no support for its efforts, organic agriculture has been growing and blooming; and with it a new ideal of decentralized markets, low energy inputs, and local self-reliance. Here is democracy in its purest form, and prospects for a truly sustainable, peaceful future. This is a Positive movement, with a capital "P," and deserves every available cent of support.

Hopefully yours,

Chris Geiger

225

COMMISSIONER
OF AGRICULTURE
P O BOX 12847
AUSTIN, TEXAS 78711 · (512) 475-2760

October 3, 1983

The Hon. George Brown, Jr., Chairman
Dept. Operations, Research &
  Foreign Agriculture
1301 Longworth Office Bldg.
Washington, D.C. 20515

Dear Congressman Brown:

As Texas Agriculture Commissioner, I wholeheartedly endorse the Agricultural
Productivity Act of 1983, HR 2714.

The United States has a tremendously successful record in agricultural research.
We have perhaps the most productive farmers in the world, due largely to our
country's commitment to agricultural research. Yet, today we also recognize
that our research focus needs to be expanded to help farmers and ranchers adapt
to a more efficient use of such scarce natural resources as water, energy and
topsoil. Our rising productivity stands on a foundation of massive energy
inputs, of petro-chemical based fertilizers and pesticides, and of capital
intensive operations which too often have abused the soil and squandered
precious water resources. Energy prices promise to continue their ascent,
interest rates are pressed upward by a general shortage of capital and national
deficits. In Texas, according to a USDA study, we have lost nearly 18 tons per
acre of topsoil on more than 19 million acres of farmland, more than three times
the level defined as acceptable by USDA. Similarly, the vast majority of our
agricultural irrigation systems are so inefficient that 40% of the water pumped
through them is wasted.

Clearly, there is an urgent need for a research program specifically designed to
help our farmers begin a careful transition to a less energy and resource
intensive agriculture. A common-sense, coordinated program of research is
required to fully address the many elements involved in such a transition (e.g.
integrated pest management, soil and water protection and conservation, and
other production practices). Farmers are aware of the problems they face, but
the vast majority of farmers depend on the outcome and reliability of government
sponsored production research to modify their operations. Natural farming is a
tremendously complex process, and in spite of its potential benefits, a
transition to such practices may pose an unacceptable financial risk for
conventional farmers without the concerted assistance of the agricultural
research community.

The Agricultural Productivity Act of 1983 is a step in the right direction; it
provides the impetus for action which has been lacking at USDA. We can no
longer ignore the need for such an effort, and I sincerely hope this is only the
beginning of an ongoing, national effort. I urge you to support its passage.

Best regards,

JIM HIGHTOWER

WHITEFLY CONTROL COMPANY
Box 986
Milpitas, CA 95035

Dear Chairman Brown and Subcommittee Members:

Thank you for this opportunity to address the need for passage of
the Agricultural Productivity Act. This bill would move the USDA
toward a balanced agricultural policy.

My biological control business produces and distributes a hymenop-
terous parasite of the pest whitefly. The growth of my business
and the biological control industry in general indicates a strong
desire of the farming and consuming communities for more organic
agricultural practices. The USDA at present does not reflect this
desire in its programs. This bill begins to rectify the gap
between federal policy and the "state-of-the-art" in the agricultural industry.

There are many important reasons to support development of organic
farming for America:

● Water Conservation - 600 tons of water are required to manu-
    facture just one (1) ton of nitrate (chemical) fertilizer.
    (Bruce K. Ferguson, "Whither Water?" The Futurist, April
    1983, p. 29.)

● Fossil Fuel Conservation - as is well known, pesticides and
    chemical fertilizers are petroleum based.

● Soil Conservation - organic practices result in the conserva-
    tion or improvement of the physical and chemical structure
    of the soil, which directly relates to its sustained (not
    quick-fix) fertility. Every nation has always been
    directly dependent upon the fertility of its top-soil.

● Biological Control of insect pests is a cornerstone of Inte-
    grated Pest Management. Passage of the APA will strengthen
    Biological Control which will in turn strengthen IPM pro-
    grams already in operation.

● Jobs - the impact of the APA on employment would be positive
    because organic agriculture is labor intensive and in
    jobs that do not expose these workers to hazardous chem-
    icals.

WHITEFLY CONTROL COMPANY
Box 986
Milpitas, CA 95035

* Public Health - increased organic practices would increase
  the public health by lowering possible agri-chemical
  residues on food sources.

Your concerns about toxics will be reflected in a favorable vote
for this bill.

Respectfully submitted,

John A. Morris

John A. Morris
Whitefly Control Company

228

Statement of the Natural Resources Defense Council, Inc.

on

H.R. 2714, The Agricultural Productivity Act of 1983

Submitted to the House Agriculture Subcommittee on
Department Operations, Research, and Foreign Agriculture

F. Kaid Benfield
Senior Staff Attorney

Justin Ward
Agriculture Project Assistant

August 3, 1983

The Natural Resources Defense Council, Inc. (NRDC)[*] is
pleased to register its strong support for H.R. 2714, the
"Agricultural Productivity Act of 1983." The bipartisan backing
of this legislation in both houses of Congress, combined with the
impressive array of supporting individuals and organizations,
testify amply to its merit.

In essence, Congressman Weaver's bill can be regarded as a
research and assistance measure which calls for the badly needed
development of more complete information on promising farm
techniques in the face of a range of challenges to the viability
and sustainability of modern agriculture. By seeking to improve
upon our imperfect understanding of issues like energy
availability and the hazards of pesticides and herbicides, the
research program contained in the bill represents a prudent
course of action and, in a fundamental sense, a sort of insurance
policy for the future. Our statement will briefly address the
conceptual and practical advantages of the bill.

First, the proposal is predicated on the welcome recognition
that desirable farmer and social objectives need not be mutually
exclusive. For instance, the stated purpose of the Act (Section
3(1)) is to simultaneously promote increased productivity,
environmental conservation, and cost-effectiveness. This
thoughtful premise challenges traditional assumptions about
trade-offs among competing goals, and we commend it heartily.

Second, the proposed research program in H.R. 2714 is wisely
designed to encourage the development and integration of
environmentally superior farming practices into the existing
framework of modern agricultural technologies -- a preferable and
practical option to offering them as comprehensive substitutes

---

[*] NRDC is a non-profit corporation with more than 43,000
members and contributors, dedicated to the preservation,
enhancement, and defense of the natural resources of the United
States and the world. Through the efforts of its agriculture
project, NRDC supports the maintenance and improvement of the
productive capacity and soils of our nation's valuable
agricultural lands as well as the protection of environmental
quality and human health.

for systems already in place. Through pilot research, the Act
comtemplates an examination of the effects of a transition from
chemical-intensive farm practices to organic farming based upon
crop rotation, the use of manure, and other techniques. The
proposed legislation in no way advocates an across-the-board
replacement of existing systems.

The advantages of such techniques are well identified in the
U.S. Department of Agriculture (USDA) "Report and Recommendations
on Organic Farming." That July 1980 study addressed various
issues of concern to NRDC including topsoil loss, declining soil
productivity, and environmental degradation with accompanying
human health risks from pesticide use -- topics which were
further discussed in the 1980 USDA appraisal conducted under the
Soil and Water Resources Conservation Act (RCA).—/

Third, the major operative provisions of the bill are
sound. The contemplated information study (Section 4) would
provide a mechanism for systematically taking stock of what is
currently known about organic farming techniques. This study
would also be useful as a means of identifying gaps in scientific
knowledge and thereby focusing future research. The pilot
research projects (Section 5) would serve as a valuable
supplement to the existing research identified in the information
study. The intercropping assistance provision (Section 10) would
clarify that, for the purposes of federal conservation aid,
farmers who utilize this highly beneficial technique to reduce
erosion and promote soil fertility are on an equal footing with
those who utilize other methods of conservation.

Finally, the proposal is not inordinately expensive; it
constitutes but a modest approach to a large issue. Indeed, the
proposed funding allocation of $2.1 million annually for 5 years
represents only a tiny fraction of the overall USDA research
budget and would not drain money devoted to other vital USDA
research needs. As Congressman Weaver suggested in his
introductory remarks on the floor of the House, the funding is
absolutely necessary to carry out the [January] 1983
recommendations of the Agricultural Research Service on the
development of superior farm technologies.

In sum, the Act would simply assist USDA in fulfilling its
basic responsibility to provide support to American farmers. It
is clearly a necessary and proper function of the Department to
serve as a catalyst for the development of, and a clearinghouse
for information about, cost-effective, conservation-oriented
agricultural techniques. The bill is a sensitive and
constructive response to the problems facing American farmers
today.

**/ U.S., Department of Agriculture, 1980 Appraisal, Parts I and
II, Soil, Water, and Related Resources in the United States:
Status, Condition, and Trends, March 1981.

Rural Advancement Fund National Sharecroppers Fund

PO Box 1029, Pittsboro, North Carolina 27312, USA

919-542-5292

TESTIMONY BY
THE RURAL ADVANCEMENT FUND/NATIONAL SHARECROPPERS FUND
submitted to
THE HOUSE AGRICULTURE SUBCOMMITTEE on
DEPARTMENT OPERATIONS, RESEARCH AND FOREIGN AGRICULTURE
August 15, 1983

The Rural Advancement Fund/National Sharecroppers Fund
is a 46-year old, non-profit organization based in Charlotte
and Pittsboro, North Carolina. Today we see our mission as
serving and promoting the well-being of the family farm and
a healthy agricultural system. To this end we conduct a
variety of programs working directly with small farmers in
rural communities in the Southeast. We work on public policy
issues which affect family farmers, and we produce a variety
of educational materials.

Thank you for the opportunity to express our views on
H.R. 2714, The Agricultural Productivity Act of 1983.

RAF/NSF supports H.R. 2714, the Agricultural Productivity

Act. This bill aims to promote innovative agricultural research

and provide information to farmers who want to know more about

energy-saving, ecological farming methods. It would develop a

broader base of scientific information and establish regional

demonstration projects to assist with the practical application

of farming methods which are less dependent on capital and

energy intensive farm inputs.

In 1980, the U.S. Department of Agriculture released
an extensive study, Report and Recommendations on Organic
Farming. USDA's report confirmed that organic farming methods
are being used successfully by both large and small-scale farm
operators in many areas of the country. The Report called for
the development of new research and educational programs to
address the needs of U.S. farmers who are working to reduce their
dependency on energy-intensive farming methods.

But despite solid evidence of promising new technology in
this area, the U.S. Dept. of Agriculture has actually taken steps
to curtail innovative research on organic farming methods.
At a minimal cost, H.R. 2714 would ensure USDA's commitment to
research on alternative farming methods. And it would not divert
funds from existing agricultural research programs.

Members of this Subcommittee are well aware that our
nation's family farmers are now facing a fourth straight year
of declining farm income. Record numbers of farm bankruptcies
and foreclosure sales plague every region of the country.
Here in North Carolina, net farm income dropped 34 percent
over the last five years while production costs shot up 30 percent
during the same period. In South Carolina, net farm income plunged
54 percent from 1978-82. Clearly, we are in desperate need
of new solutions to address the chronic ills facing American
agriculture. And we must look beyond traditional answers.

The Agricultural Productivity Act will not solve the farm
crisis, but it is an important step in the right direction.

H.R. 2714 will begin to help U.S. farmers cut soaring
production costs and lessen their dependency on energy
and capital intensive farm inputs. Ultimately, this will
mean increasing profitability for farmers while promoting
an environmentally sound and sustainable system of
agriculture.

We believe that H.R. 2714 deserves your support.
Thank you for your careful consideration of this important
legislation.

O

DEPOSIT

APR 0 4 1984

Lightning Source UK Ltd.
Milton Keynes UK
UKHW020647061218
333419UK00012B/1639/P